Flying Witch

Ishizuka

Contents

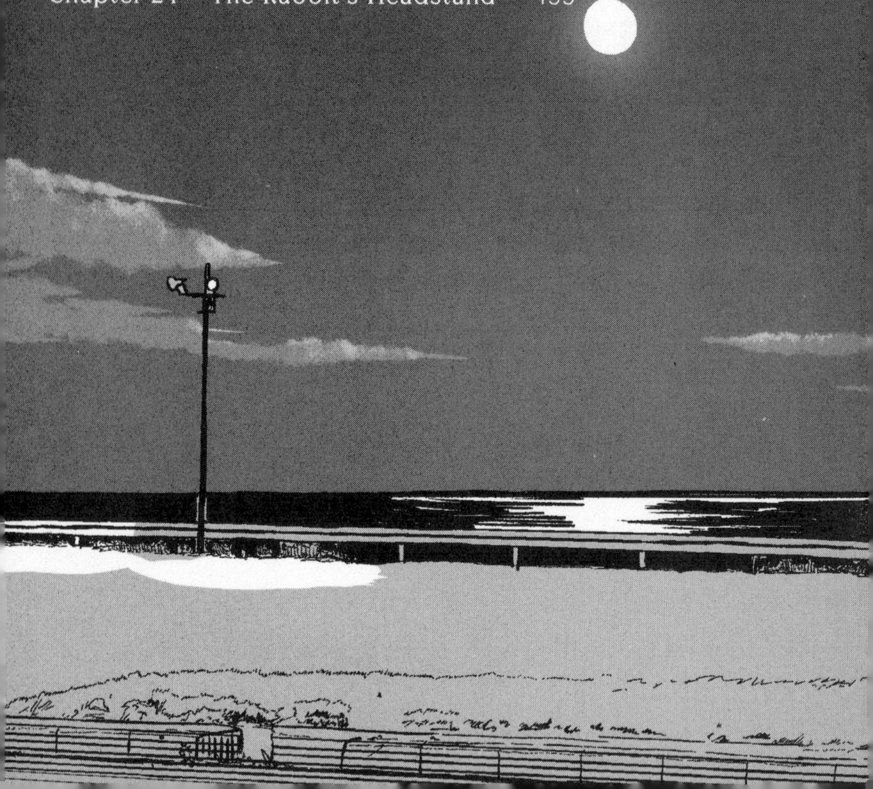

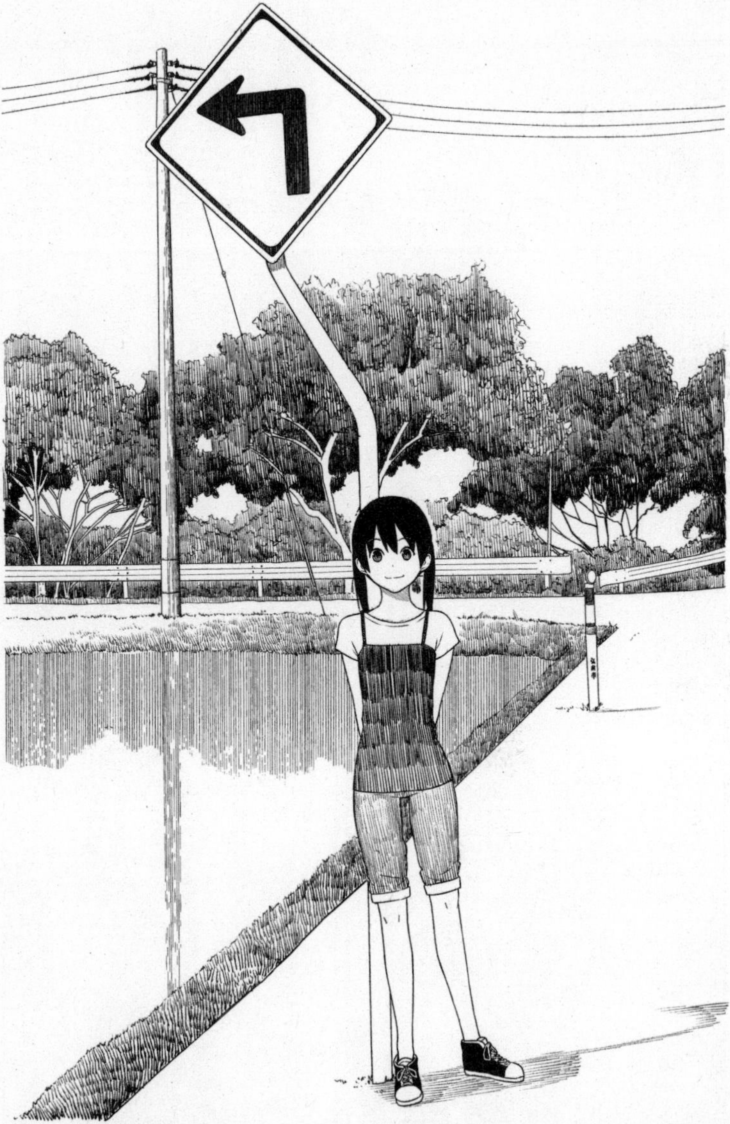

Chapter 19
To Each Witch Her Own Robe

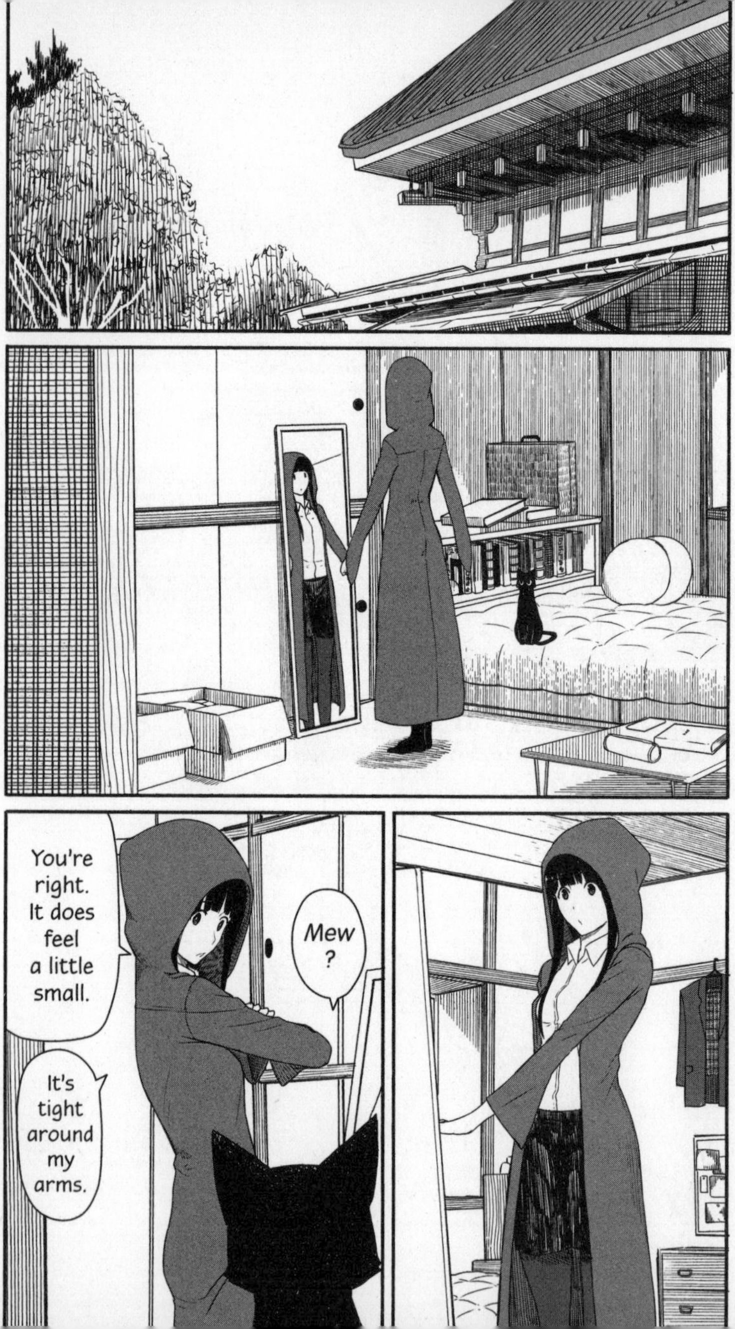
Mew?
You're right. It does feel a little small.
It's tight around my arms.

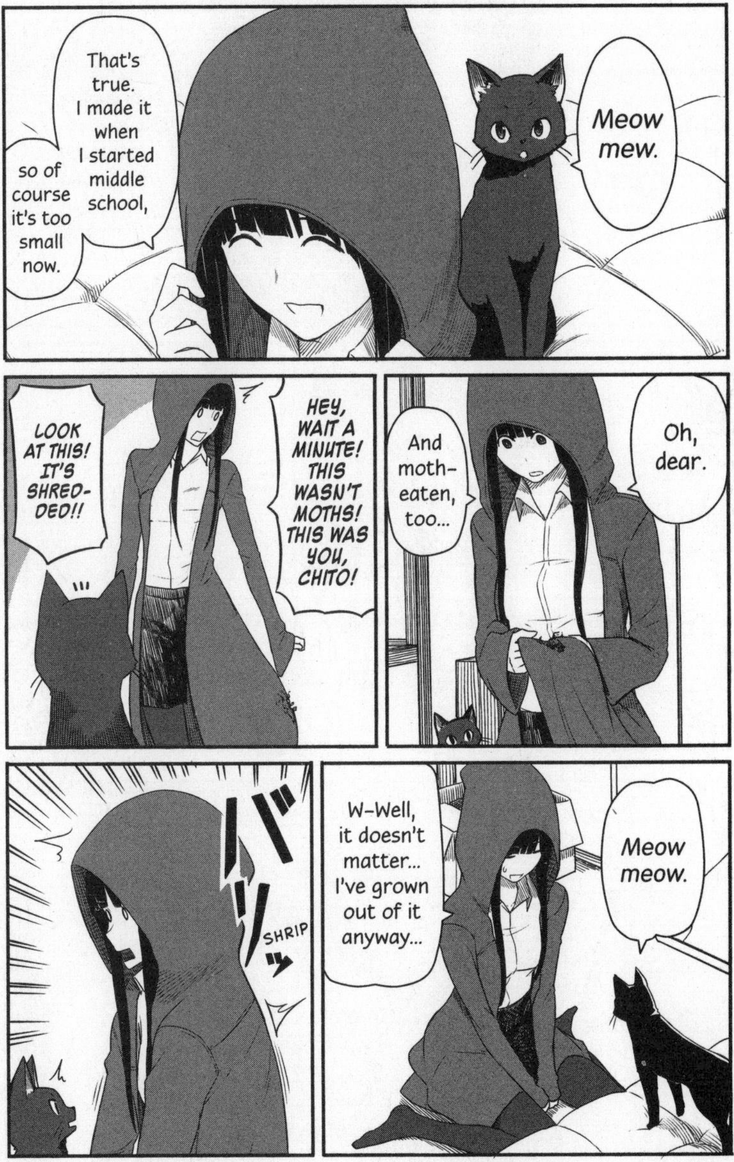
Meow mew.
That's true. I made it when I started middle school,
so of course it's too small now.
Oh, dear.
And moth-eaten, too...
HEY, WAIT A MINUTE! THIS WASN'T MOTHS! THIS WAS YOU, CHITO!
LOOK AT THIS! IT'S SHREDDED!!
Meow meow.
W-Well, it doesn't matter... I've grown out of it anyway...
バッ
SHRIP

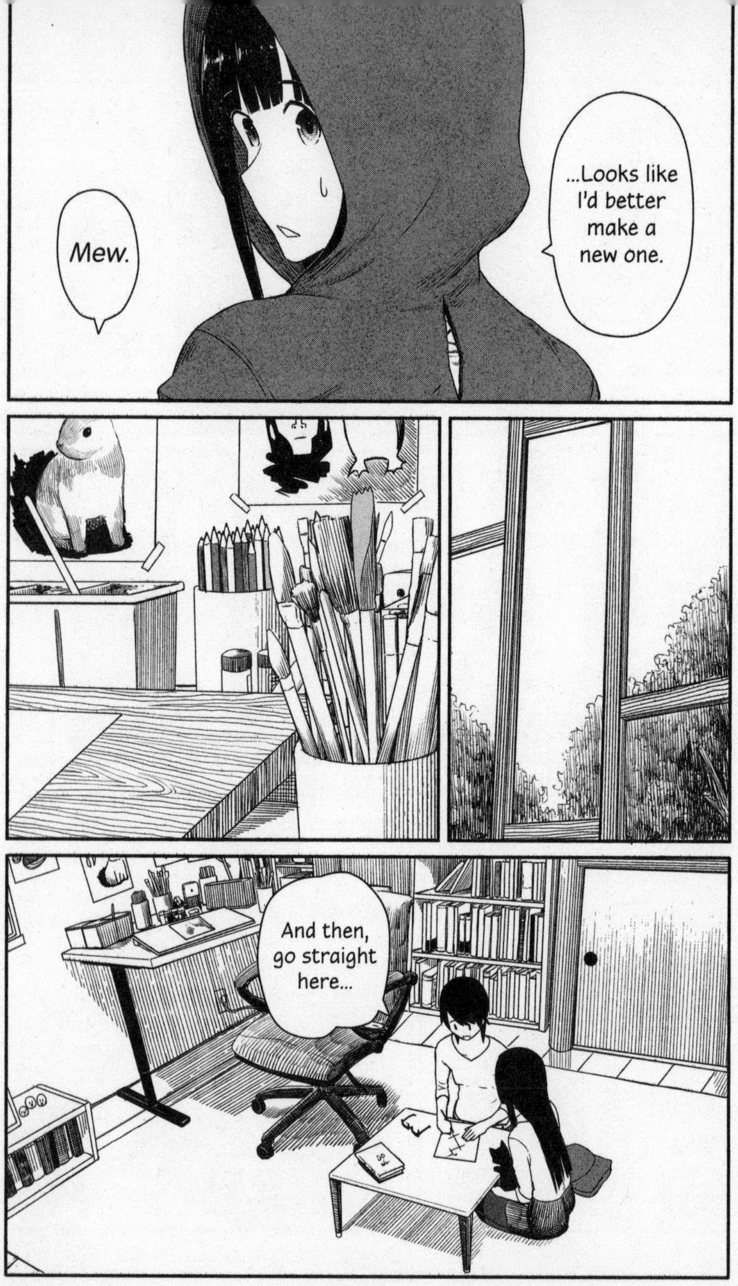
...Looks like I'd better make a new one.
Mew.
And then, go straight here...

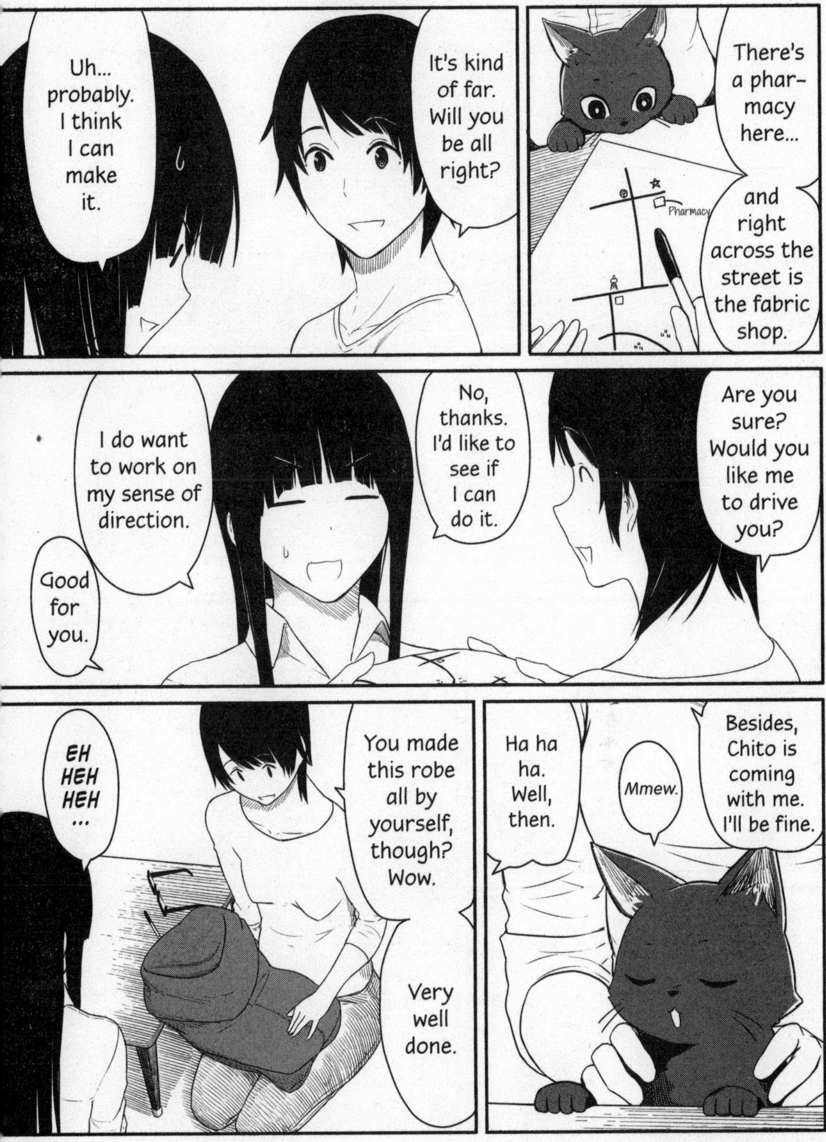
There's a phar-macy here...
Pharmacy
and right across the street is the fabric shop.
It's kind of far. Will you be all right?
Uh... probably. I think I can make it.
Are you sure? Would you like me to drive you?
No, thanks. I'd like to see if I can do it.
I do want to work on my sense of direction.
Good for you.
Besides, Chito is coming with me. I'll be fine.
Mmew.
Ha ha ha. Well, then.
You made this robe all by yourself, though? Wow.
Very well done.
EH HEH HEH...

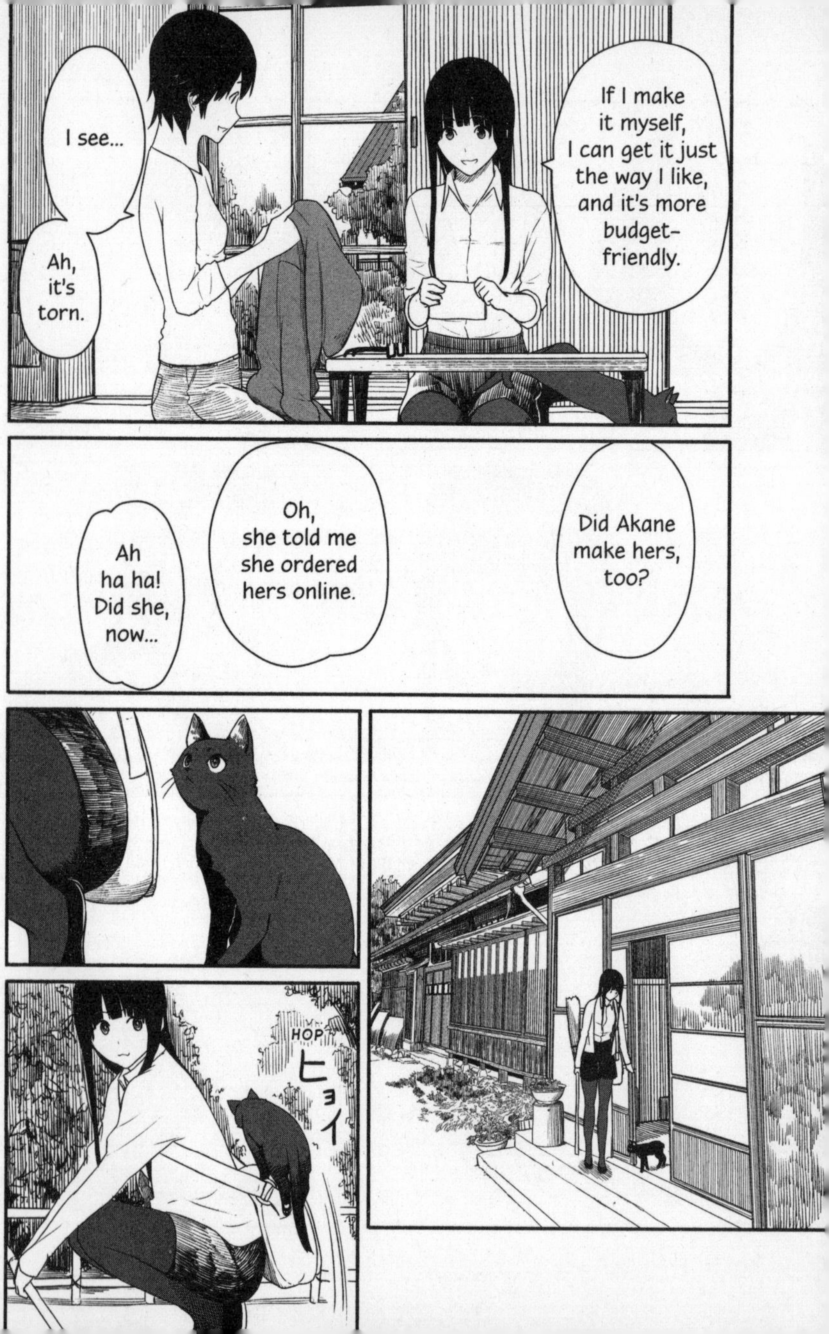
If I make it myself, I can get it just the way I like, and it's more budget-friendly.
I see...
Ah, it's torn.
Did Akane make hers, too?
Oh, she told me she ordered hers online.
Ah ha ha! Did she, now...
HOP
ヒョイ

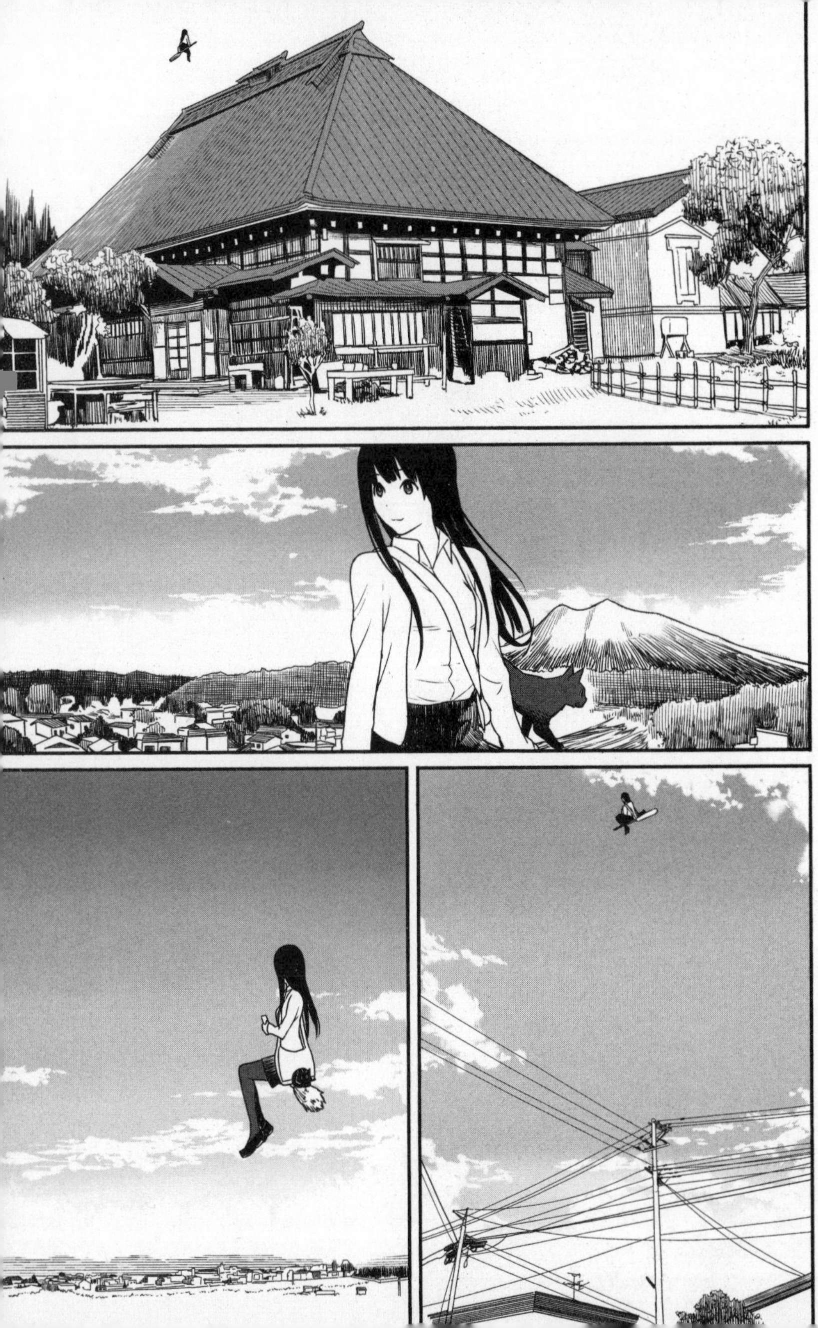

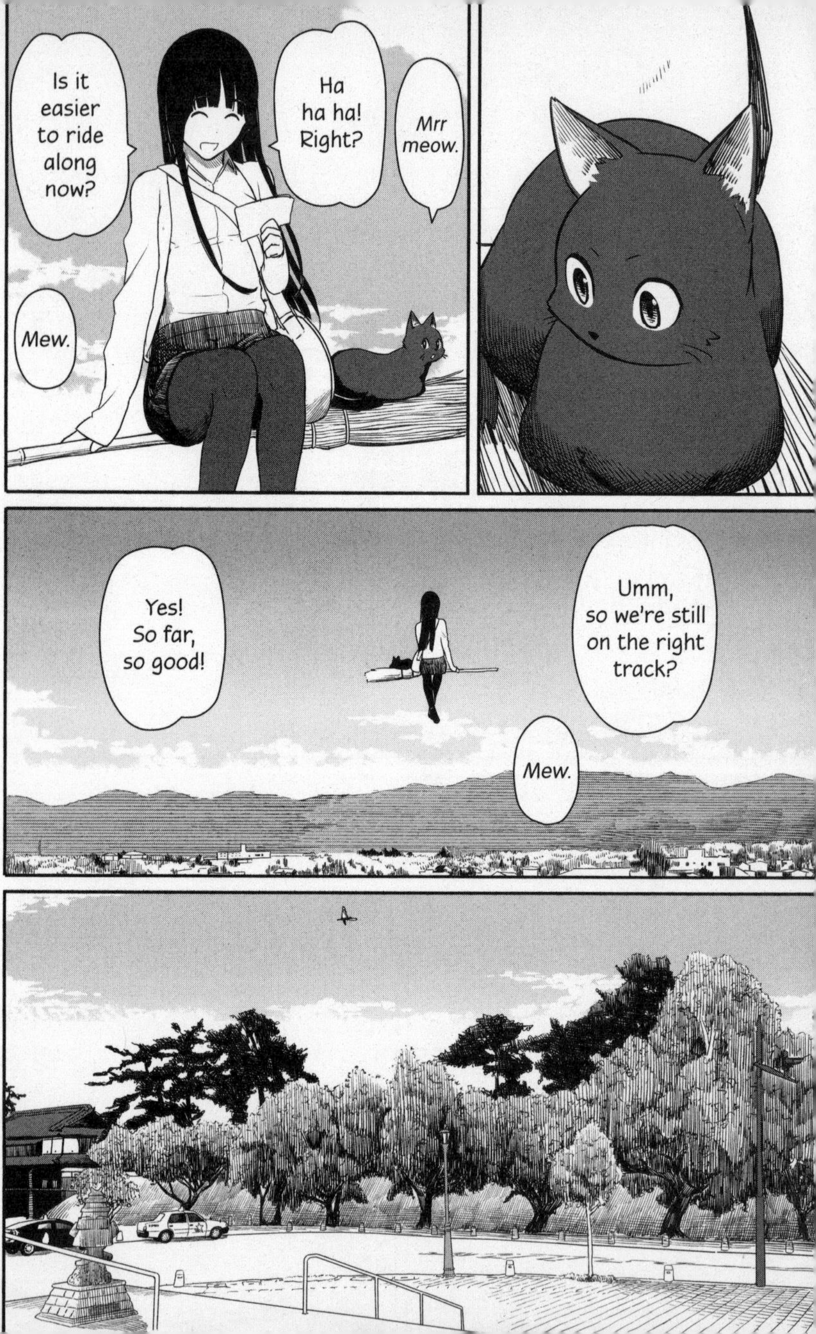
Mrr meow.
Ha ha ha! Right?
Is it easier to ride along now?
Mew.
Umm, so we're still on the right track?
Mew.
Yes! So far, so good!

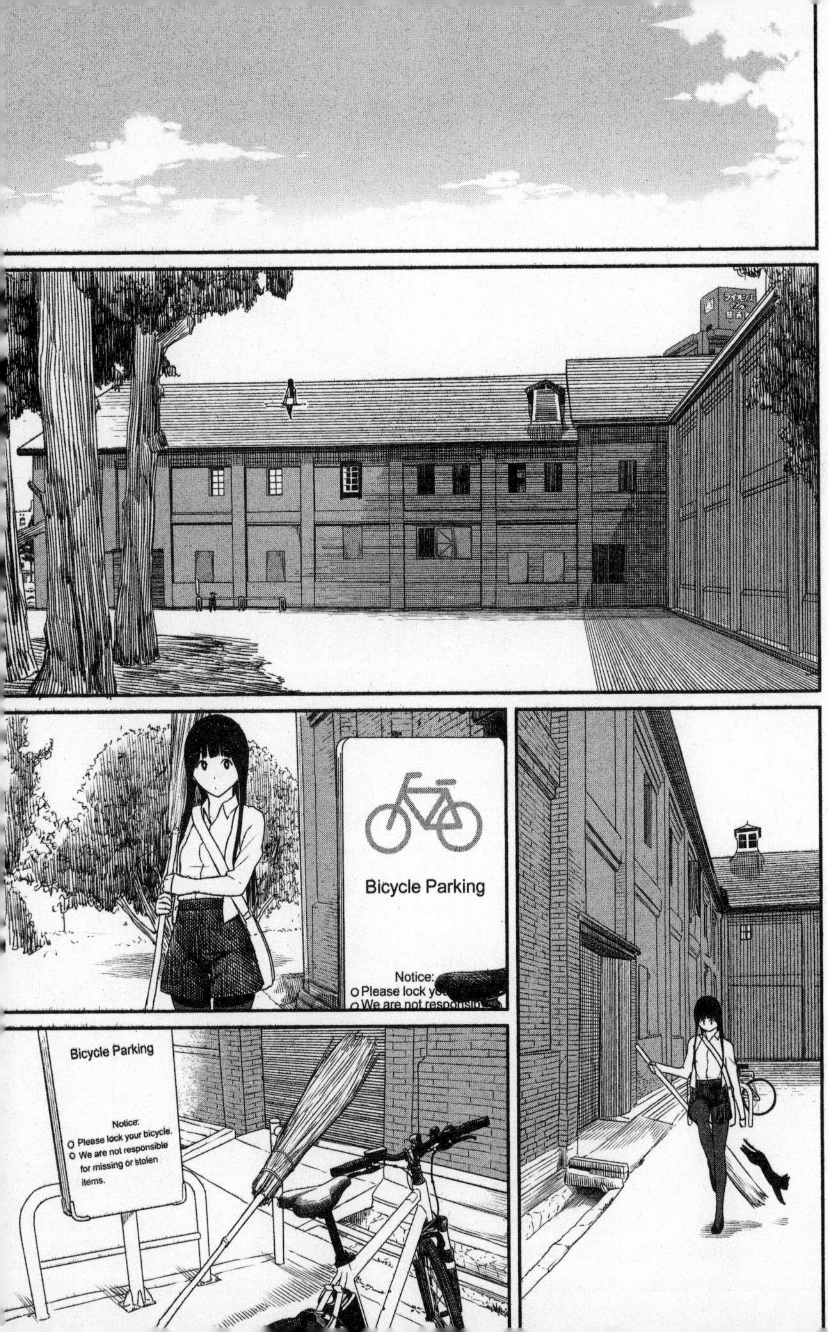
Bicycle Parking
Notice:
Bicycle Parking
Notice:
Please lock your bicycle.
We are not responsible for missing or stolen items.

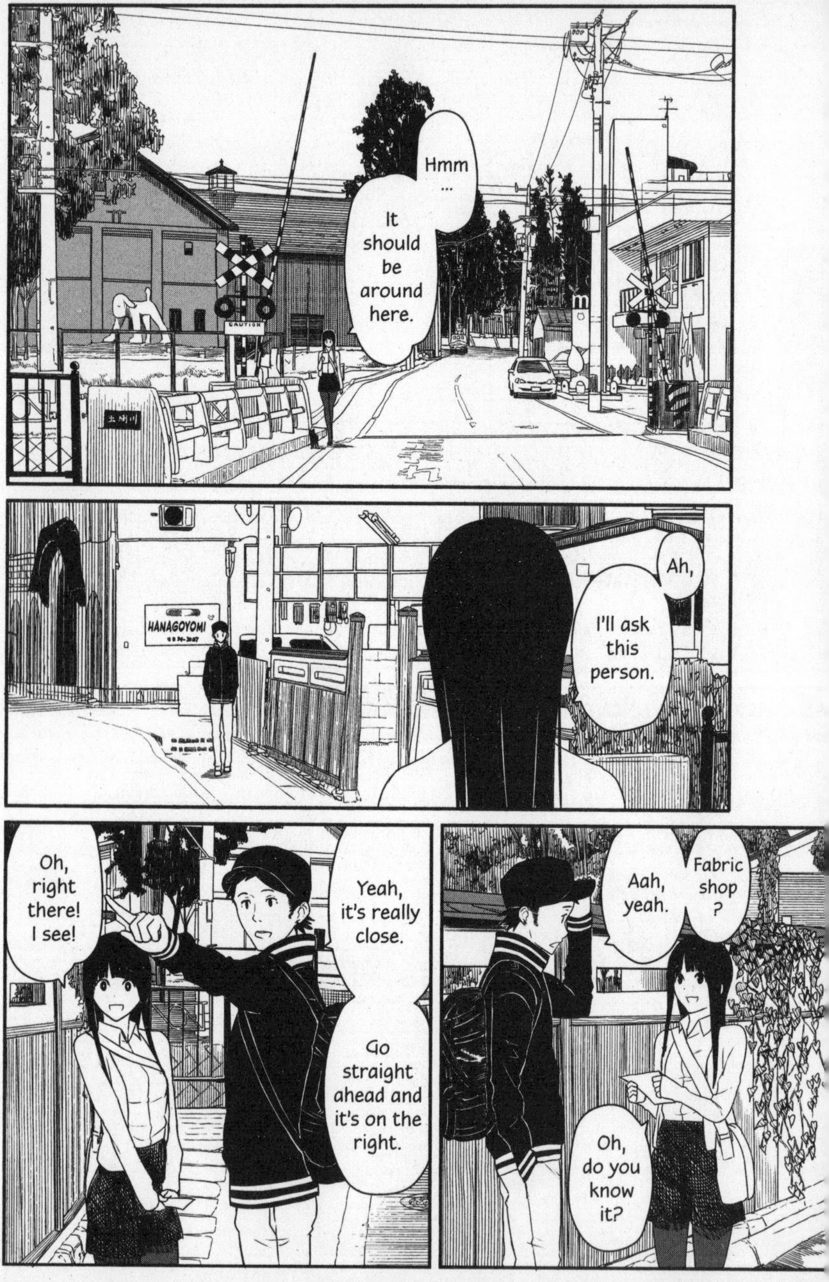
Hmm ...
It should be around here.
CAUTION
Ah,
I'll ask this person.
HANAGOYOMI
Fabric shop ?
Aah, yeah.
Oh, do you know it?
Yeah, it's really close.
Go straight ahead and it's on the right.
Oh, right there! I see!

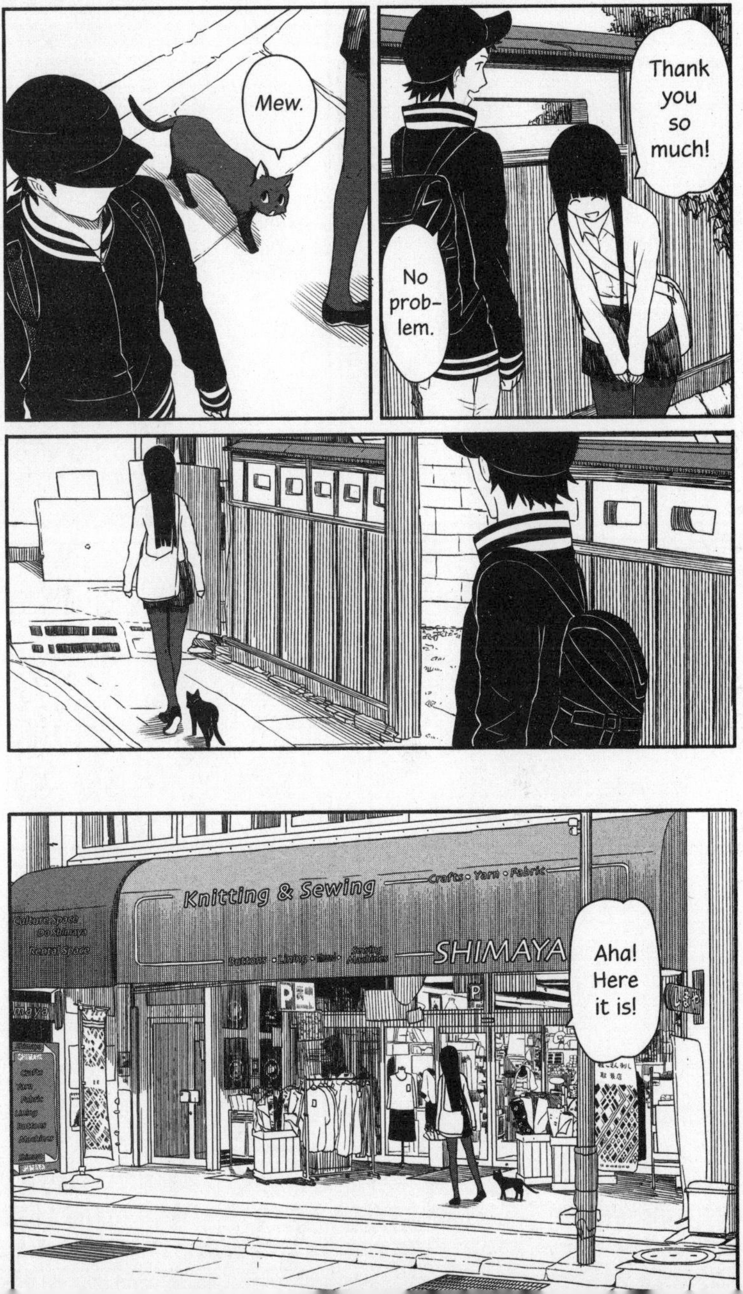
Thank you so much!
No problem.
Mew.
Knitting & Sewing
Crafts • Yarn • Fabric
SHIMAYA
Culture Space
Do Shimaya
Rental Space
Aha! Here it is!

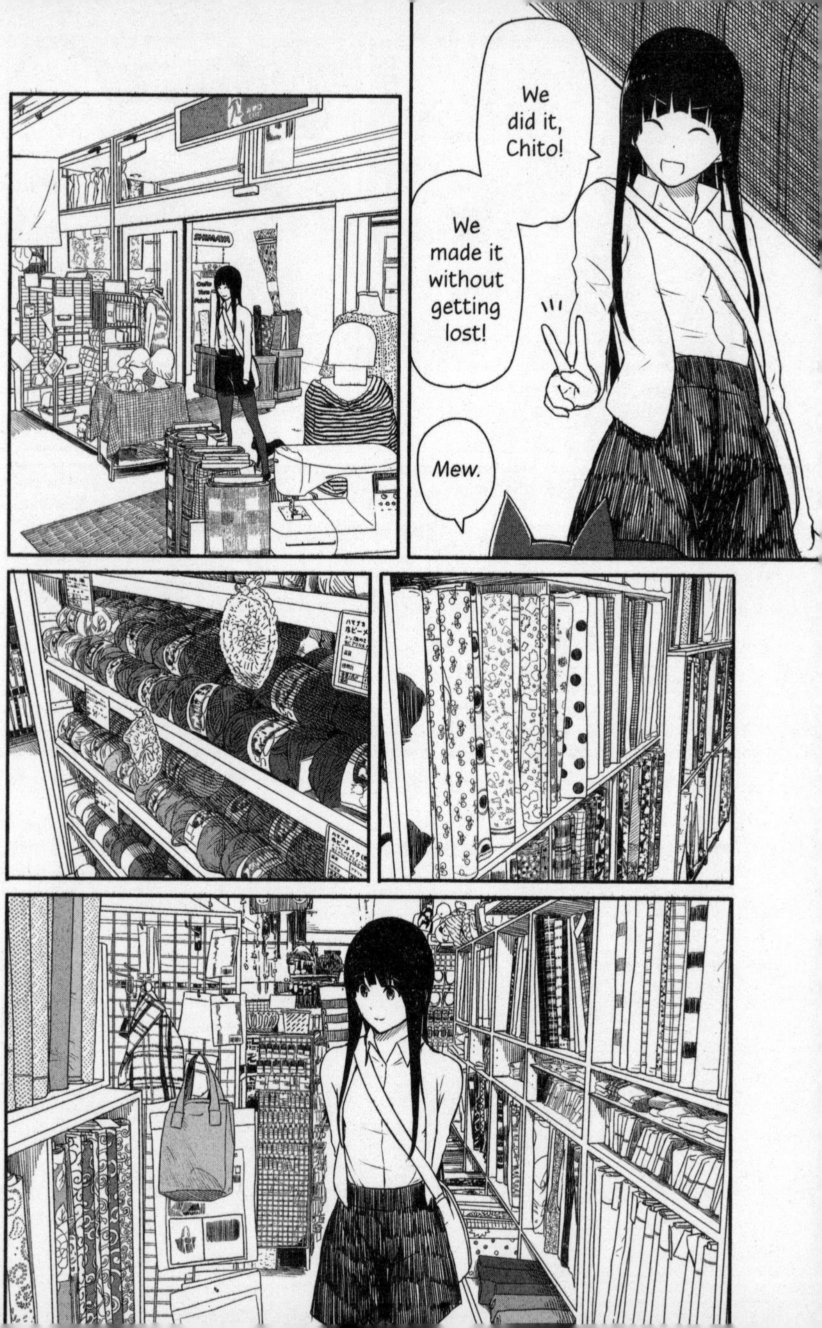

We did it, Chito!
We made it without getting lost!
Mew.
SHIMAYA

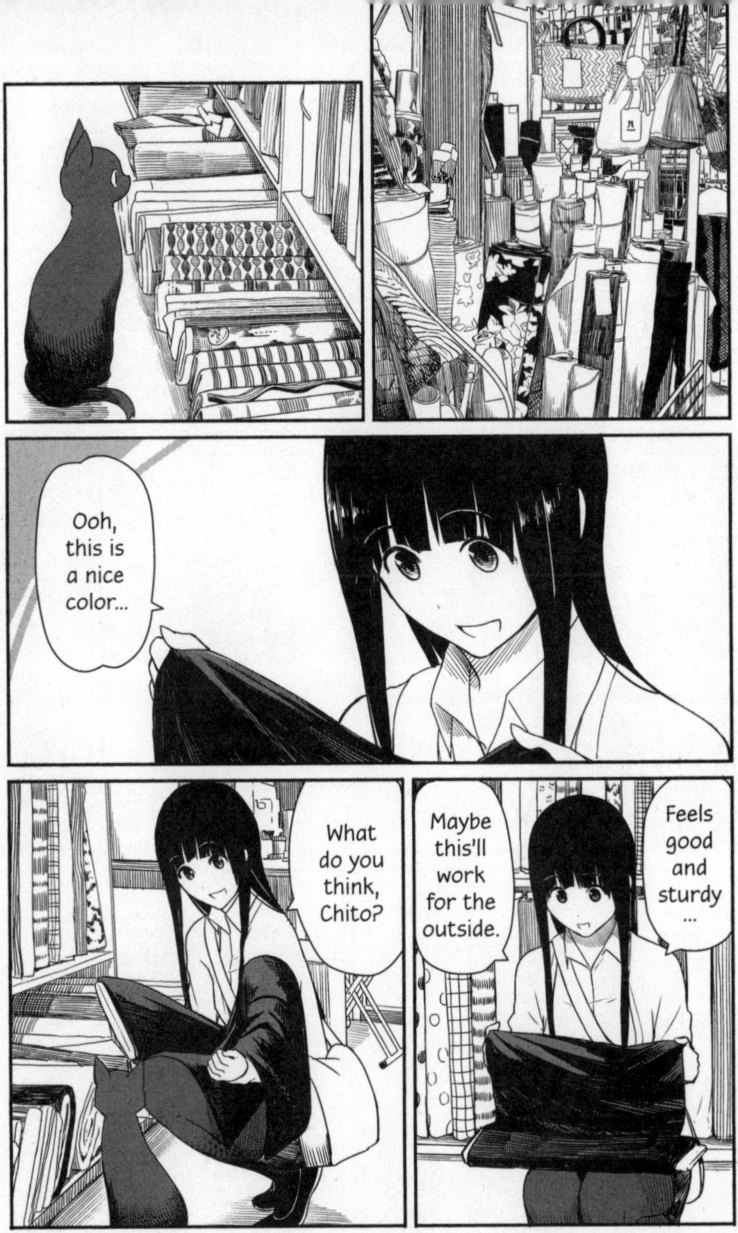
Ooh, this is a nice color...
Feels good and sturdy ...
Maybe this'll work for the outside.
What do you think, Chito?

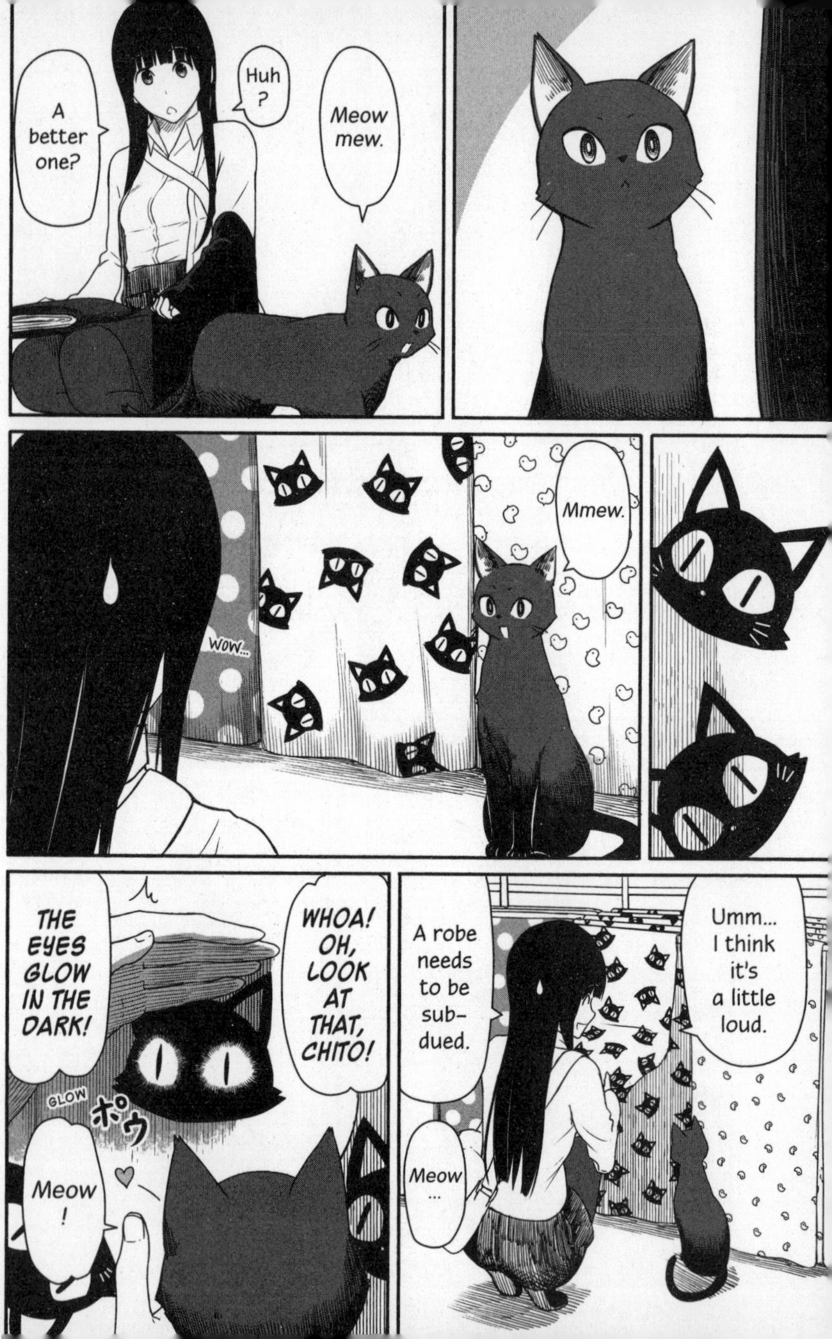
Meow mew.
Huh?
A better one?
Mmew.
WOW...
Umm... I think it's a little loud.
A robe needs to be sub-dued.
Meow...
WHOA! OH, LOOK AT THAT, CHITO!
THE EYES GLOW IN THE DARK!
GLOW
ポウ
Meow!

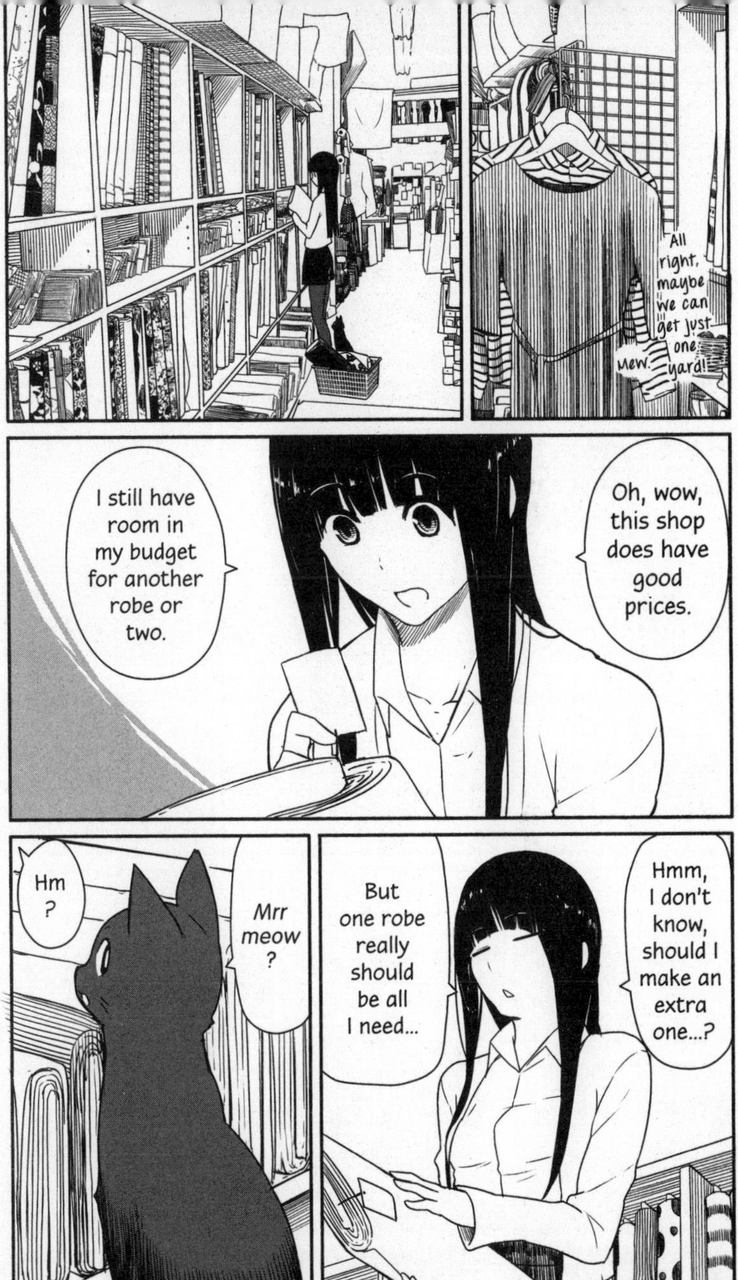
All right, maybe we can get just one yard!
Mew.
Oh, wow, this shop does have good prices.
I still have room in my budget for another robe or two.
Hmm, I don't know, should I make an extra one...?
But one robe really should be all I need...
Mrr meow?
Hm?

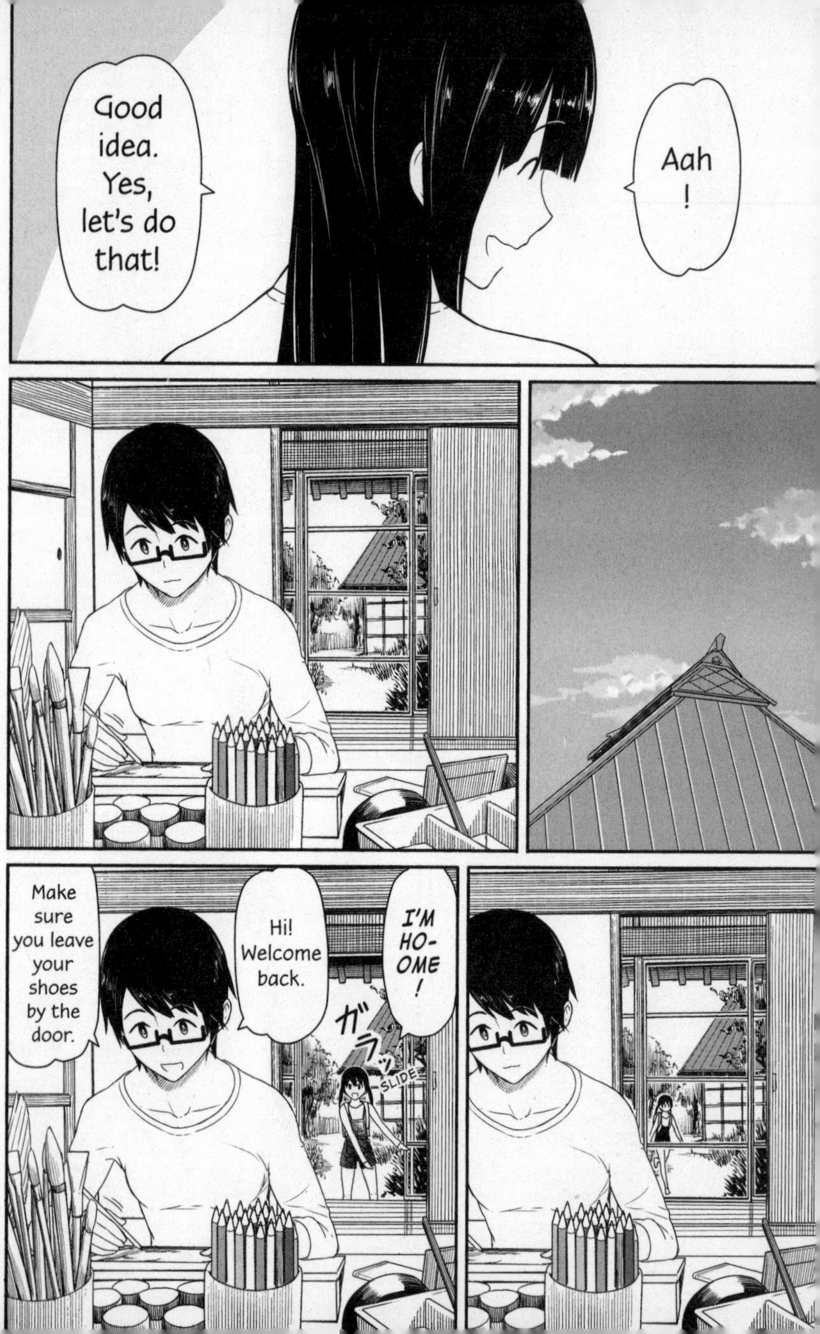
Aah!
Good idea. Yes, let's do that!
I'M HO-OME!
ガラッ
SLIDE
Hi! Welcome back.
Make sure you leave your shoes by the door.

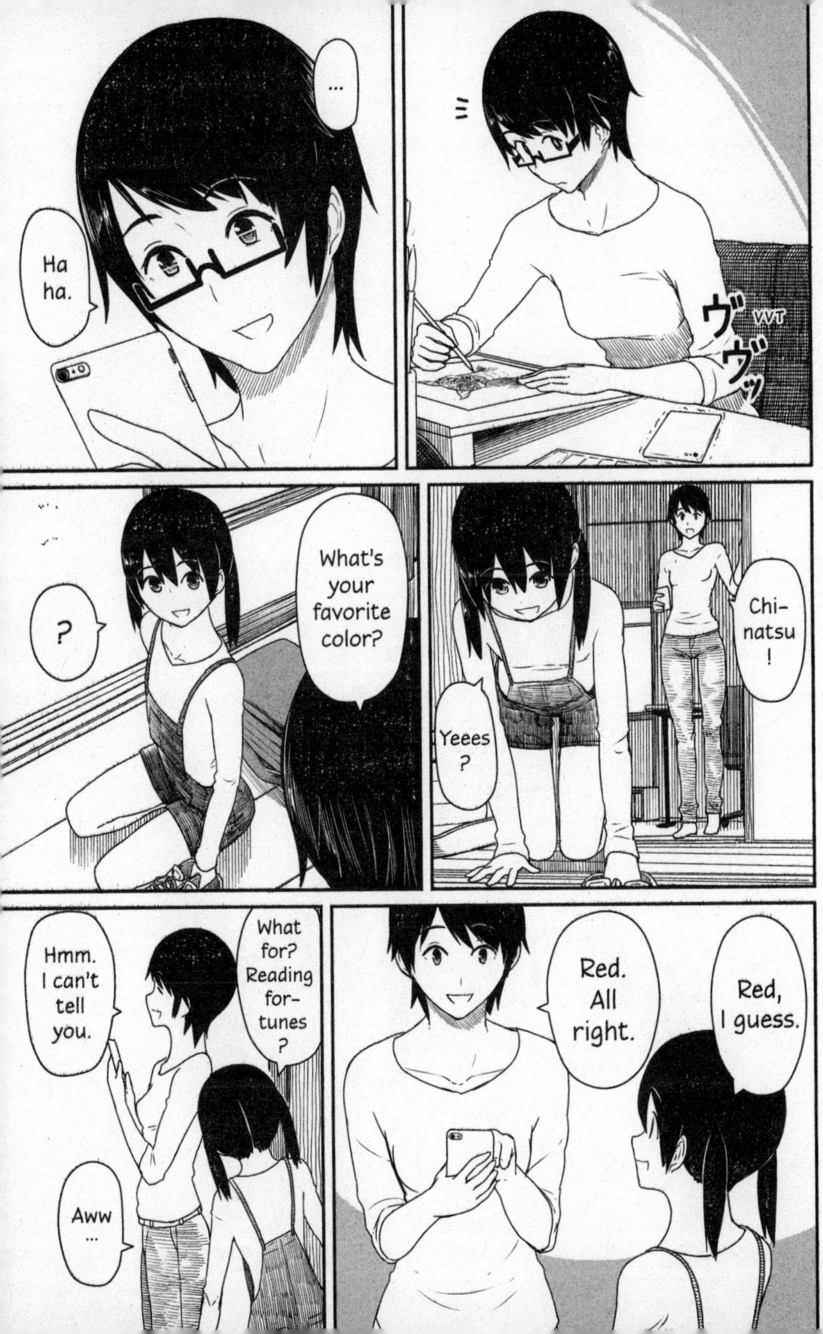
ヴヴッ
VVT
...
Ha ha.
Chi-natsu!
Yeees?
What's your favorite color?
?
Red, I guess.
Red. All right.
What for? Reading for-tunes?
Hmm. I can't tell you.
Aww...

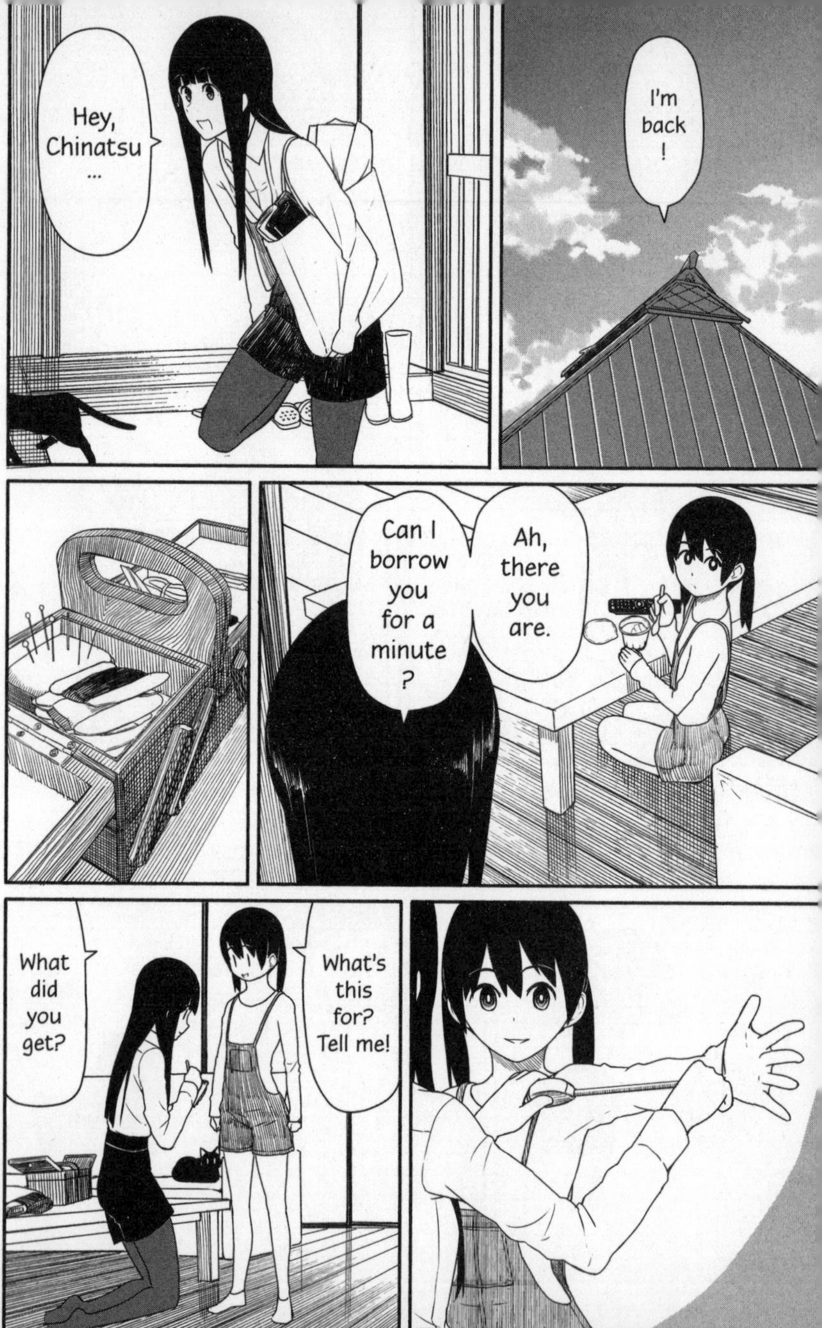
I'm back!
Hey, Chinatsu...
Ah, there you are.
Can I borrow you for a minute?
What's this for? Tell me!
What did you get?

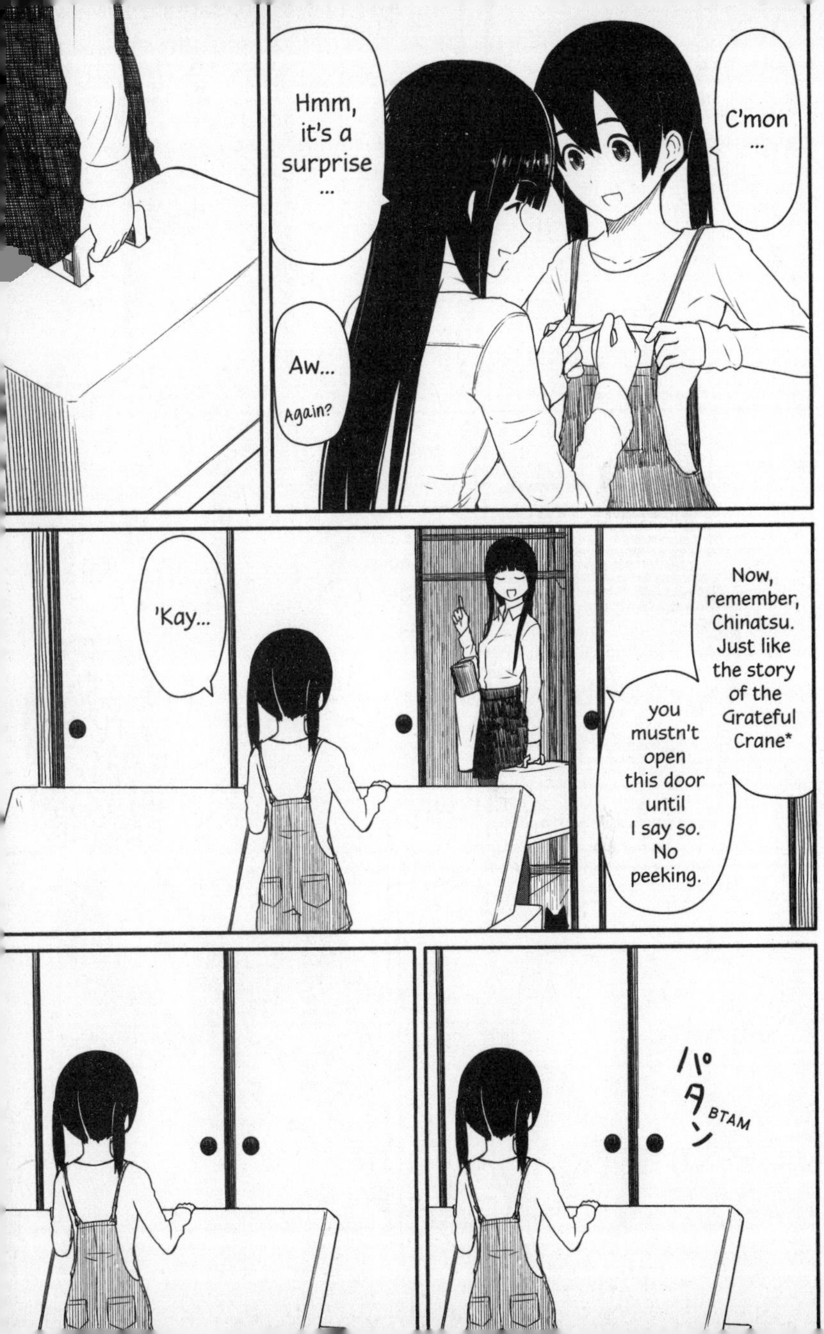
C'mon ...
Hmm, it's a surprise ...
Aw... Again?
Now, remember, Chinatsu. Just like the story of the Grateful Crane*
you mustn't open this door until I say so. No peeking.
'Kay...
パタン BTAM

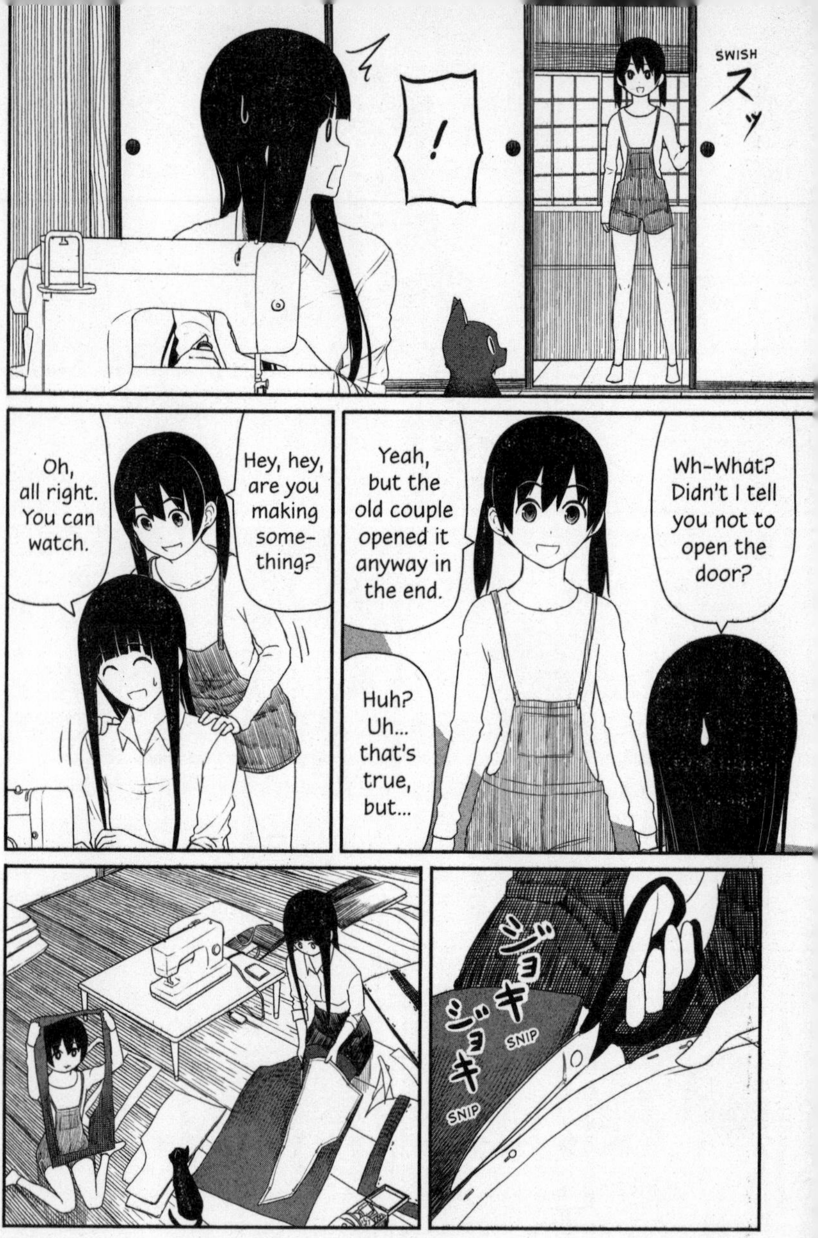
SWISH
スッ
!
Wh-What? Didn't I tell you not to open the door?
Yeah, but the old couple opened it anyway in the end.
Huh? Uh... that's true, but...
Hey, hey, are you making some-thing?
Oh, all right. You can watch.
ジョキ
ジョキ
SNIP
SNIP

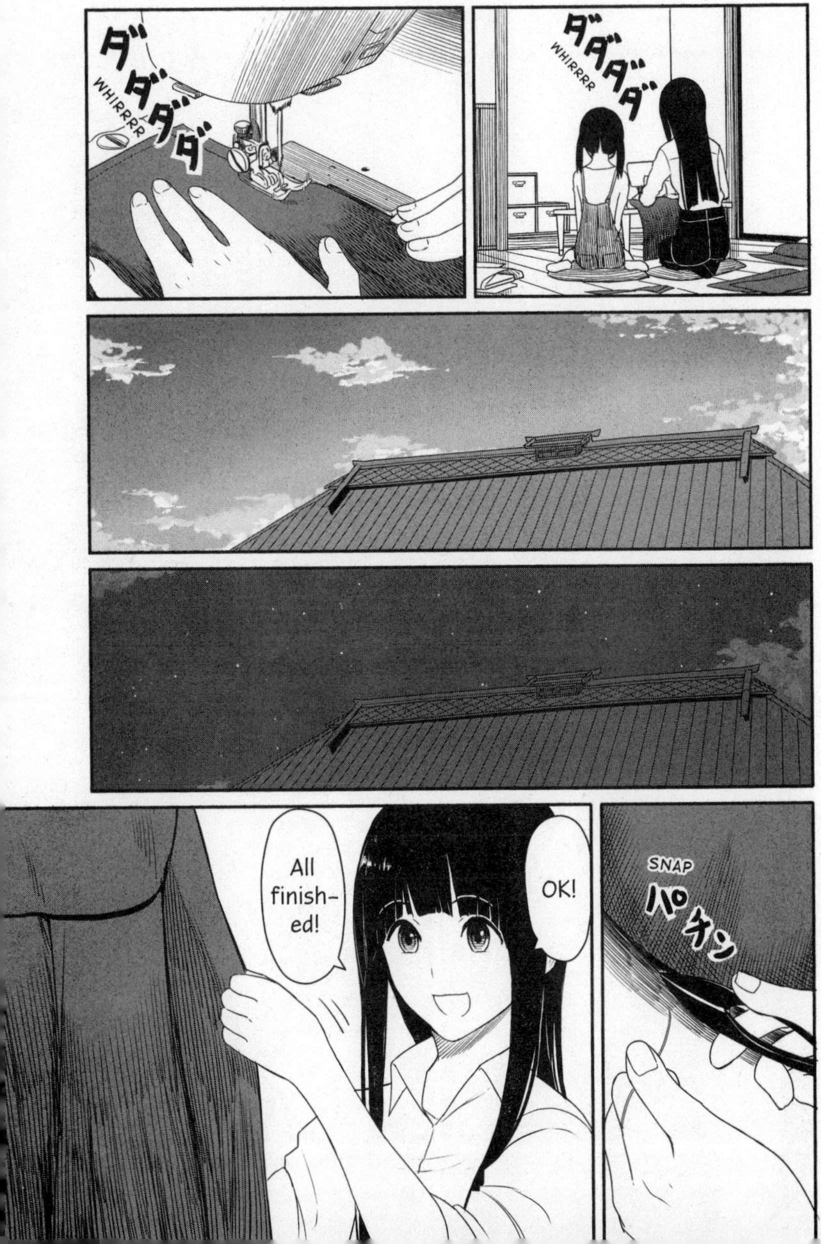

ダダダダ
WHIRRRR
ダダダダ
WHIRRRR
SNAP
パチン
OK!
All finish-ed!

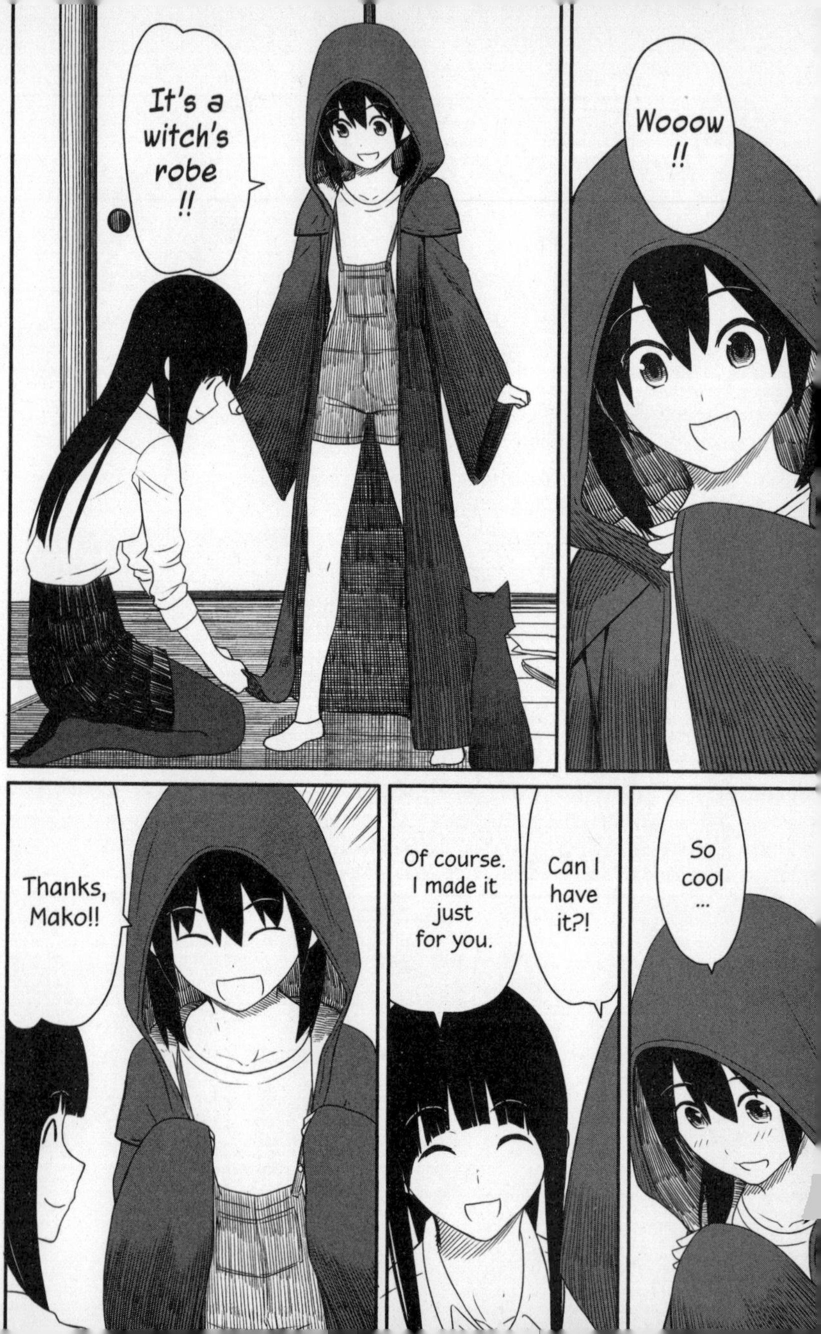
Wooow !!
It's a witch's robe !!
So cool ...
Can I have it?!
Of course. I made it just for you.
Thanks, Mako!!

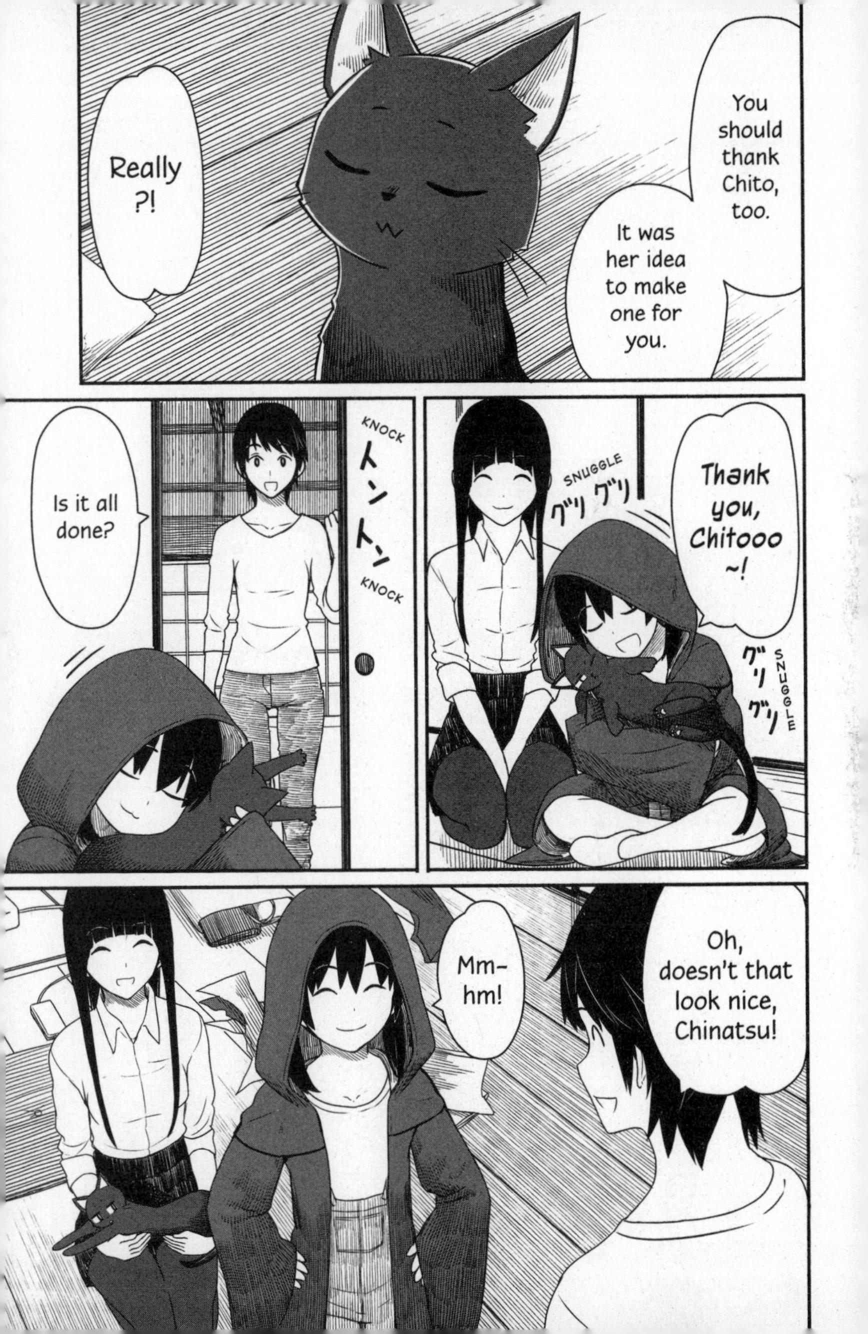
You should thank Chito, too.
It was her idea to make one for you.
Really?!
Thank you, Chitooo ~!
SNUGGLE
グリグリ
グリグリ
SNUGGLE
KNOCK
トントン
KNOCK
Is it all done?
Oh, doesn't that look nice, Chinatsu!
Mm-hm!

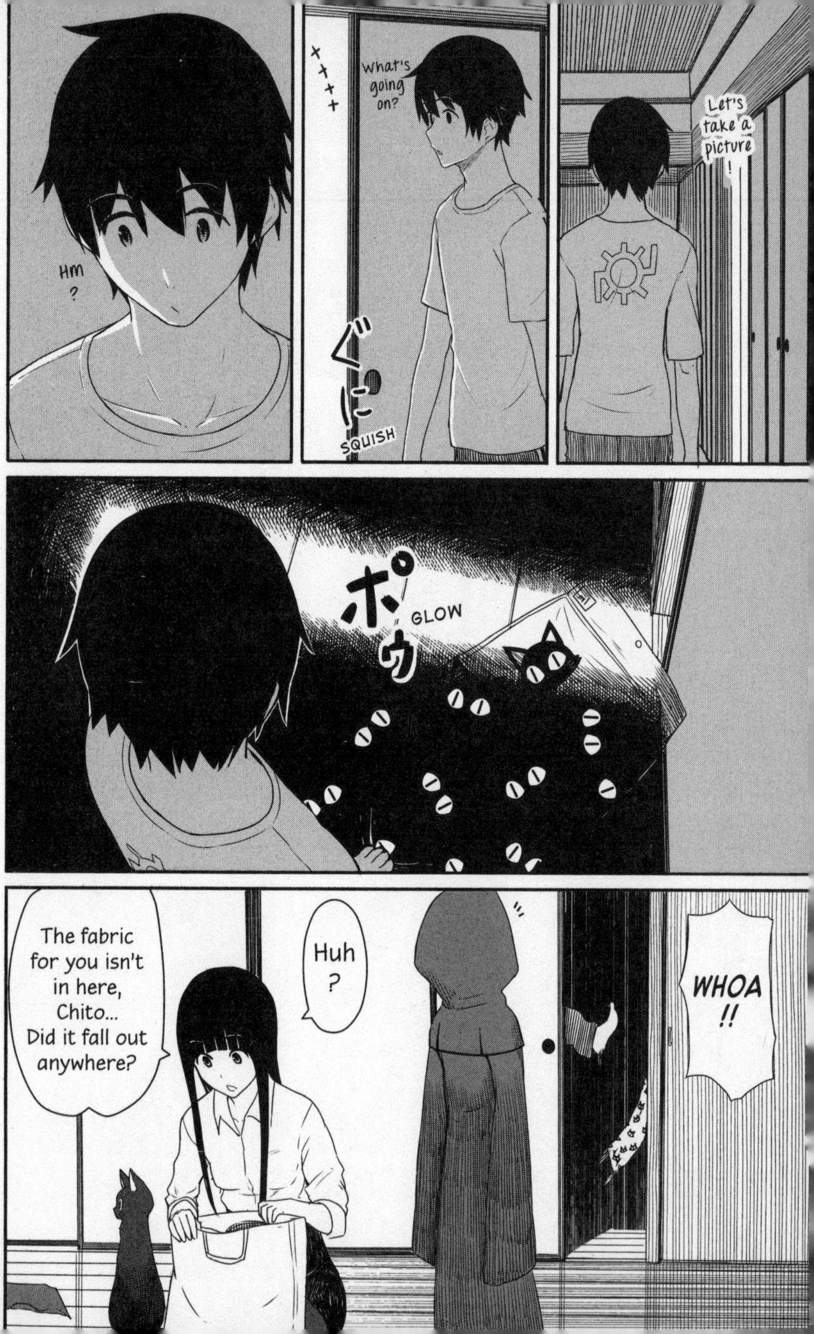
Let's take a picture!
What's going on?
SQUISH
Hm?
ポゥ
GLOW
WHOA!!
Huh?
The fabric for you isn't in here, Chito... Did it fall out anywhere?

*The Grateful Crane is a folktale in which a childless old couple rescues a crane from a trap. That night, a beautiful girl comes to the couple's home in the midst of a blizzard, and they let her stay with them. She weaves splendid cloth to sell, making them rich, but warns them never to look in while she's working. But curiosity gets the better of the old couple, and one day they peek... and find a crane plucking its own feathers to produce the gleaming brocades. The girl was the crane they saved. Out of gratitude, she had wished to stay with them as their daughter and weave for their prosperity, but cannot remain now that her true nature is discovered, and so she flees.

Flying
Witch

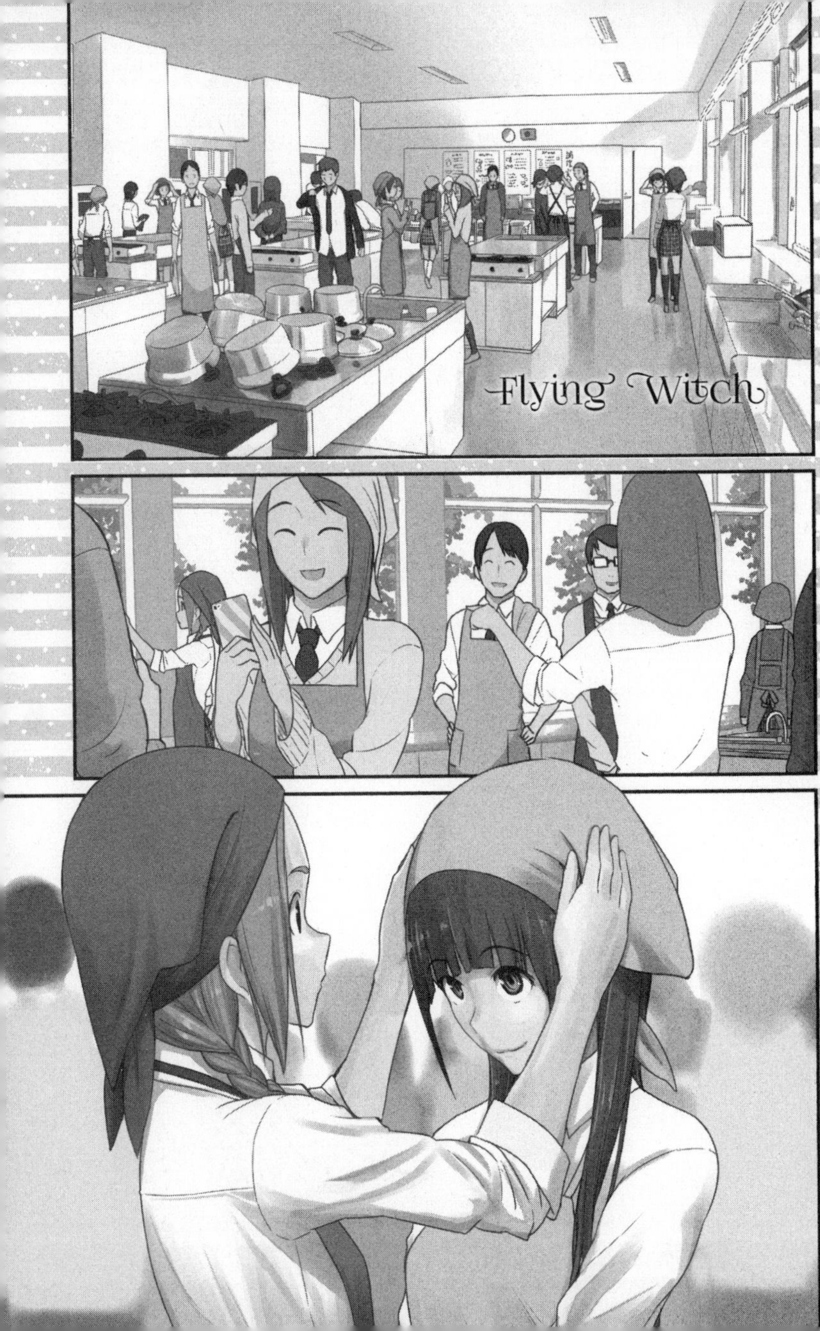
Flying Witch

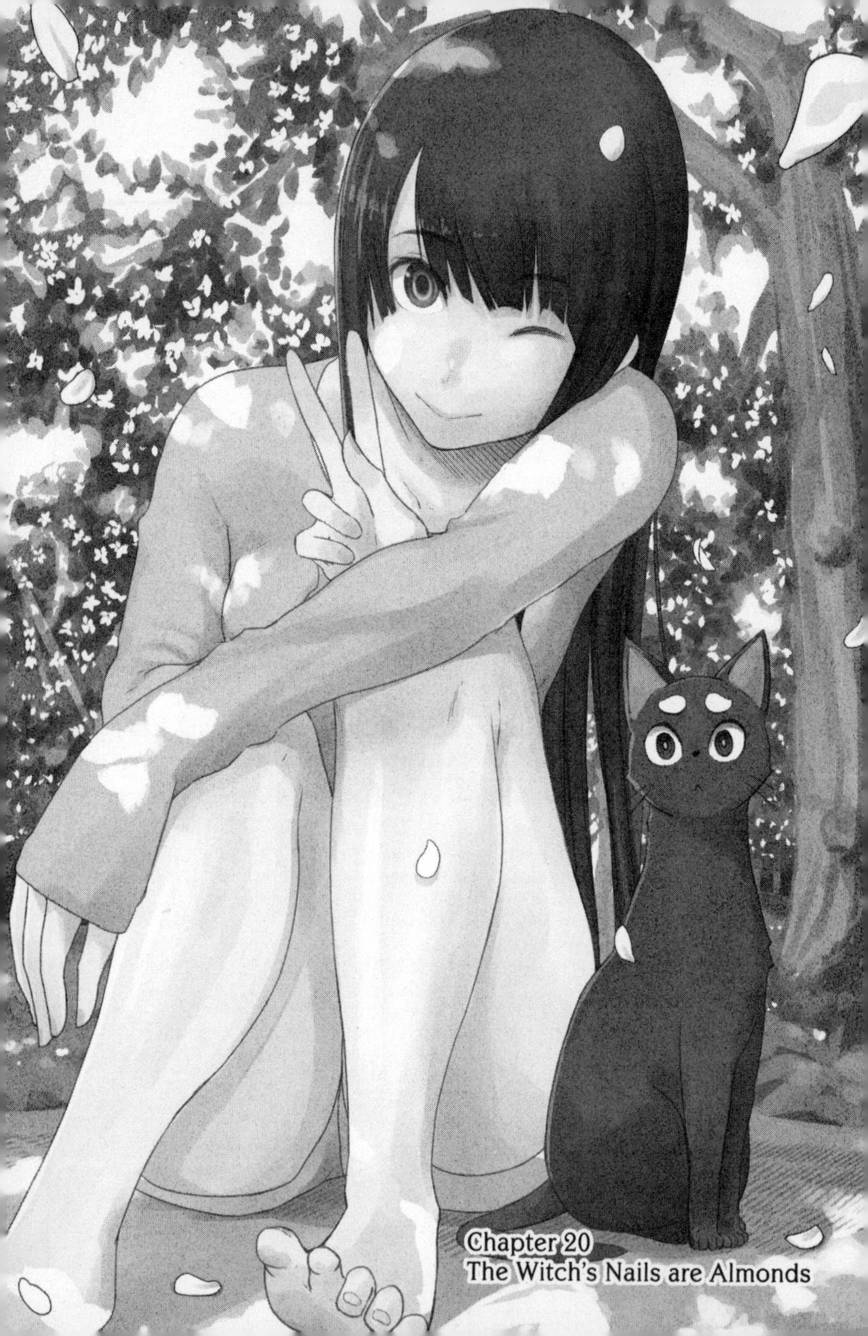

Chapter 20
The Witch's Nails are Almonds

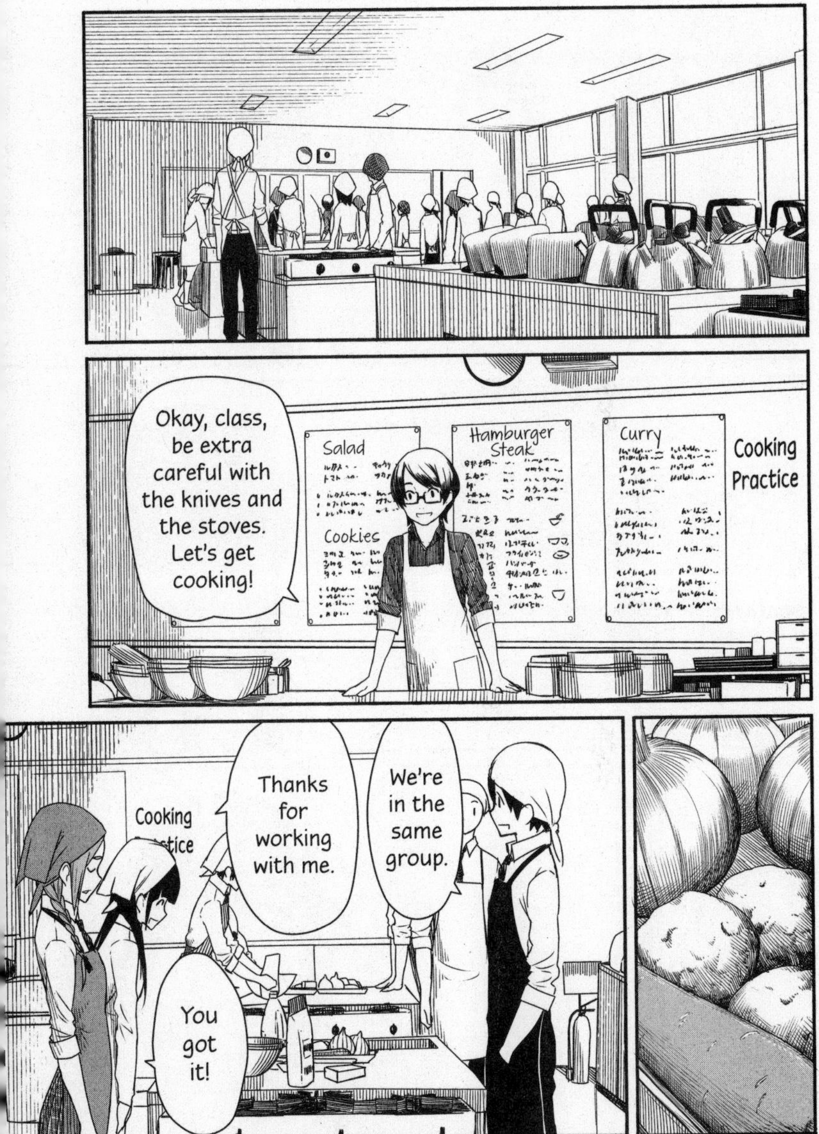
Cooking Practice
Curry
Hamburger Steak
Salad
Cookies
Okay, class, be extra careful with the knives and the stoves. Let's get cooking!
We're in the same group.
Thanks for working with me.
Cooking
You got it!

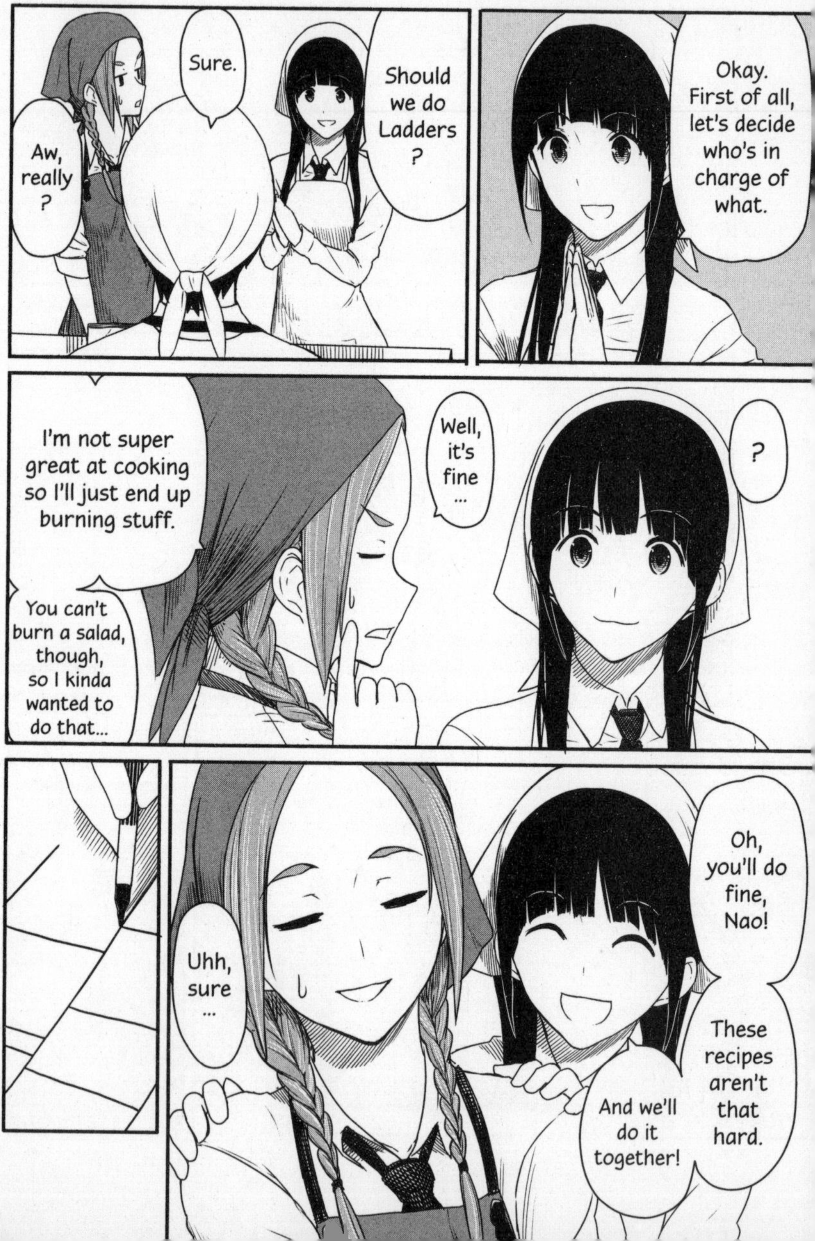
Okay. First of all, let's decide who's in charge of what.
Should we do Ladders?
Sure.
Aw, really?
?
Well, it's fine...
I'm not super great at cooking so I'll just end up burning stuff.
You can't burn a salad, though, so I kinda wanted to do that...
Oh, you'll do fine, Nao!
These recipes aren't that hard.
And we'll do it together!
Uhh, sure...

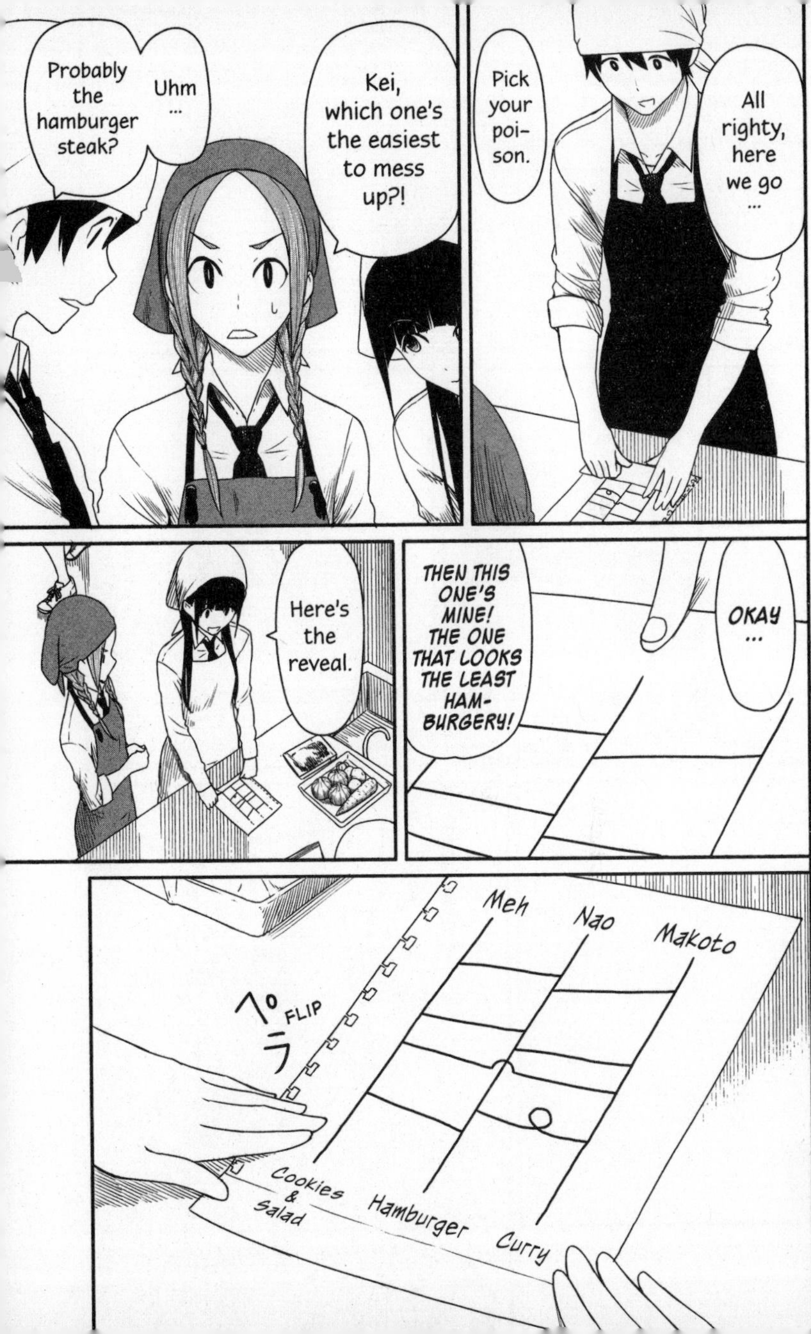

All righty, here we go ...
Pick your poi-son.
Kei, which one's the easiest to mess up?!
Uhm ...
Probably the hamburger steak?
OKAY ...
THEN THIS ONE'S MINE! THE ONE THAT LOOKS THE LEAST HAM-BURGERY!
Here's the reveal.
Makoto
Nao
Meh
ペラ FLIP
Curry
Hamburger
Cookies & Salad

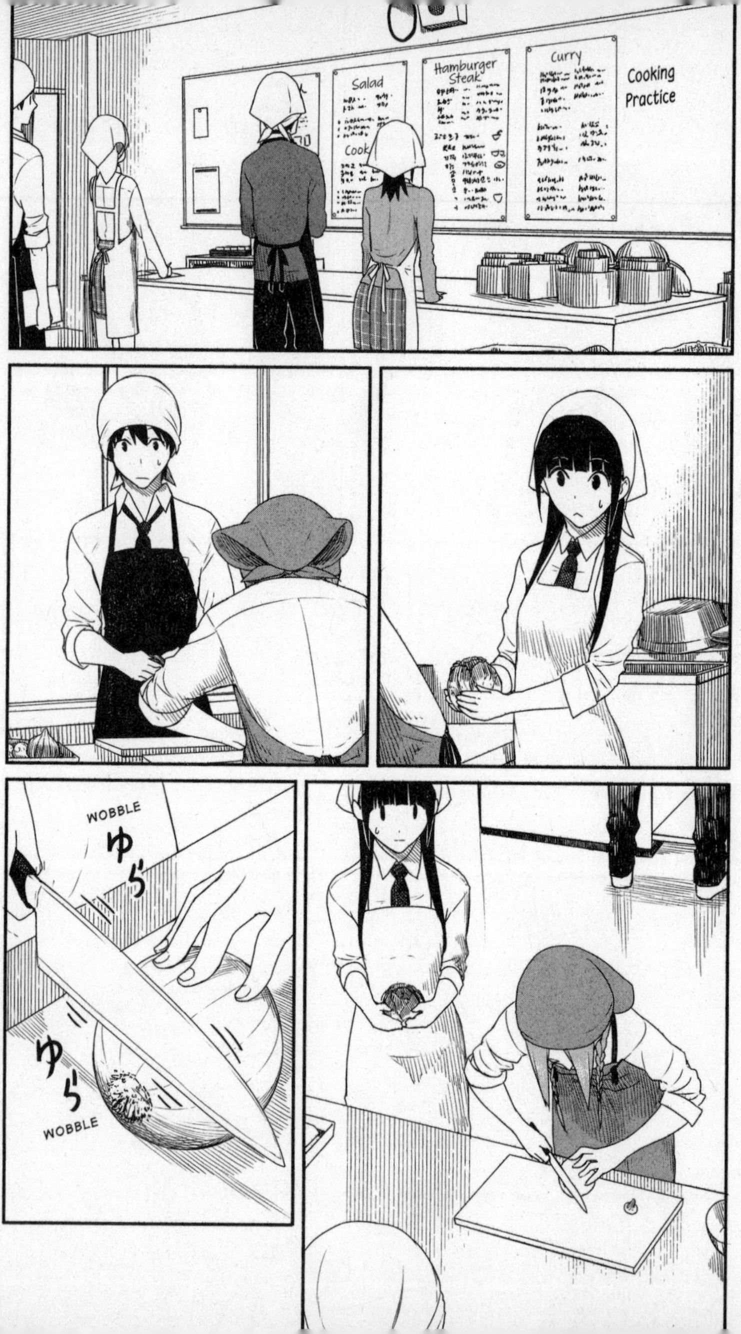
Salad
Hamburger Steak
Curry
Cooking Practice
WOBBLE
ゆら
ゆら
WOBBLE

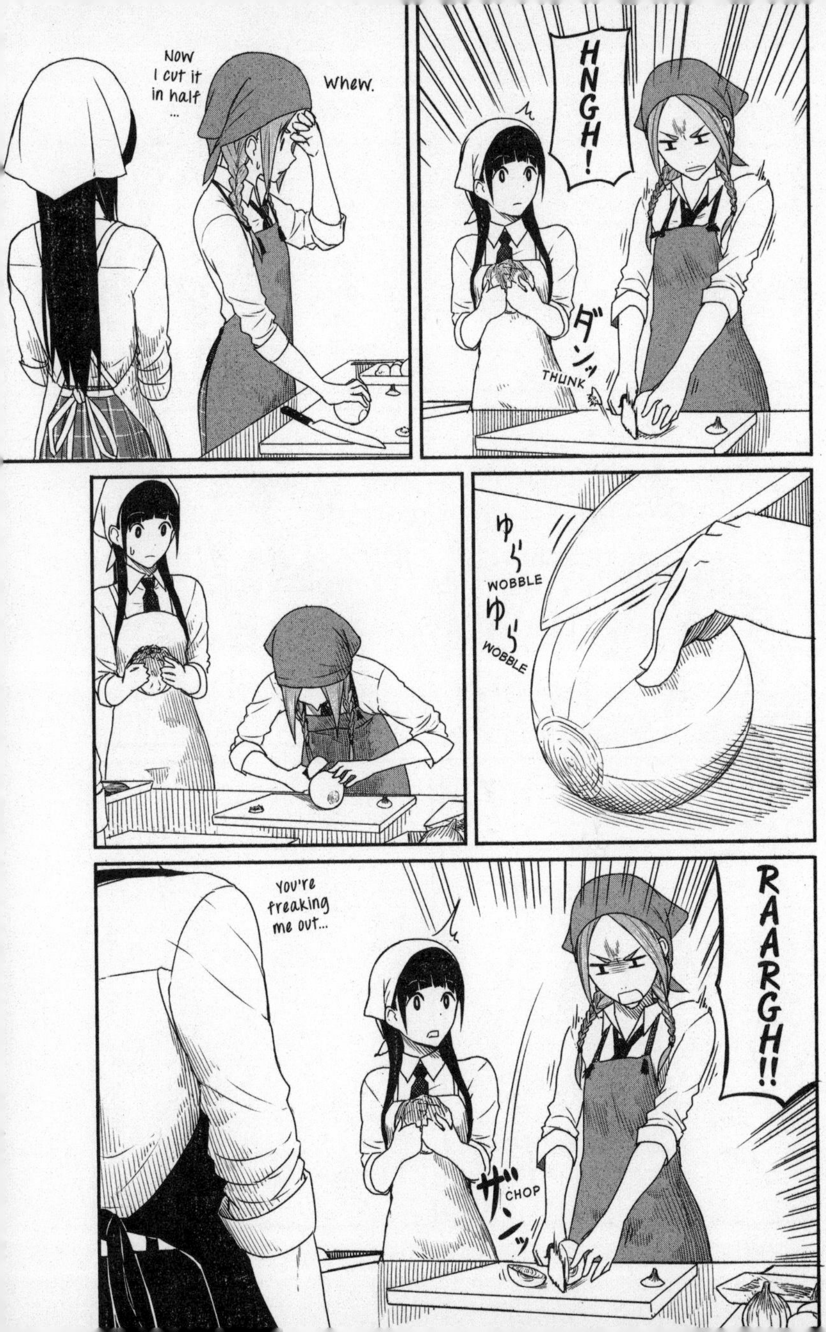
HNGH!
ダンッ
THUNK
Whew.
Now I cut it in half ...
ゆら
WOBBLE
ゆら
WOBBLE
RAARGH!!
You're freaking me out...
ザンッ
CHOP

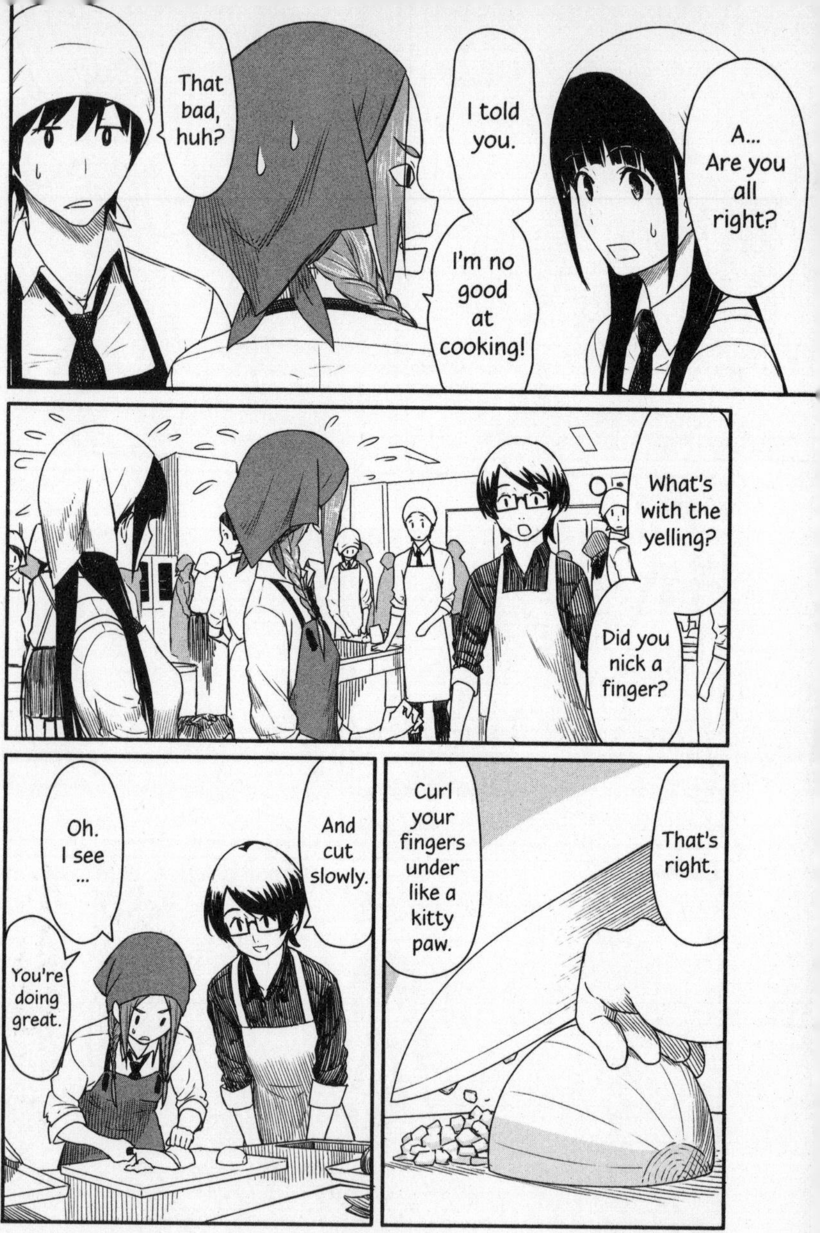
A... Are you all right?
I told you.
I'm no good at cooking!
That bad, huh?
What's with the yelling?
Did you nick a finger?
That's right.
Curl your fingers under like a kitty paw.
And cut slowly.
Oh. I see ...
You're doing great.

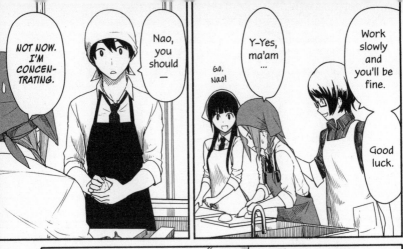

Work slowly and you'll be fine.
Good luck.
Y-Yes, ma'am ...
GO, NAO!
Nao, you should —
NOT NOW. I'M CONCEN-TRATING.
SHKK
シャク
シャク
SHKK
生もの解凍
ガパ
KPOP
Huh? You're using the micro-wave?
Yup.
ヴー
VREEEE
If you warm up an onion in the microwave before you cut it...

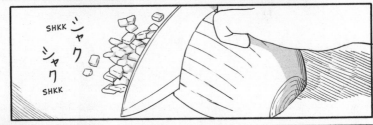

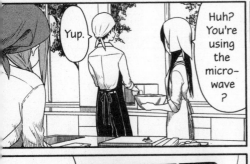

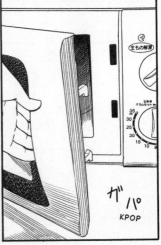

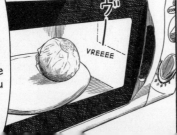

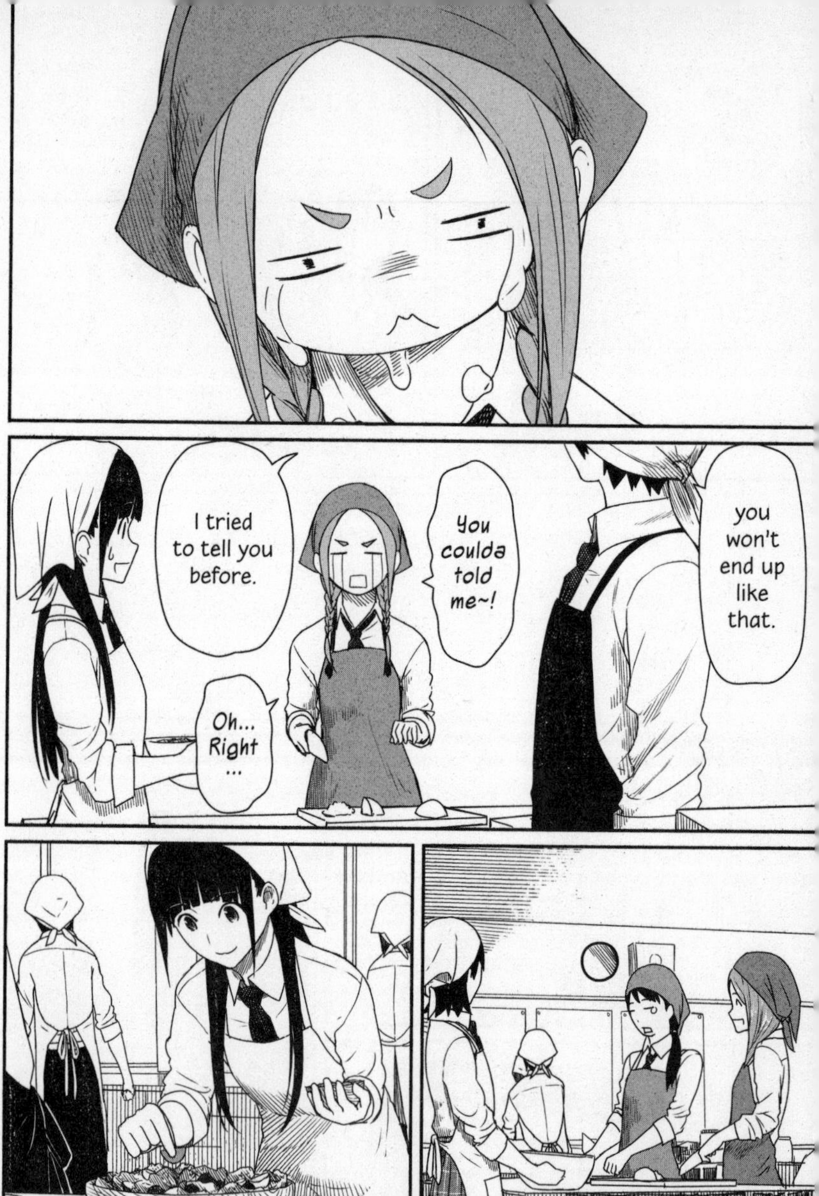
you won't end up like that.
You coulda told me~!
I tried to tell you before.
Oh... Right ...

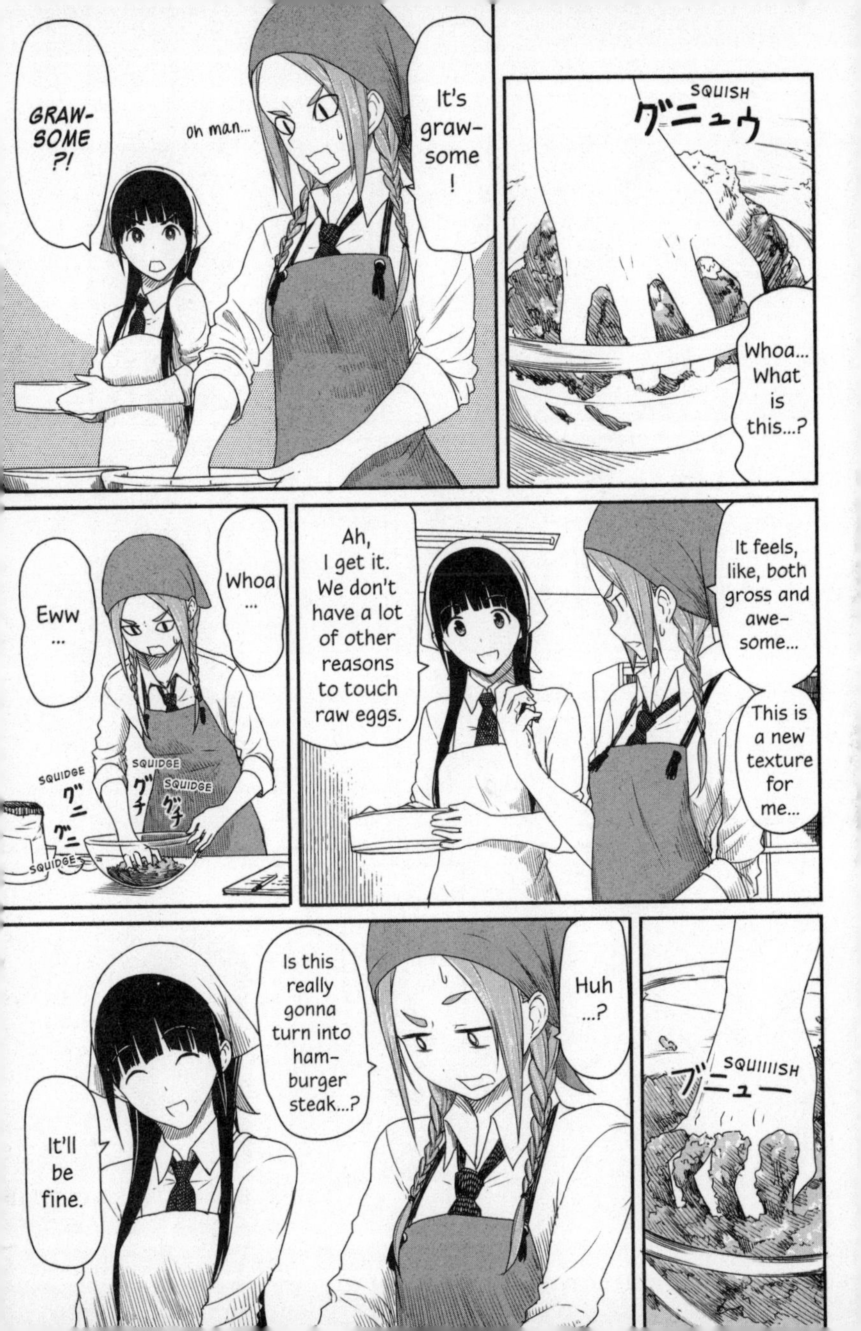
SQUISH
グニュウ
Whoa... What is this...?
It's graw-some!
oh man...
GRAW-SOME?!
It feels, like, both gross and awe-some...
This is a new texture for me...
Ah, I get it. We don't have a lot of other reasons to touch raw eggs.
Whoa...
Eww...
SQUIDGE
グチ
SQUIDGE
グチ
SQUIDGE
グニ
グニ
SQUIDGE
SQUIIIISH
ブニュー
Huh...?
Is this really gonna turn into ham-burger steak...?
It'll be fine.

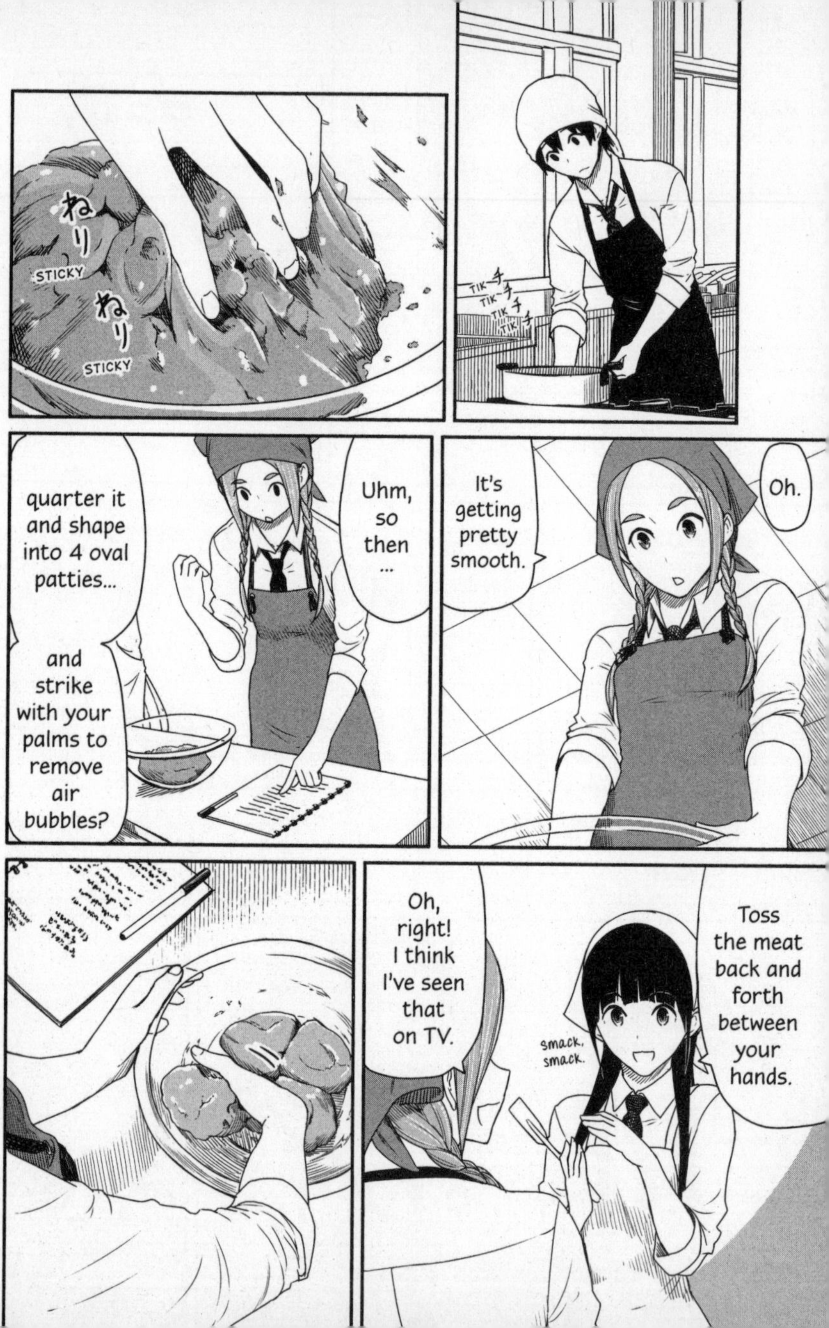

TIK チ
TIK チ
TIK チ
TIK チ
ねり
STICKY
ねり
STICKY
Oh.
It's getting pretty smooth.
Uhm, so then ...
quarter it and shape into 4 oval patties...
and strike with your palms to remove air bubbles?
Toss the meat back and forth between your hands.
Oh, right! I think I've seen that on TV.
smack, smack.

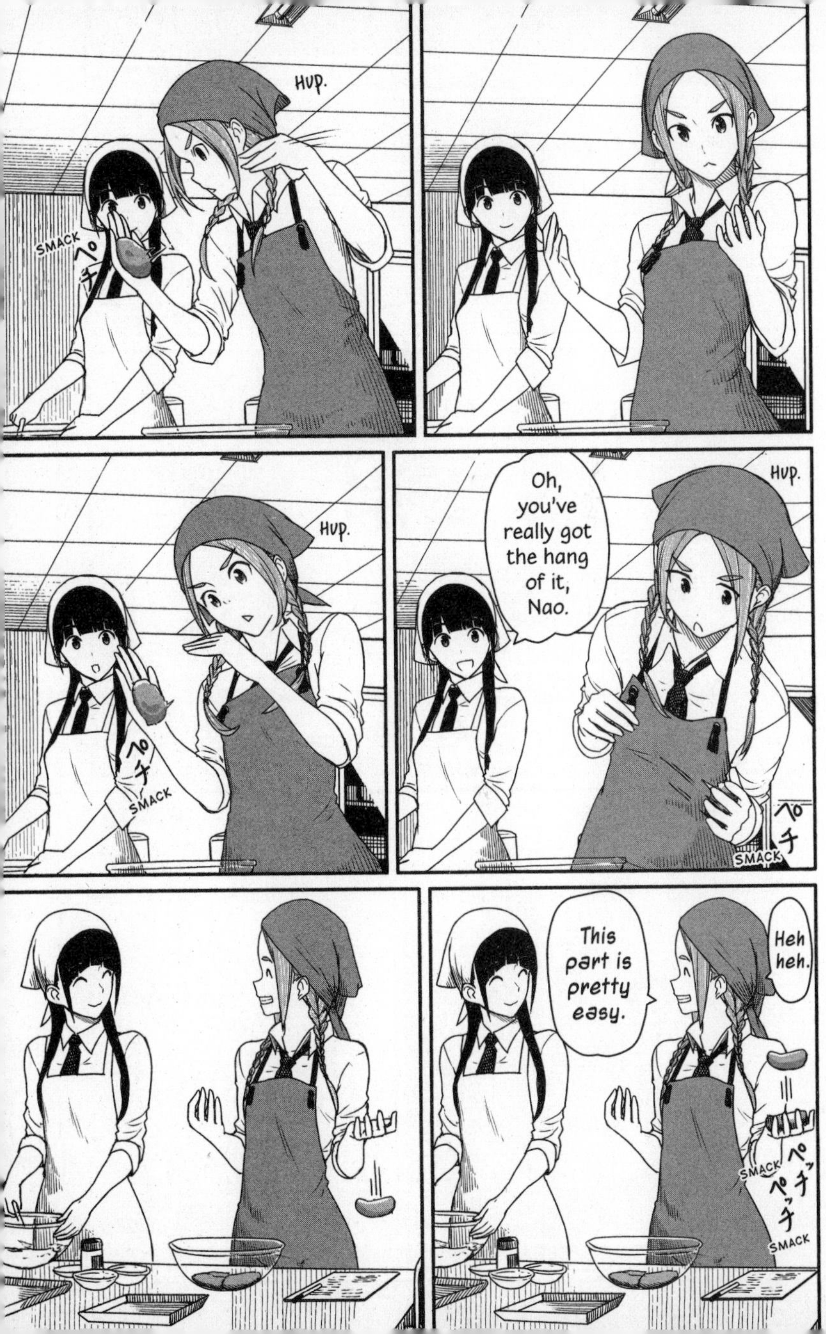

Hup.
SMACK
ペチ
Hup.
Oh, you've really got the hang of it, Nao.
ペチ
SMACK
Hup.
ペチ
SMACK
Heh heh.
This part is pretty easy.
SMACK
ペッチ
ペッチ
SMACK

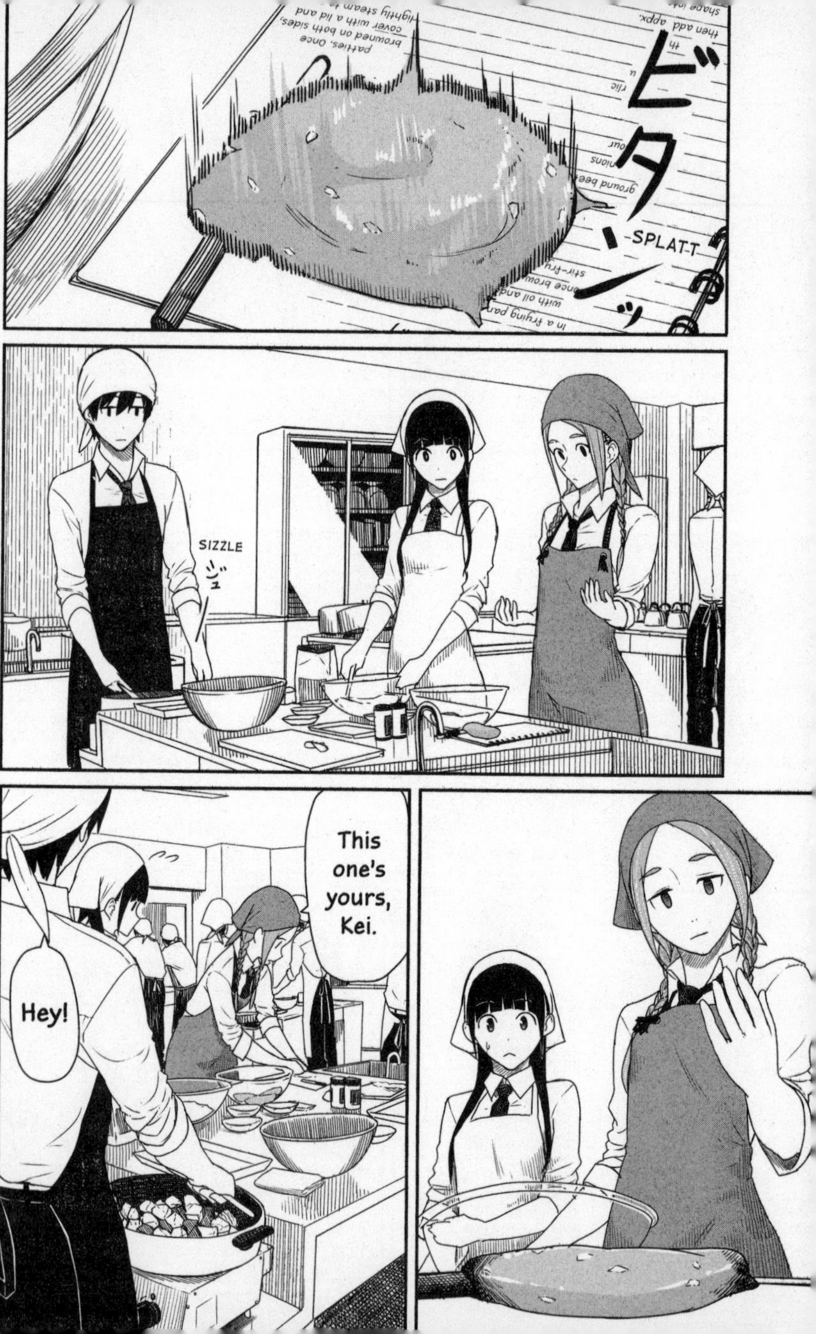

ビタッ
SPLAT-T
patties. Once
browned on both sides,
cover with a lid and
with oil and
In a frying pan
SIZZLE
ジュ
This one's yours, Kei.
Hey!

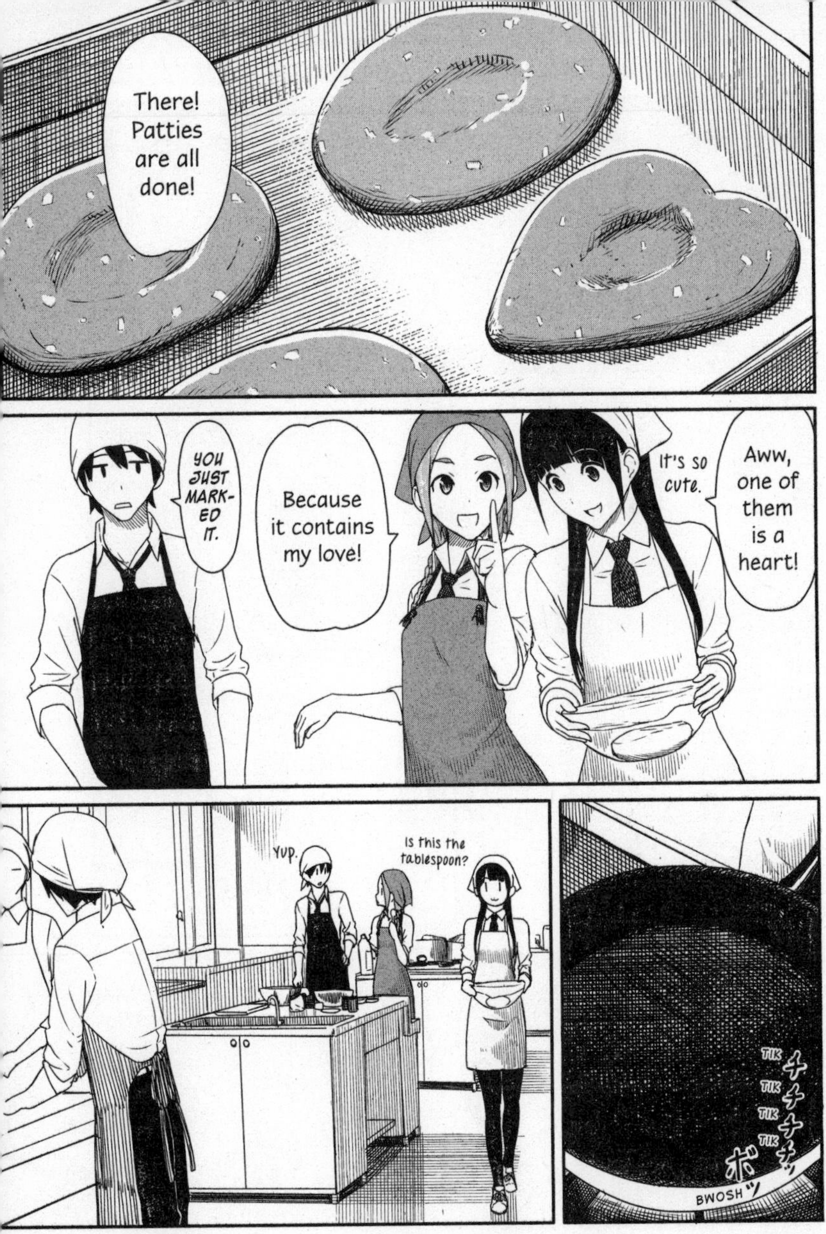
There! Patties are all done!
Aww, one of them is a heart!
It's so cute.
Because it contains my love!
YOU JUST MARK-ED IT.
TIK TIK TIK TIK
BWOSH
Is this the tablespoon?
Yup.

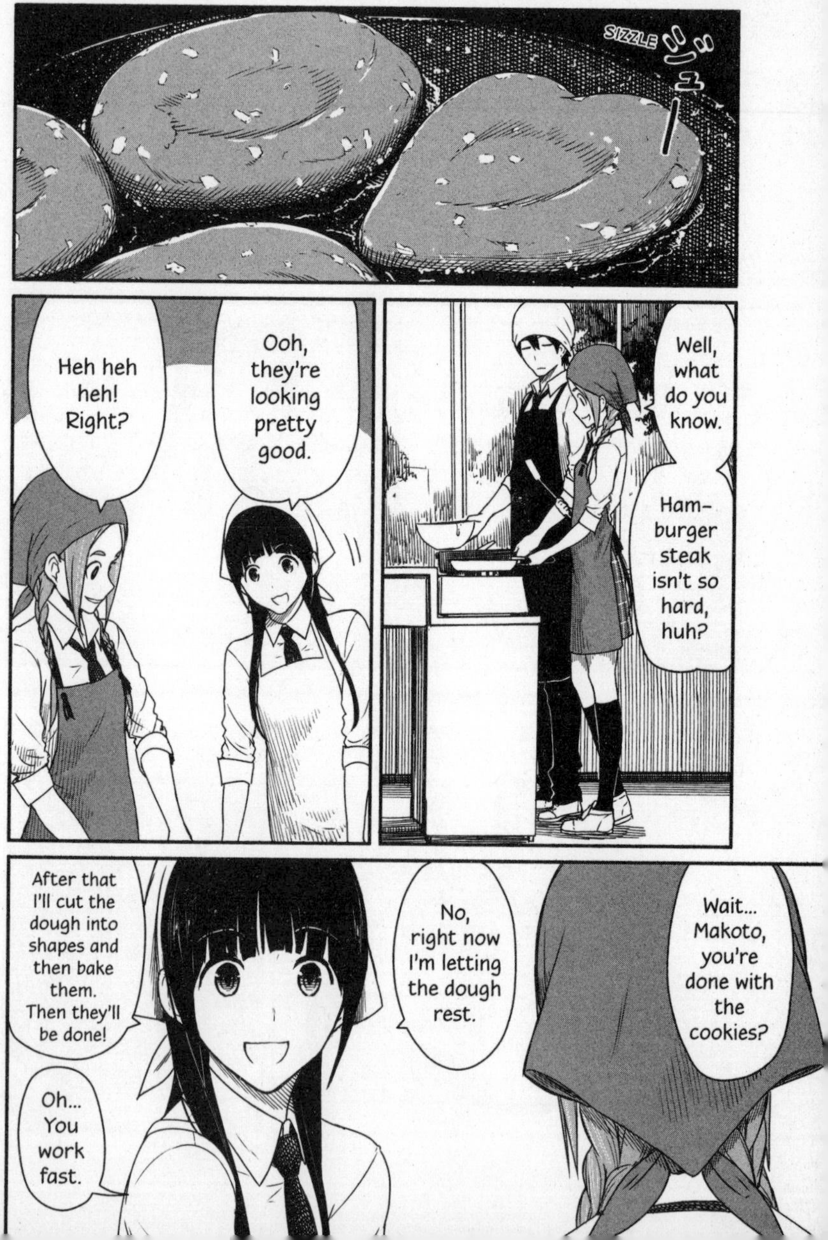
SIZZLE
Well, what do you know.
Ham-burger steak isn't so hard, huh?
Ooh, they're looking pretty good.
Heh heh heh! Right?
Wait... Makoto, you're done with the cookies?
No, right now I'm letting the dough rest.
After that I'll cut the dough into shapes and then bake them. Then they'll be done!
Oh... You work fast.

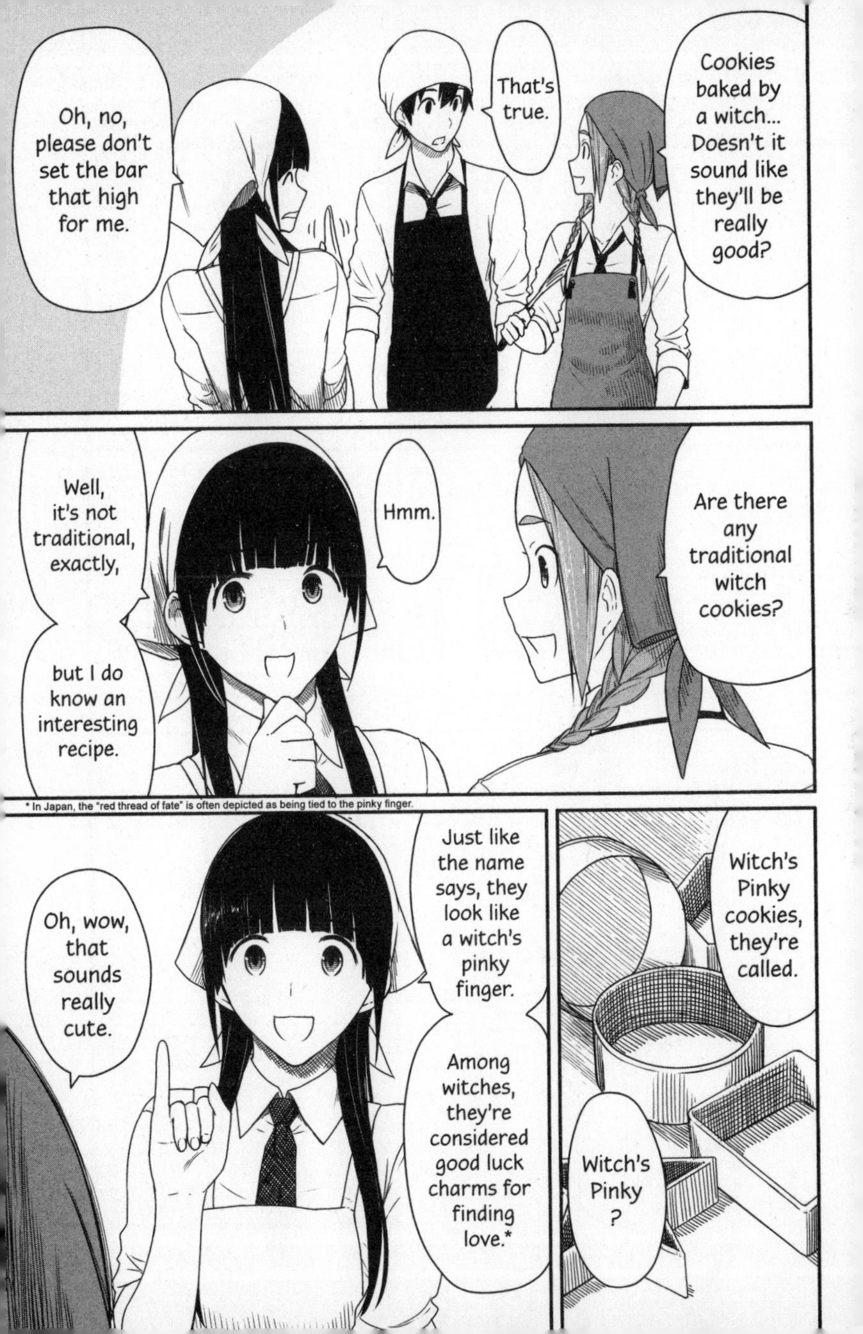
Cookies baked by a witch... Doesn't it sound like they'll be really good?
That's true.
Oh, no, please don't set the bar that high for me.
Are there any traditional witch cookies?
Hmm.
Well, it's not traditional, exactly,
but I do know an interesting recipe.
Witch's Pinky cookies, they're called.
Witch's Pinky?
Just like the name says, they look like a witch's pinky finger.
Among witches, they're considered good luck charms for finding love.*
Oh, wow, that sounds really cute.

* In Japan, the "red thread of fate" is often depicted as being tied to the pinky finger.

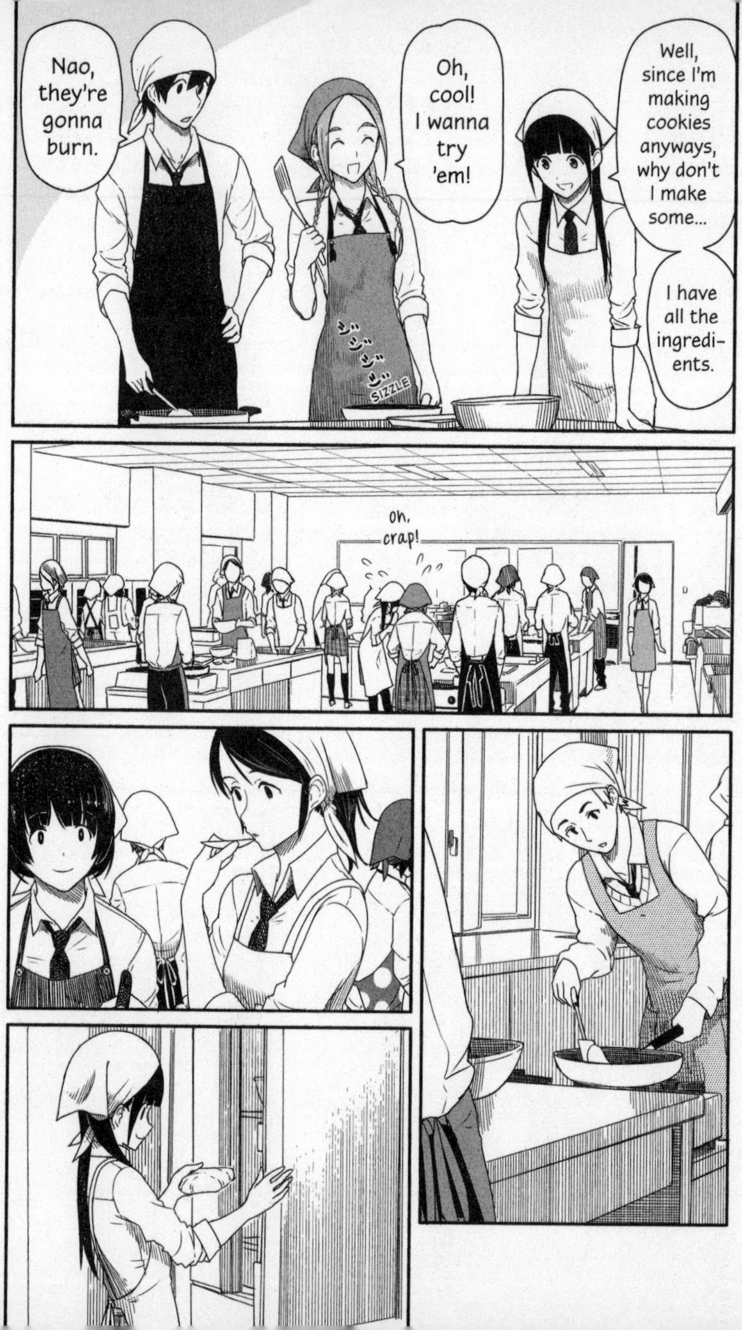
Well, since I'm making cookies anyways, why don't I make some...
I have all the ingredients.
Oh, cool! I wanna try 'em!
ジジジジ SIZZLE
Nao, they're gonna burn.
Oh, crap!

There.

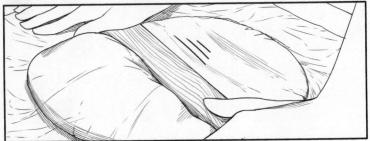

Nice work.

Ooh.

VOILÀ.

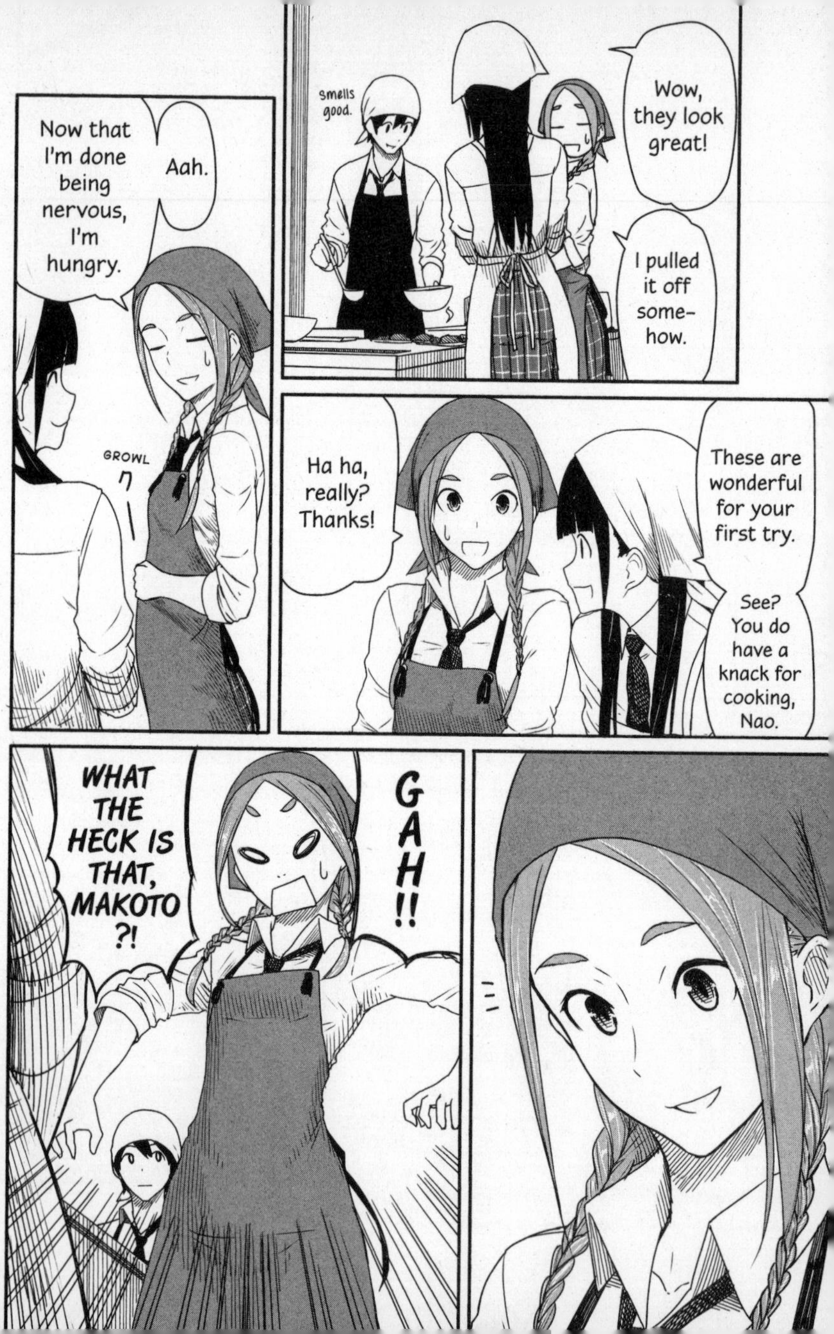
Wow, they look great!
smells good.
I pulled it off somehow.
These are wonderful for your first try.
See? You do have a knack for cooking, Nao.
Ha ha, really? Thanks!
Aah.
Now that I'm done being nervous, I'm hungry.
GROWL
GAH!!
WHAT THE HECK IS THAT, MAKOTO?!

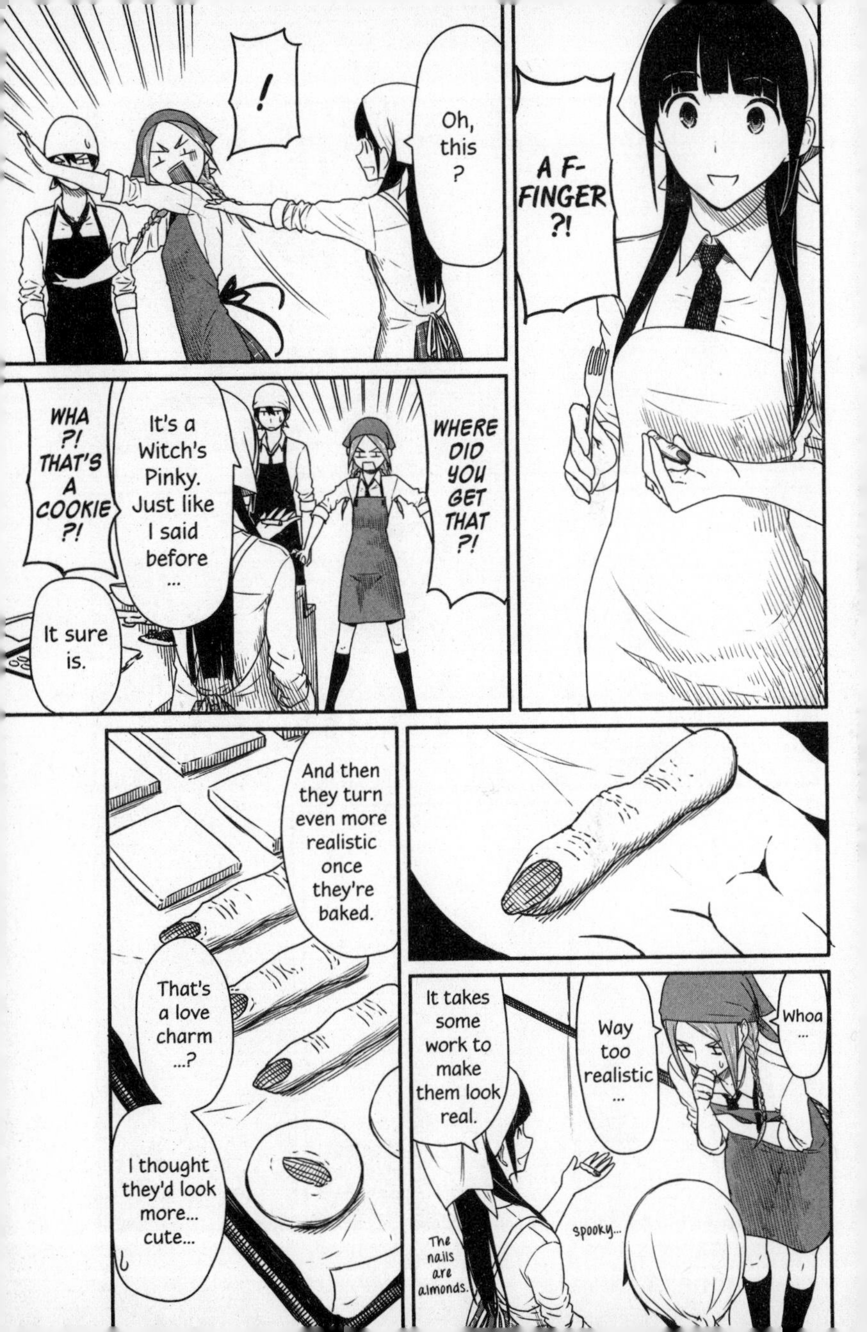
A F-FINGER ?!
Oh, this ?
!
WHERE DID YOU GET THAT ?!
It's a Witch's Pinky. Just like I said before ...
WHA ?! THAT'S A COOKIE ?!
It sure is.
Whoa ...
Way too realistic ...
It takes some work to make them look real.
spooky...
The nails are almonds.
And then they turn even more realistic once they're baked.
That's a love charm ...?
I thought they'd look more... cute...

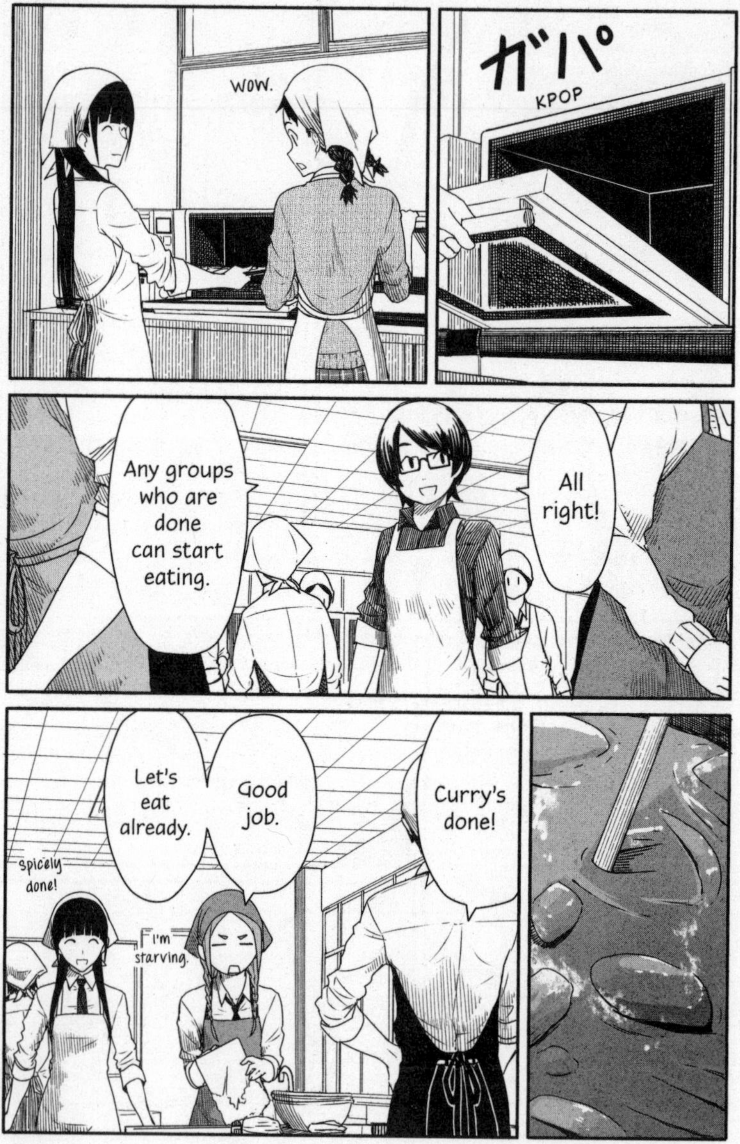
ガパ
KPOP
WOW.
All right!
Any groups who are done can start eating.
Curry's done!
Good job.
Let's eat already.
spicely done!
I'm starving.

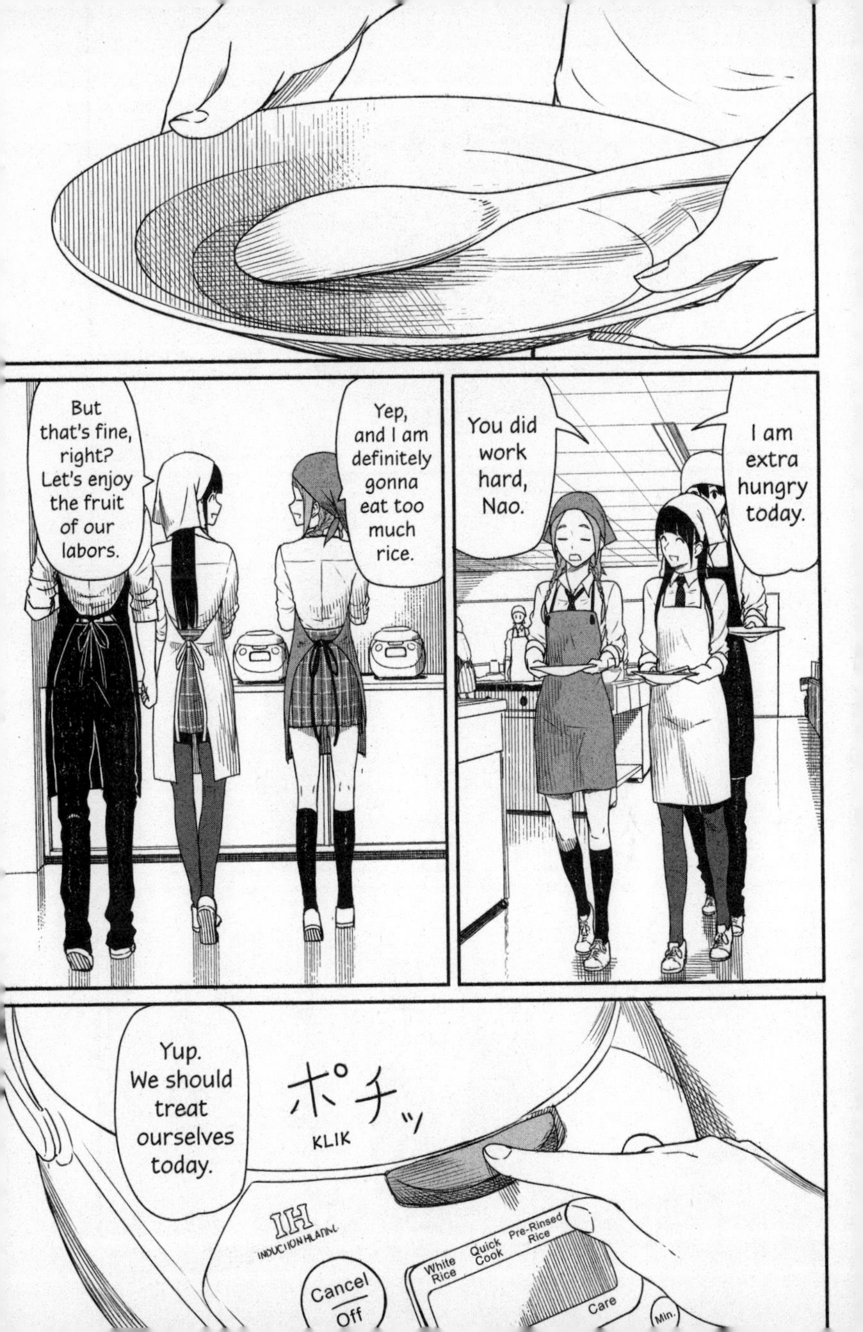
I am extra hungry today.
You did work hard, Nao.
Yep, and I am definitely gonna eat too much rice.
But that's fine, right? Let's enjoy the fruit of our labors.
ポチッ
KLIK
Yup. We should treat ourselves today.
IH
Pre-Rinsed Rice
Quick Cook
White Rice
Cancel
Off
Care
Min.

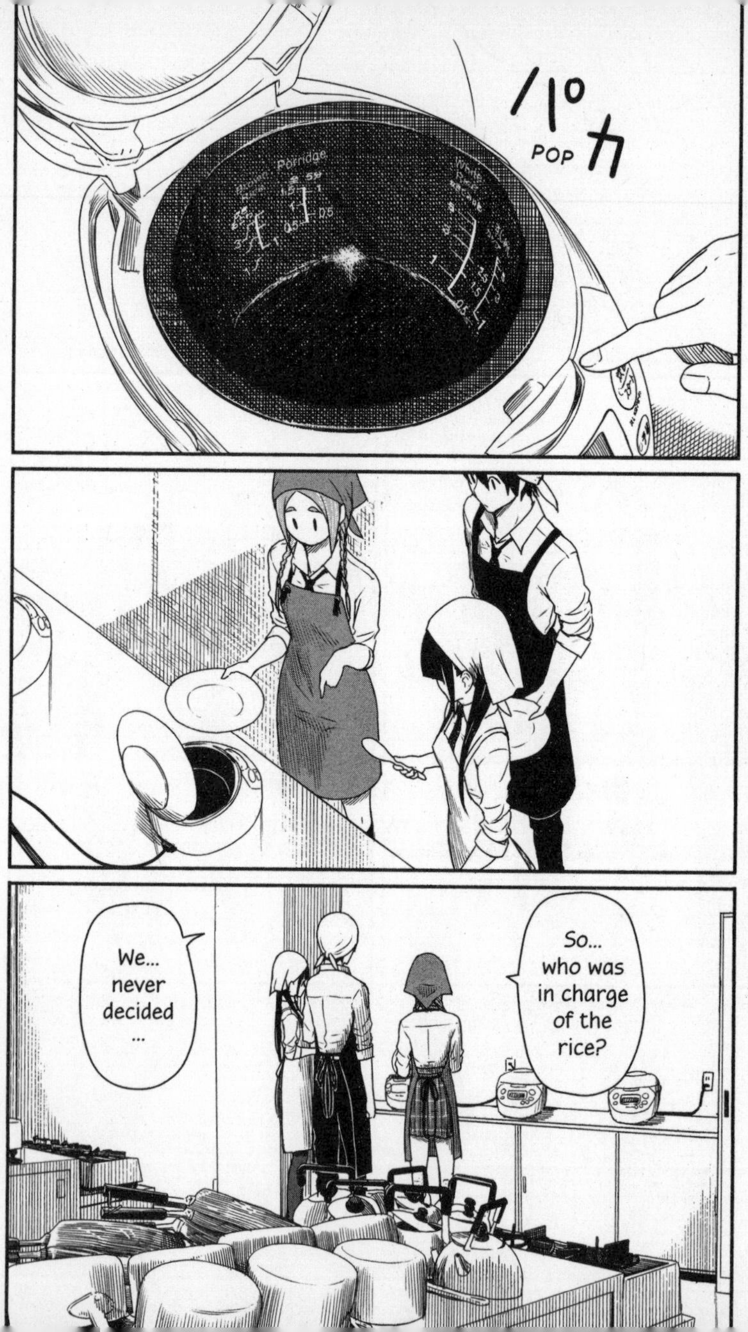
パカ
POP
Porridge
So... who was in charge of the rice?
We... never decided ...

Do you
have any
leftover
rice?

Uhm...

Flying
Witch

Chapter 21
Witches and Bees Don't Get Along

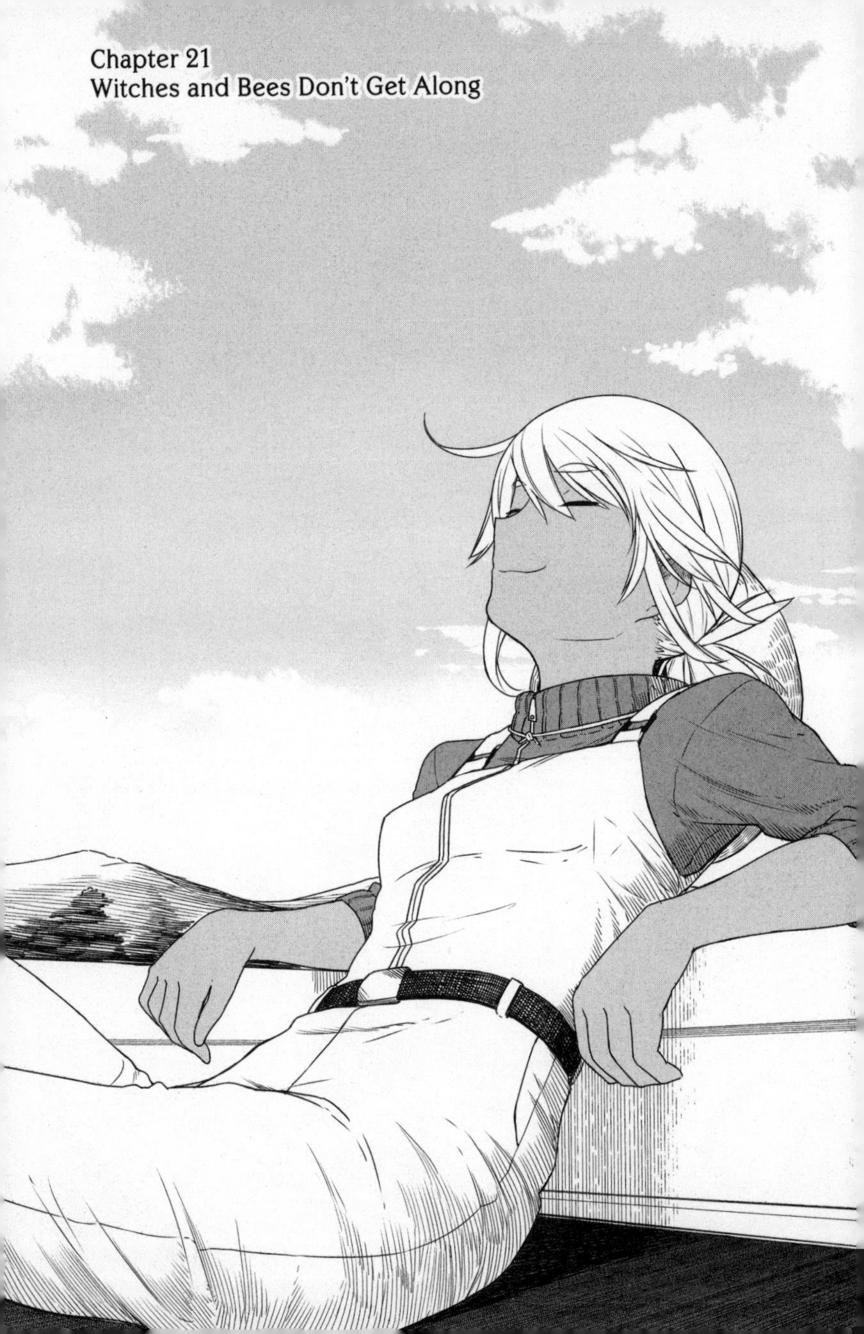

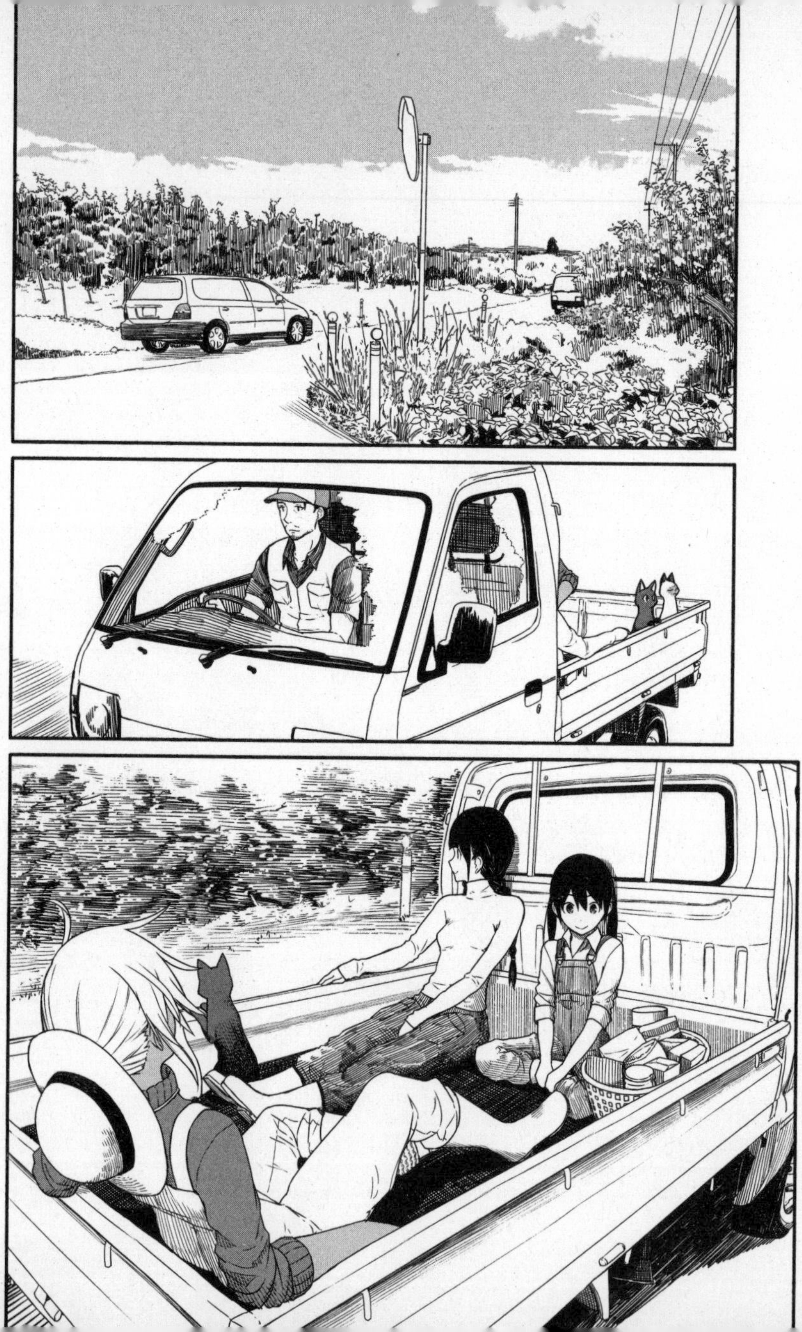

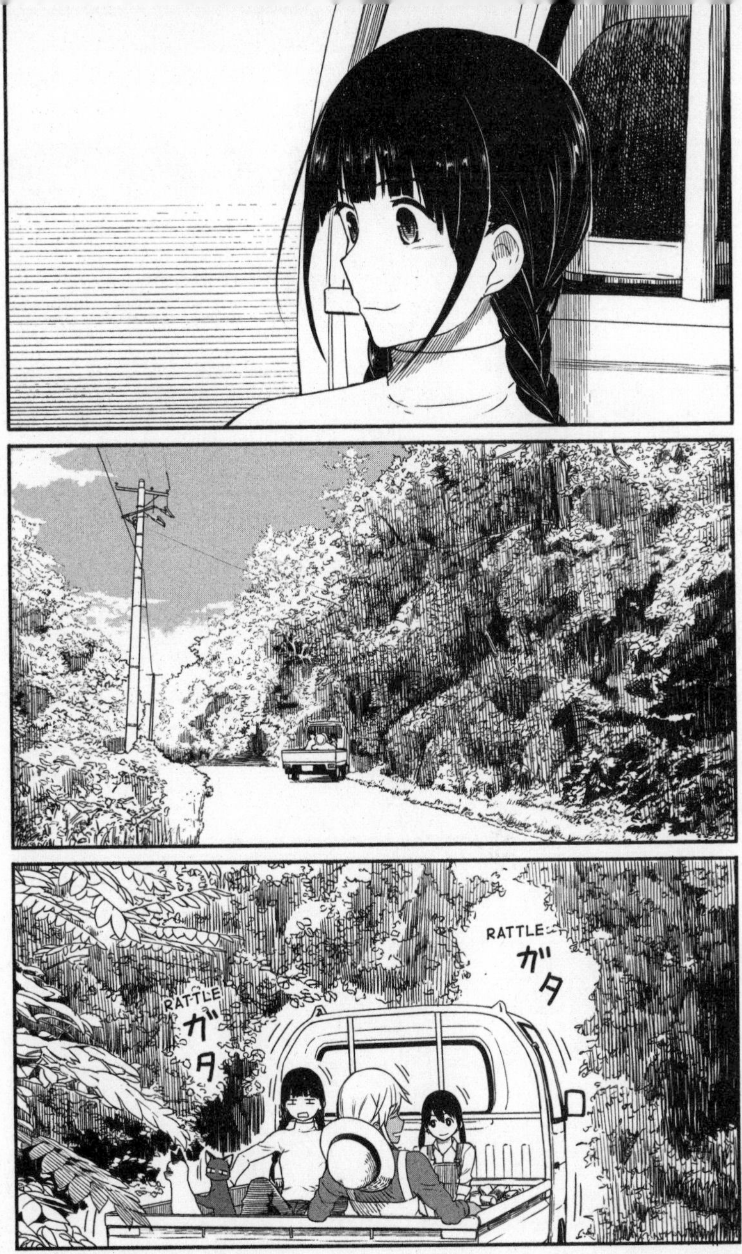
RATTLE
ガタ
RATTLE
ガタ

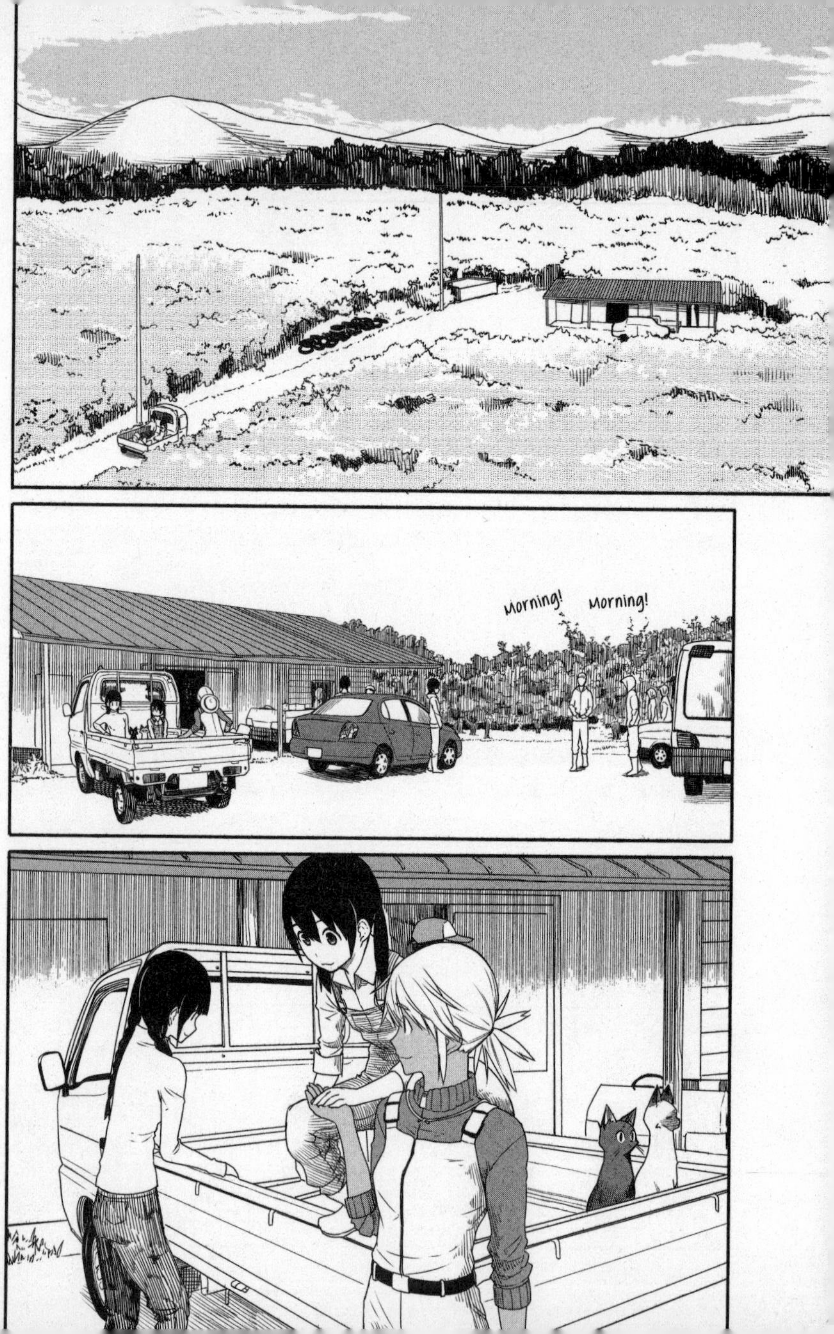
Morning!
Morning!

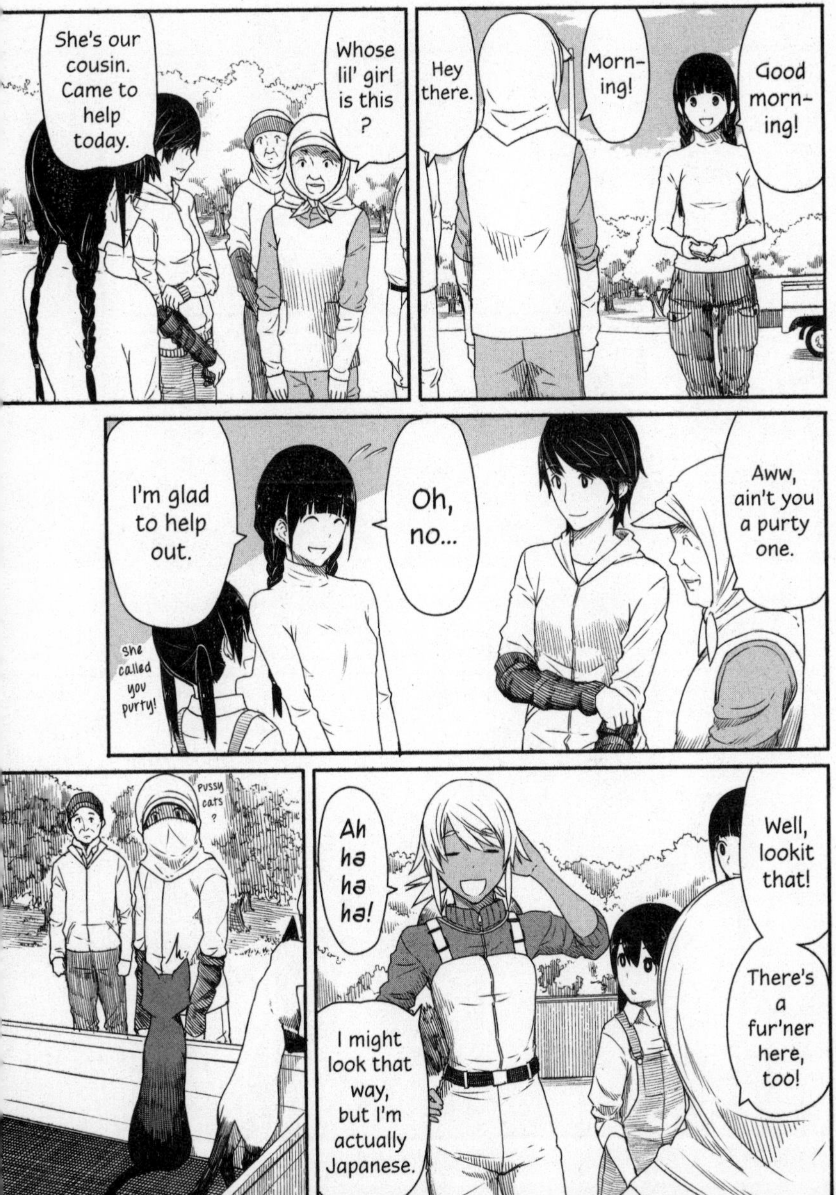
Good morn-ing!
Morn-ing!
Hey there.
Whose lil' girl is this ?
She's our cousin. Came to help today.
Aww, ain't you a purty one.
Oh, no...
I'm glad to help out.
she called you purty!
Well, lookit that!
There's a fur'ner here, too!
Ah ha ha ha!
I might look that way, but I'm actually Japanese.
pussy cats ?

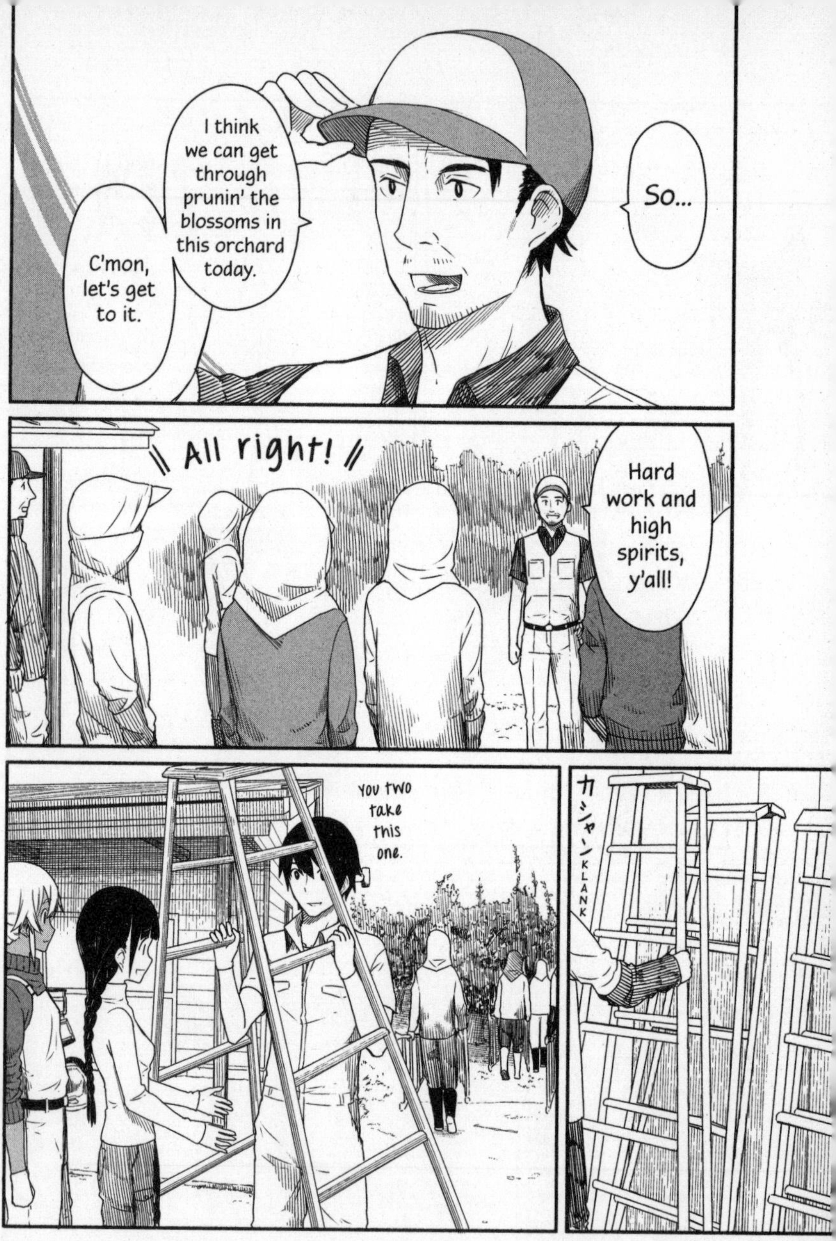
So...
I think we can get through prunin' the blossoms in this orchard today.
C'mon, let's get to it.
Hard work and high spirits, y'all!
All right!
カシャン KLANK
You two take this one.

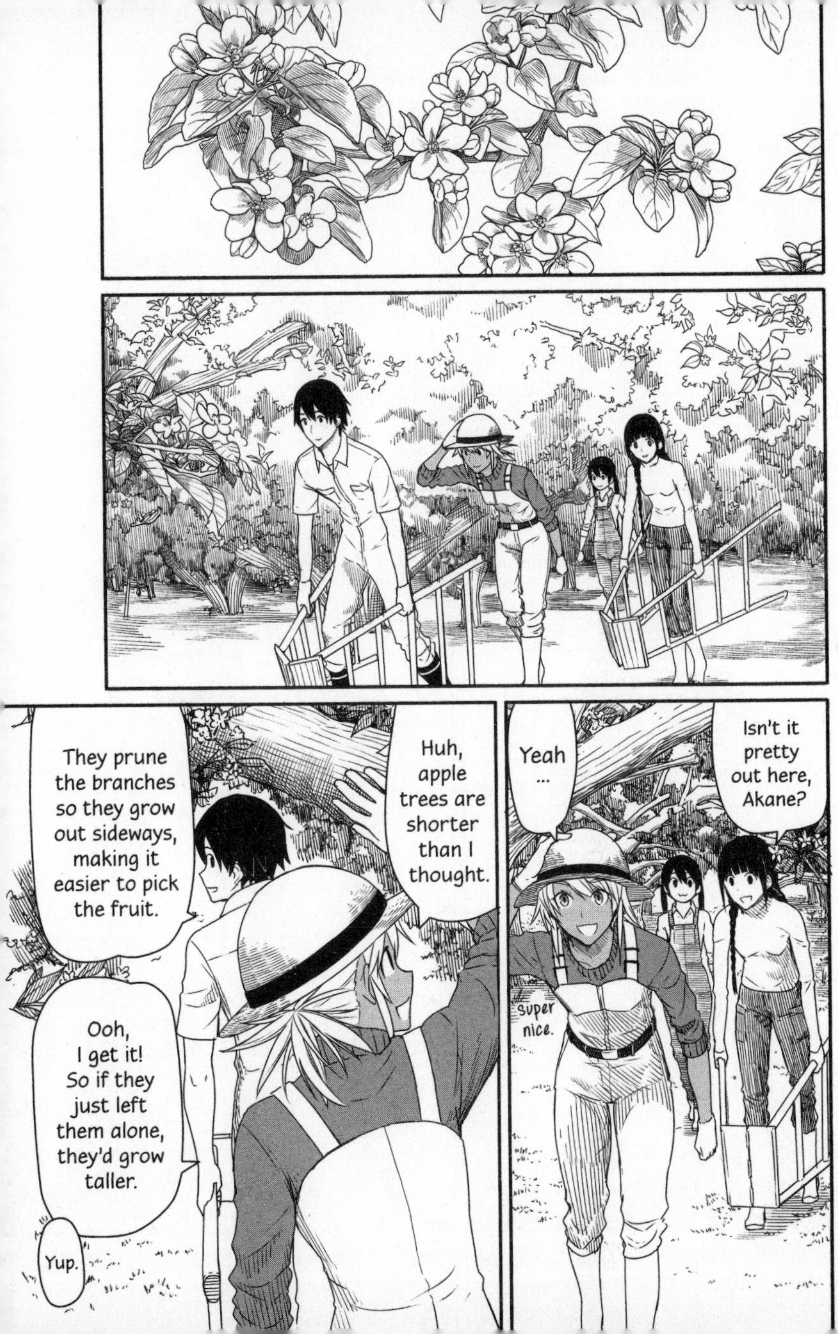
Isn't it pretty out here, Akane?
Yeah ...
super nice.
Huh, apple trees are shorter than I thought.
They prune the branches so they grow out sideways, making it easier to pick the fruit.
Ooh, I get it! So if they just left them alone, they'd grow taller.
Yup.

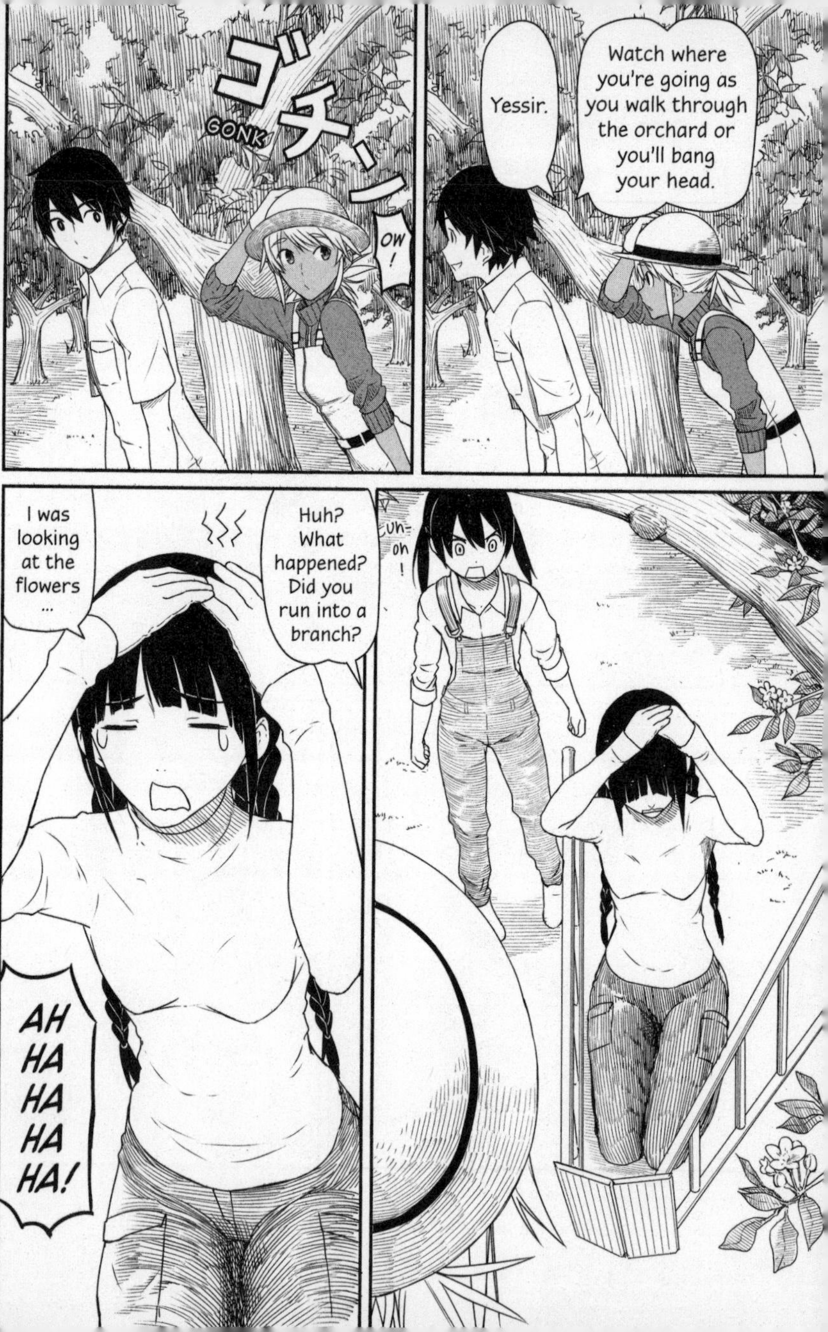
Watch where you're going as you walk through the orchard or you'll bang your head.
Yessir.
ゴチーン
GONK
OW!
uh-oh!
Huh? What happened? Did you run into a branch?
I was looking at the flowers ...
AH HA HA HA HA HA!

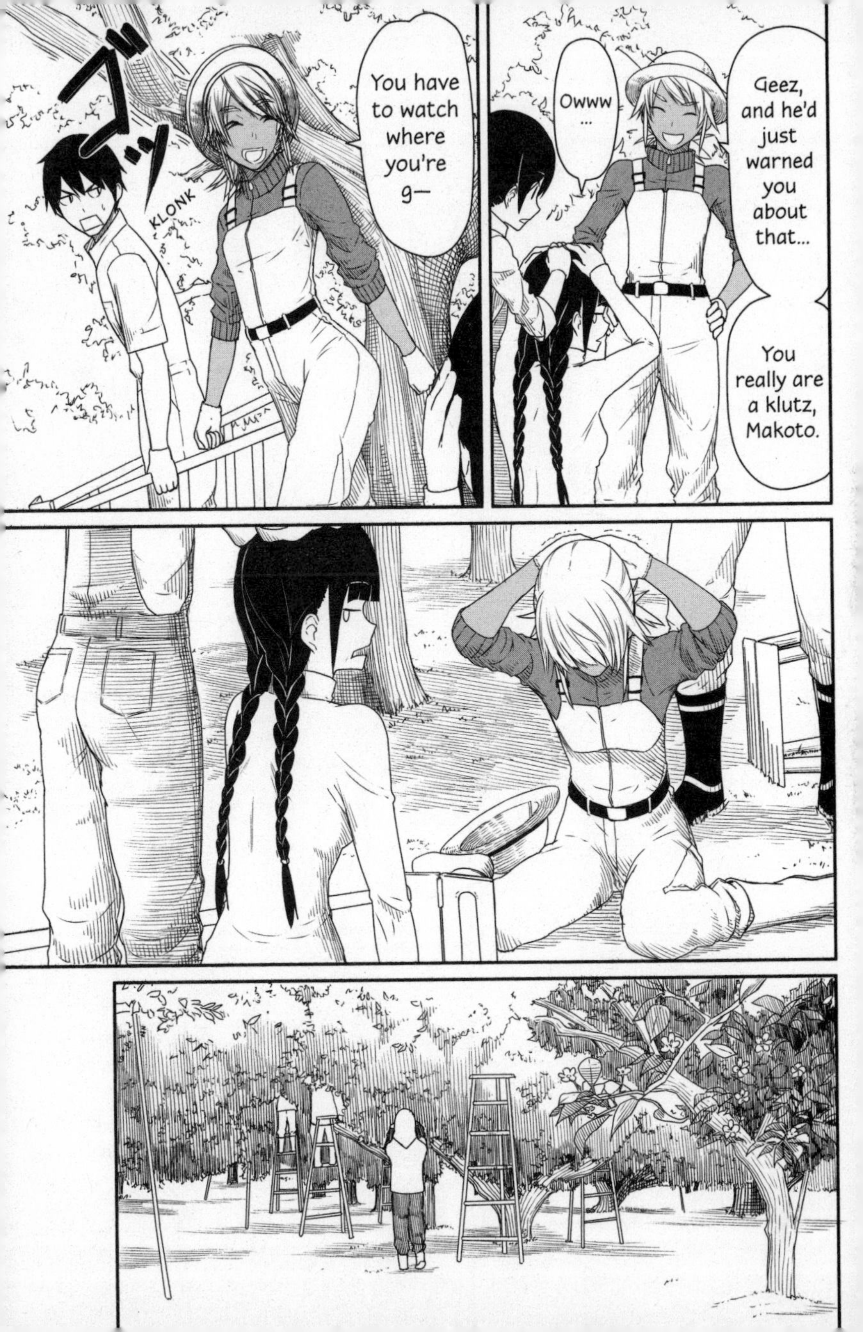
ゴッ
KLONK
You have to watch where you're g—
Owww ...
Geez, and he'd just warned you about that...
You really are a klutz, Makoto.

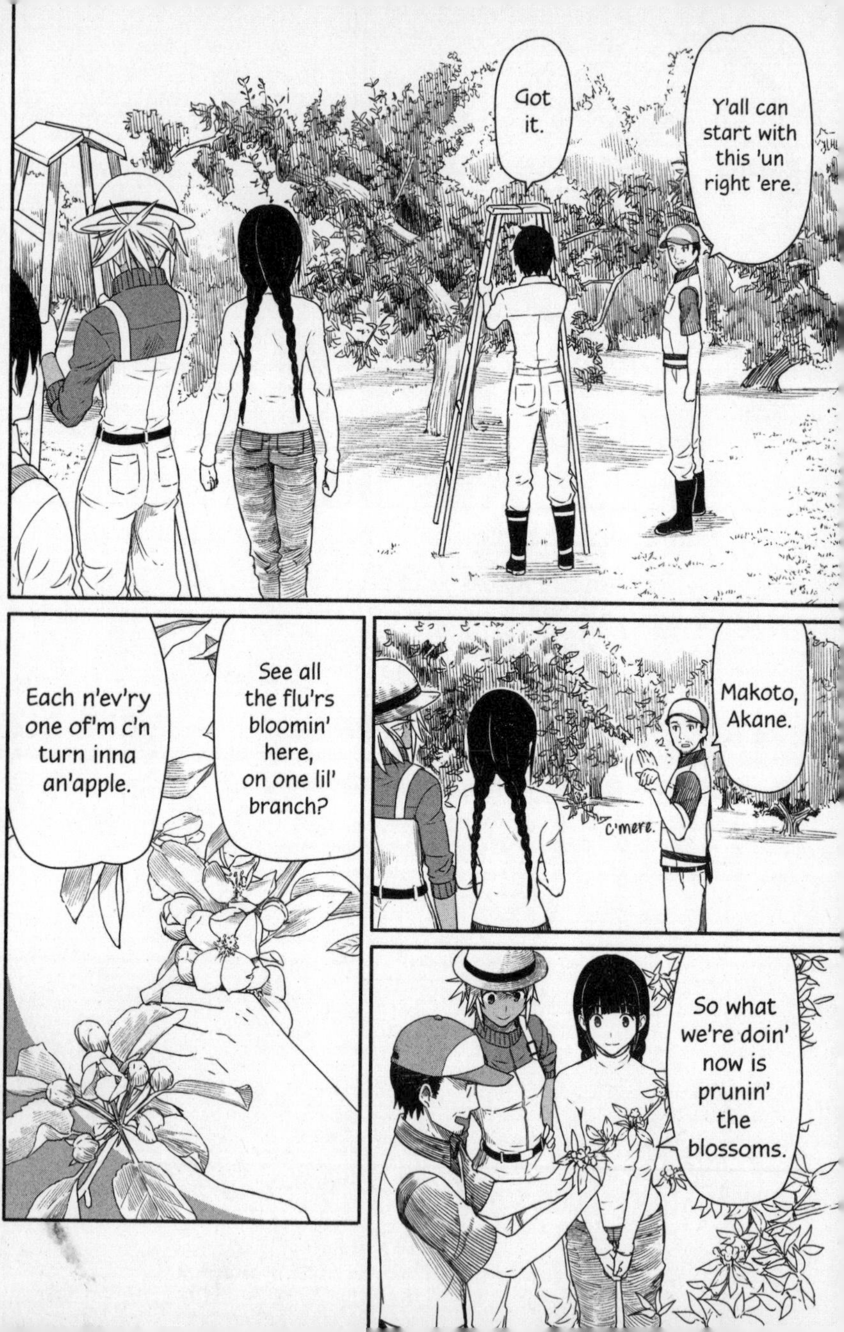
Y'all can start with this 'un right 'ere.
Got it.
Makoto, Akane.
C'mere.
So what we're doin' now is prunin' the blossoms.
See all the flu'rs bloomin' here, on one lil' branch?
Each n'ev'ry one of'm c'n turn inna an'apple.

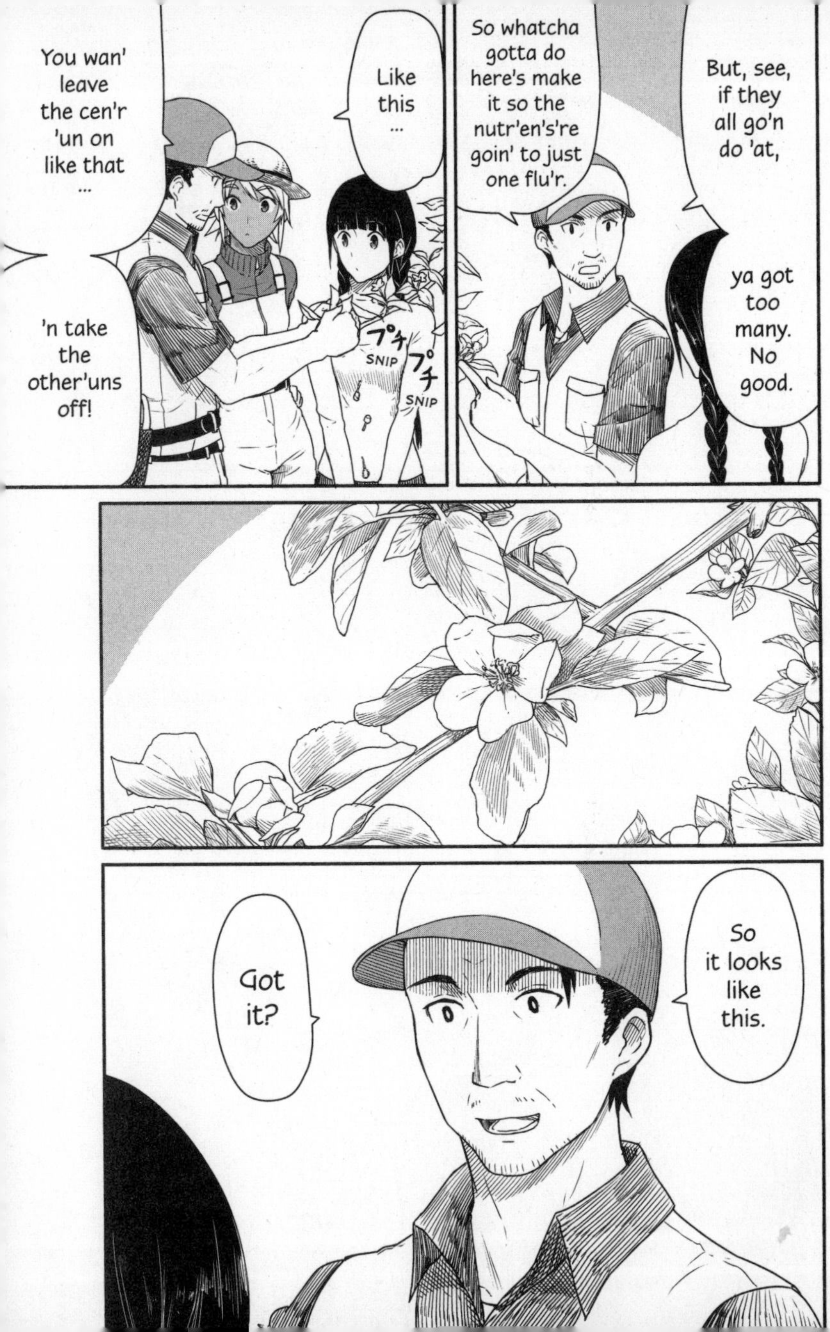
But, see, if they all go'n do 'at,
ya got too many. No good.
So whatcha gotta do here's make it so the nutr'en's're goin' to just one flu'r.
Like this ...
You wan' leave the cen'r 'un on like that ...
'n take the other'uns off!
プチ SNIP
プチ SNIP
So it looks like this.
Got it?

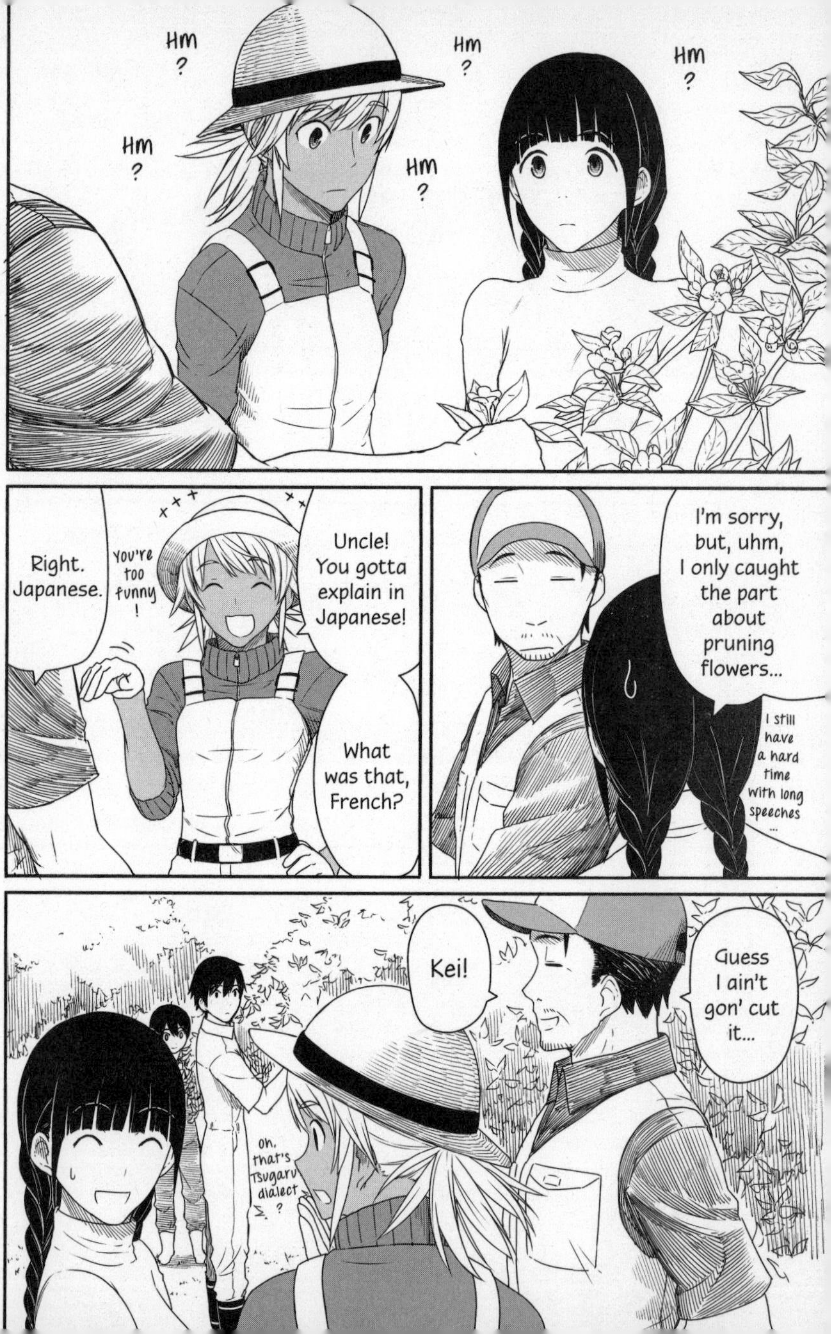
Hm ?
Hm ?
Hm ?
Hm ?
Hm ?
I'm sorry, but, uhm, I only caught the part about pruning flowers...
I still have a hard time with long speeches ...
Uncle! You gotta explain in Japanese!
What was that, French?
You're too funny !
Right. Japanese.
Guess I ain't gon' cut it...
Kei!
Oh, that's Tsugaru dialect ?

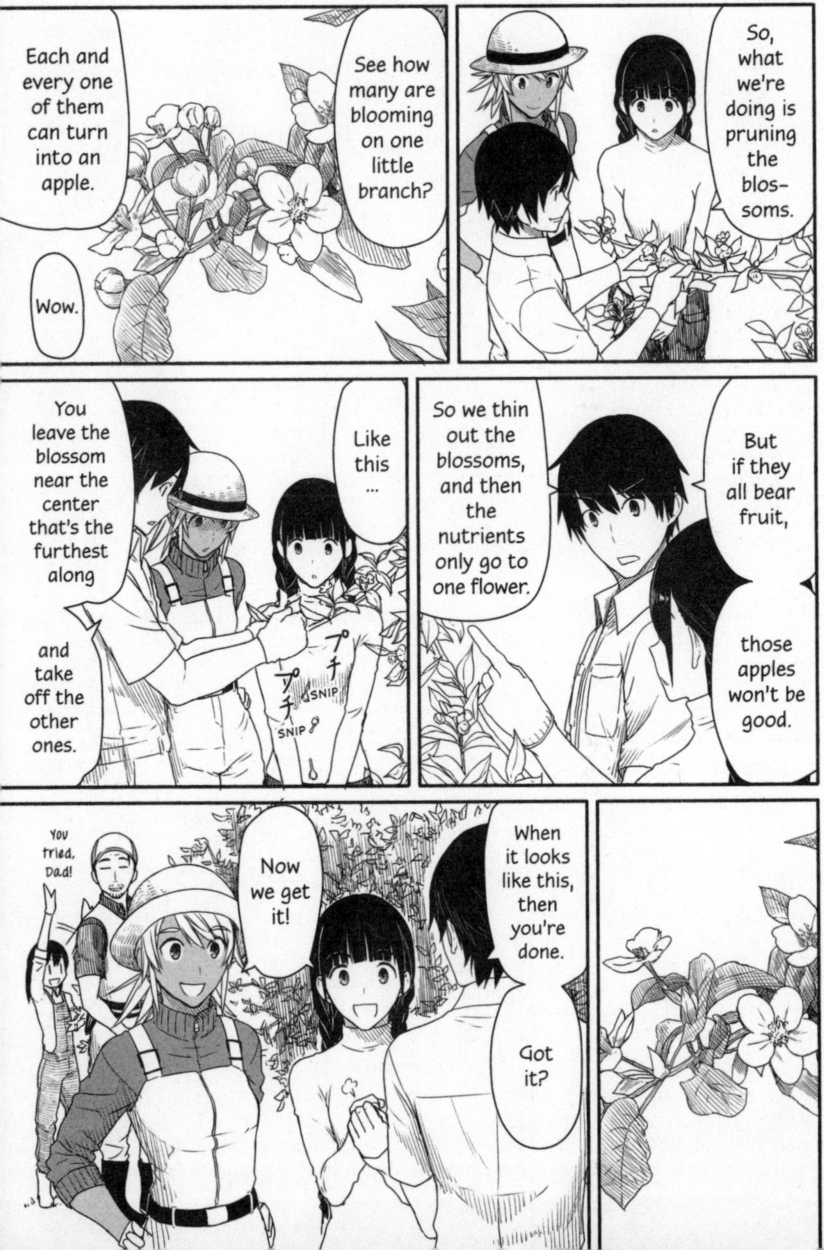
So, what we're doing is pruning the blos-soms.
See how many are blooming on one little branch?
Each and every one of them can turn into an apple.
Wow.
But if they all bear fruit,
those apples won't be good.
So we thin out the blossoms, and then the nutrients only go to one flower.
Like this ...
You leave the blossom near the center that's the furthest along
プチ
SNIP
プチ
SNIP
and take off the other ones.
When it looks like this, then you're done.
Got it?
Now we get it!
You tried, Dad!

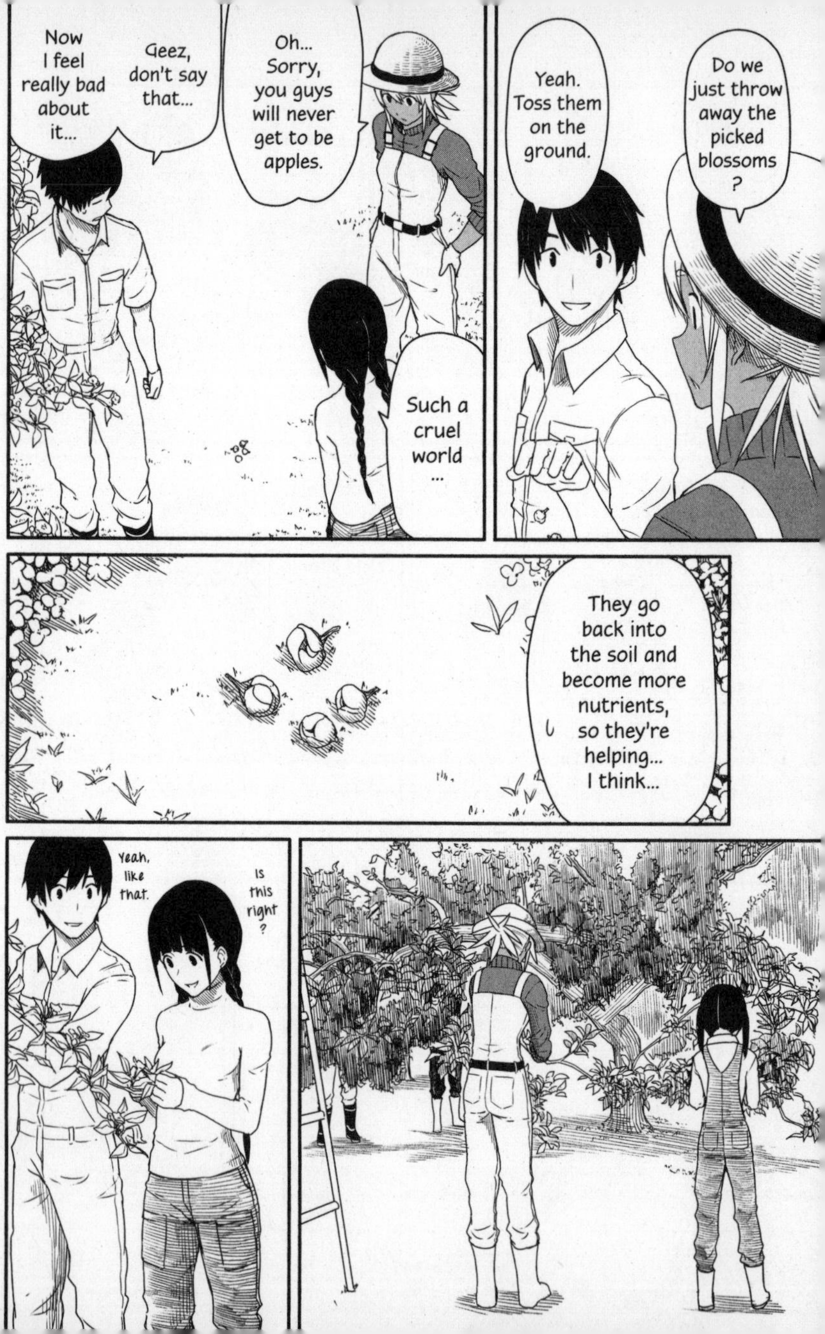

Do we just throw away the picked blossoms ?
Yeah. Toss them on the ground.
Oh... Sorry, you guys will never get to be apples.
Such a cruel world ...
Geez, don't say that...
Now I feel really bad about it...
They go back into the soil and become more nutrients, so they're helping... I think...
Is this right ?
Yeah, like that.

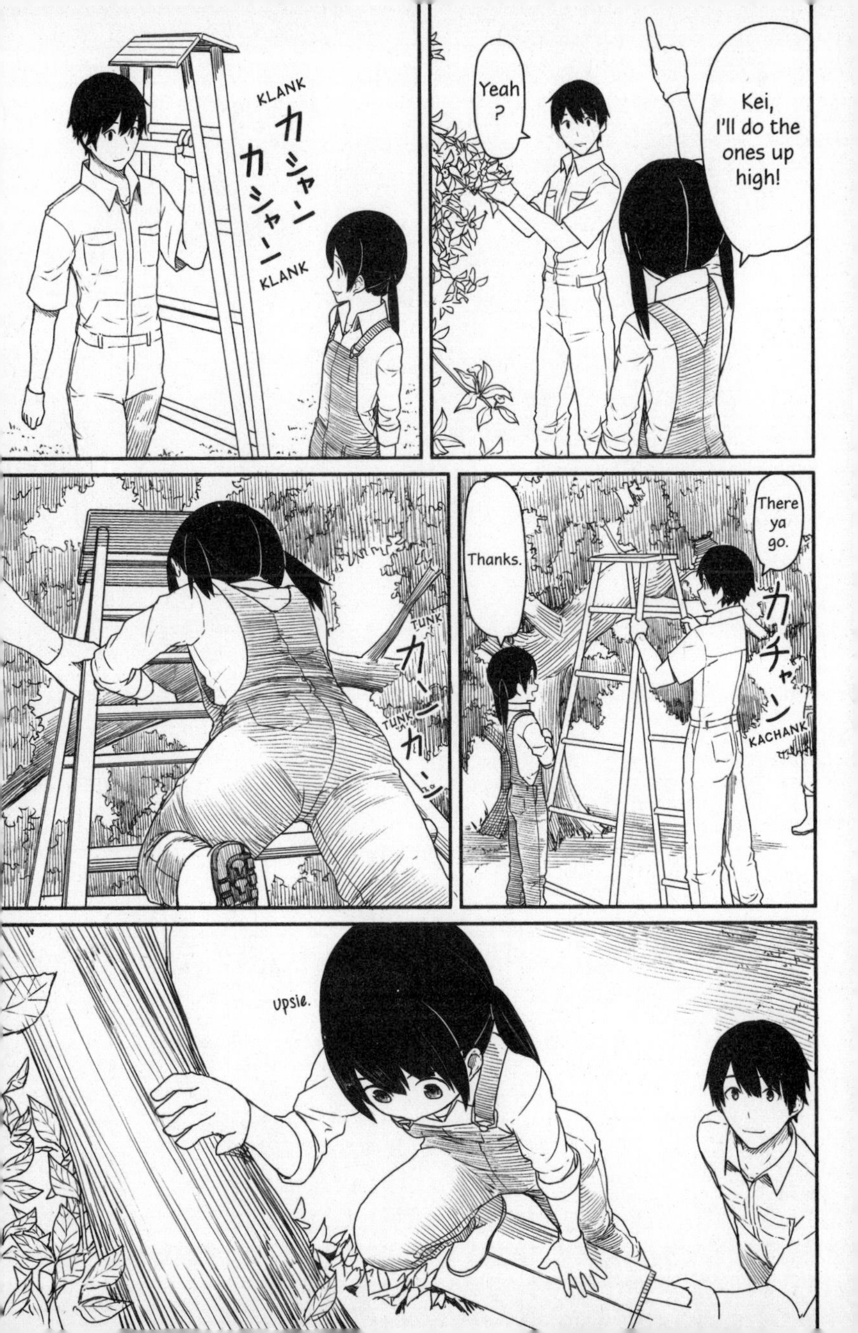
Kei, I'll do the ones up high!
Yeah?
カシャーン
KLANK
カシャーン
KLANK
There ya go.
カチャン
KACHANK
Thanks.
カーン
TUNK
カーン
TUNK
Upsie.

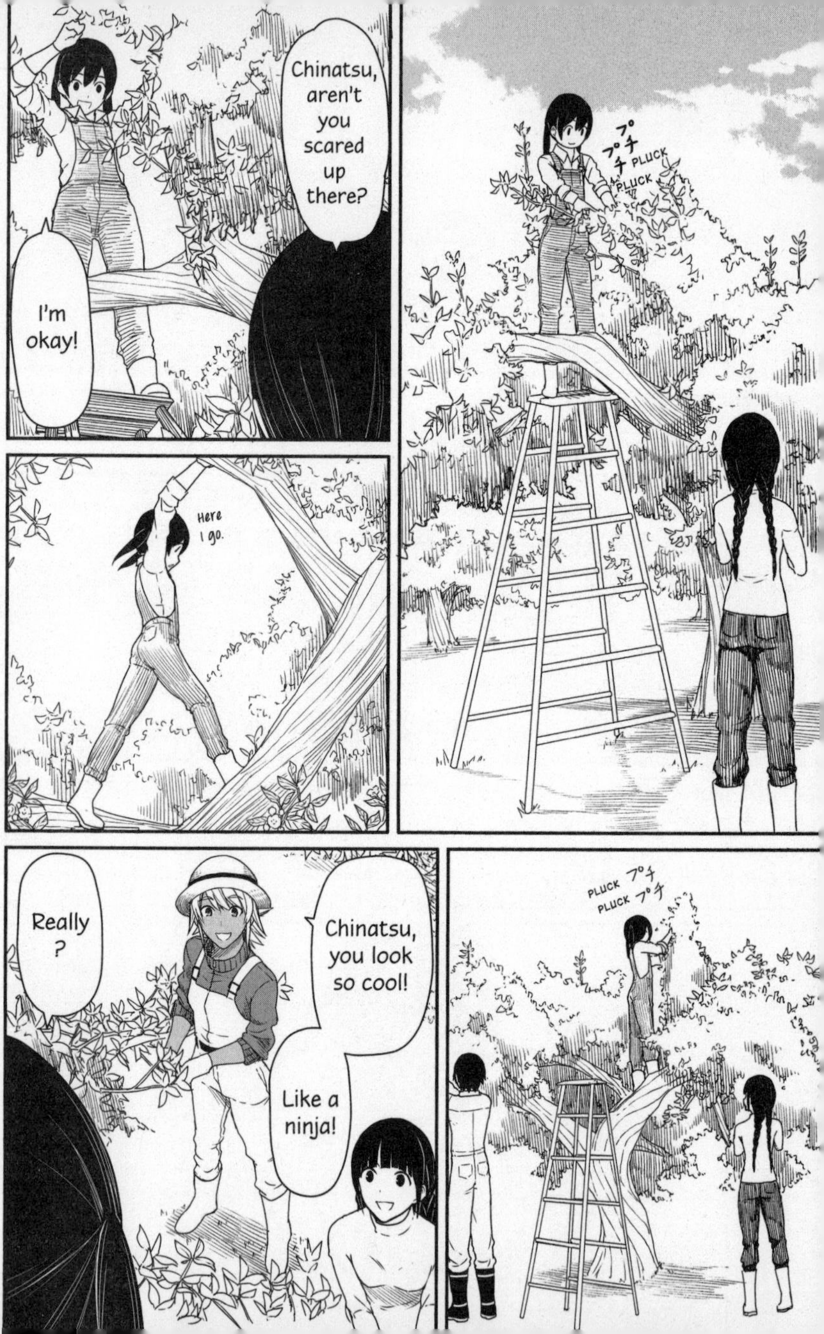
プチ
プチ
PLUCK
PLUCK
Chinatsu, aren't you scared up there?
I'm okay!
Here I go.
PLUCK プチ
PLUCK プチ
Chinatsu, you look so cool!
Like a ninja!
Really?

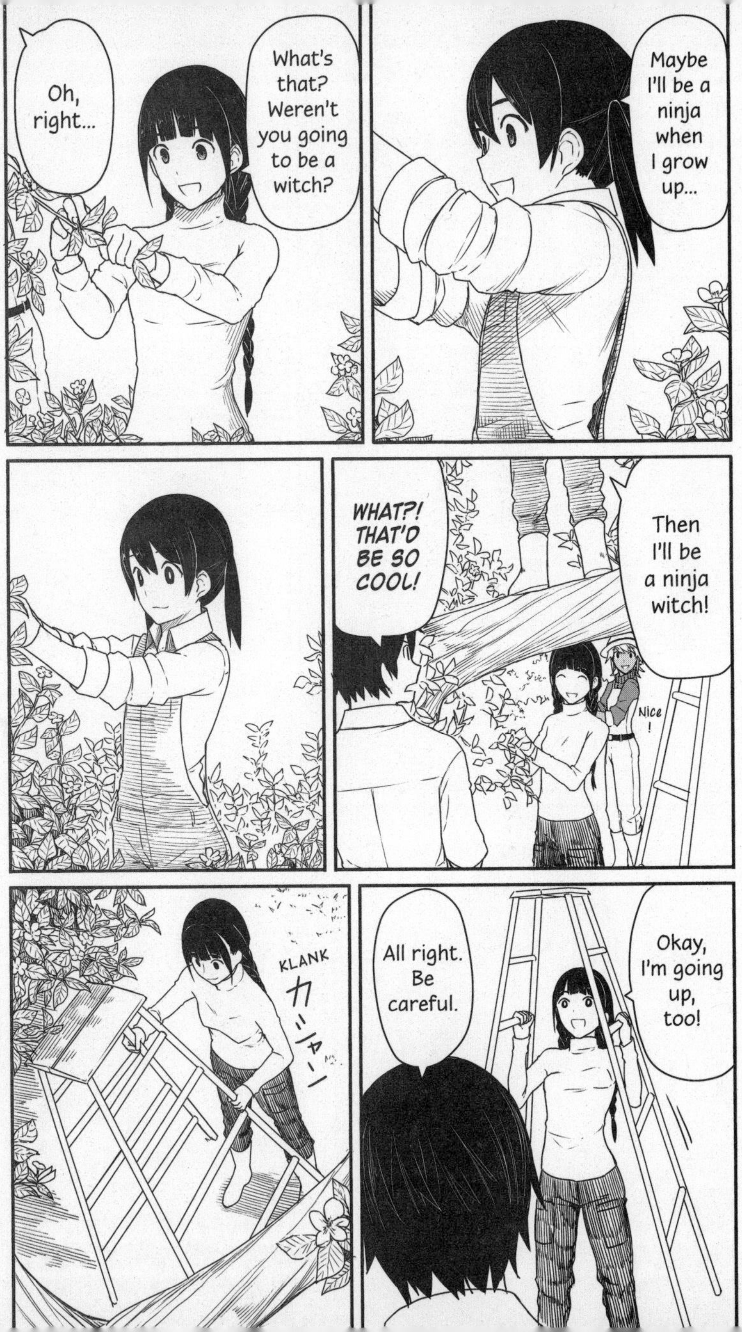
Maybe I'll be a ninja when I grow up...
What's that? Weren't you going to be a witch?
Oh, right...
Then I'll be a ninja witch!
WHAT?! THAT'D BE SO COOL!
Nice!
Okay, I'm going up, too!
All right. Be careful.
KLANK
カシャーン

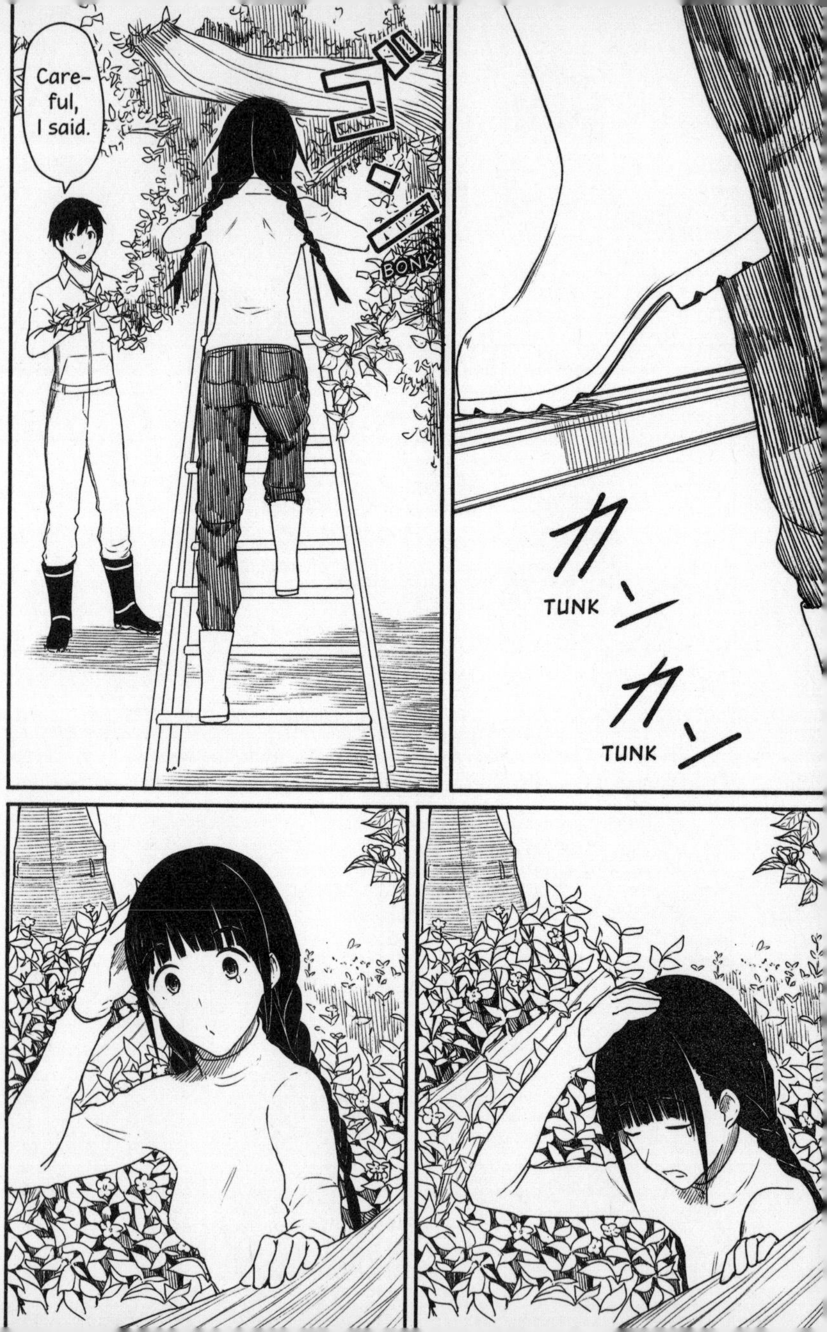
TUNK
TUNK
Careful, I said.
BONK

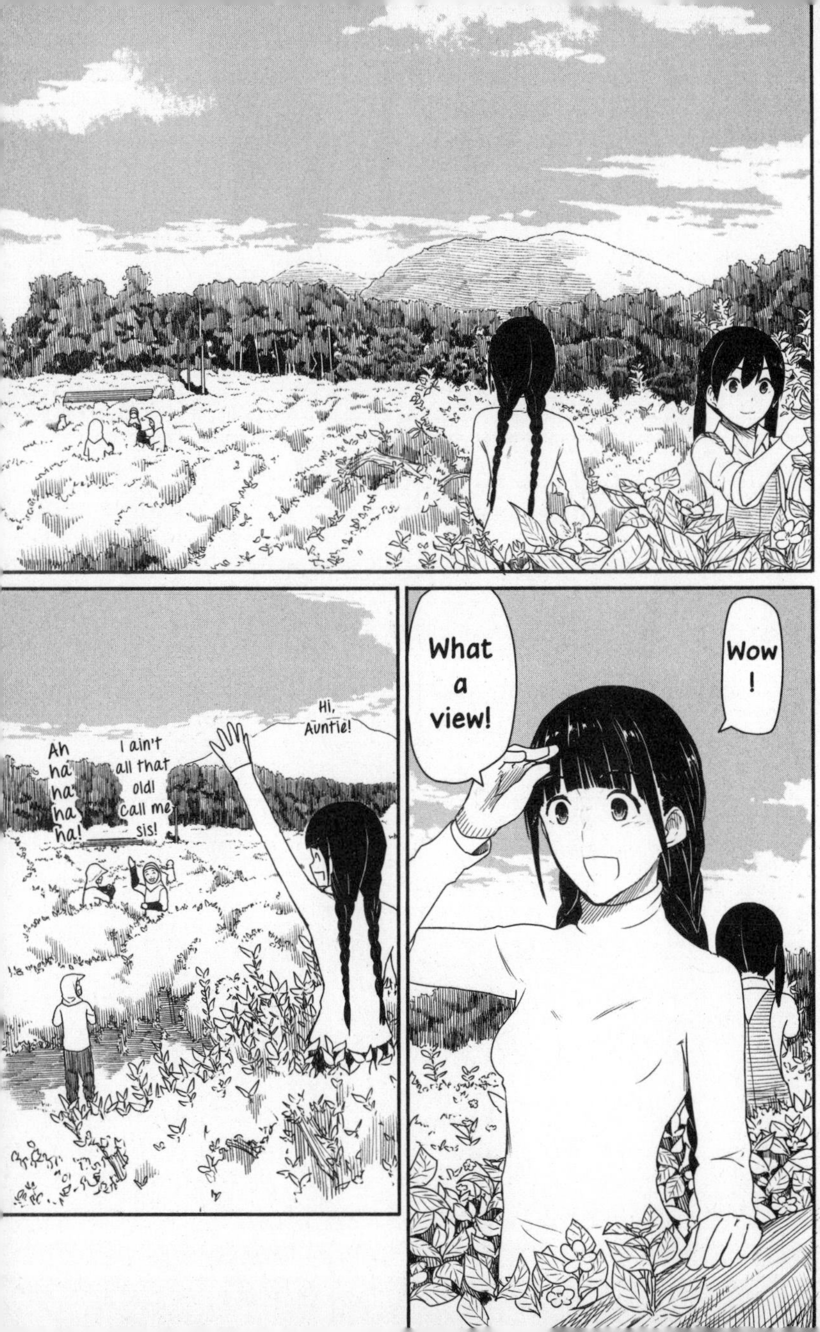
Wow!
What a view!
Hi, Auntie!
I ain't all that old! Call me sis!
Ah ha ha ha ha!

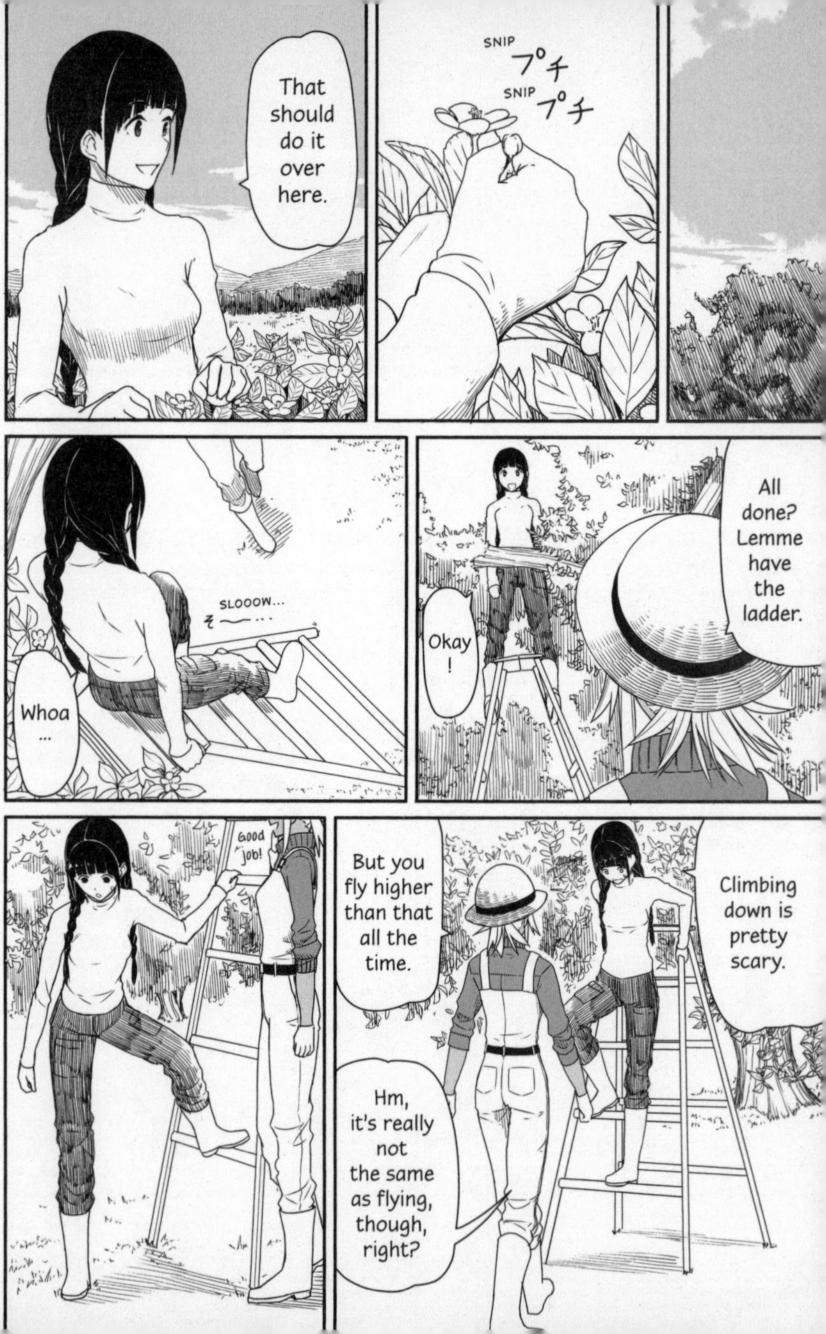
SNIP プチ
SNIP プチ
That should do it over here.
All done? Lemme have the ladder.
Okay!
SLOOOW... そ〜…
Whoa...
Climbing down is pretty scary.
But you fly higher than that all the time.
Hm, it's really not the same as flying, though, right?
Good job!

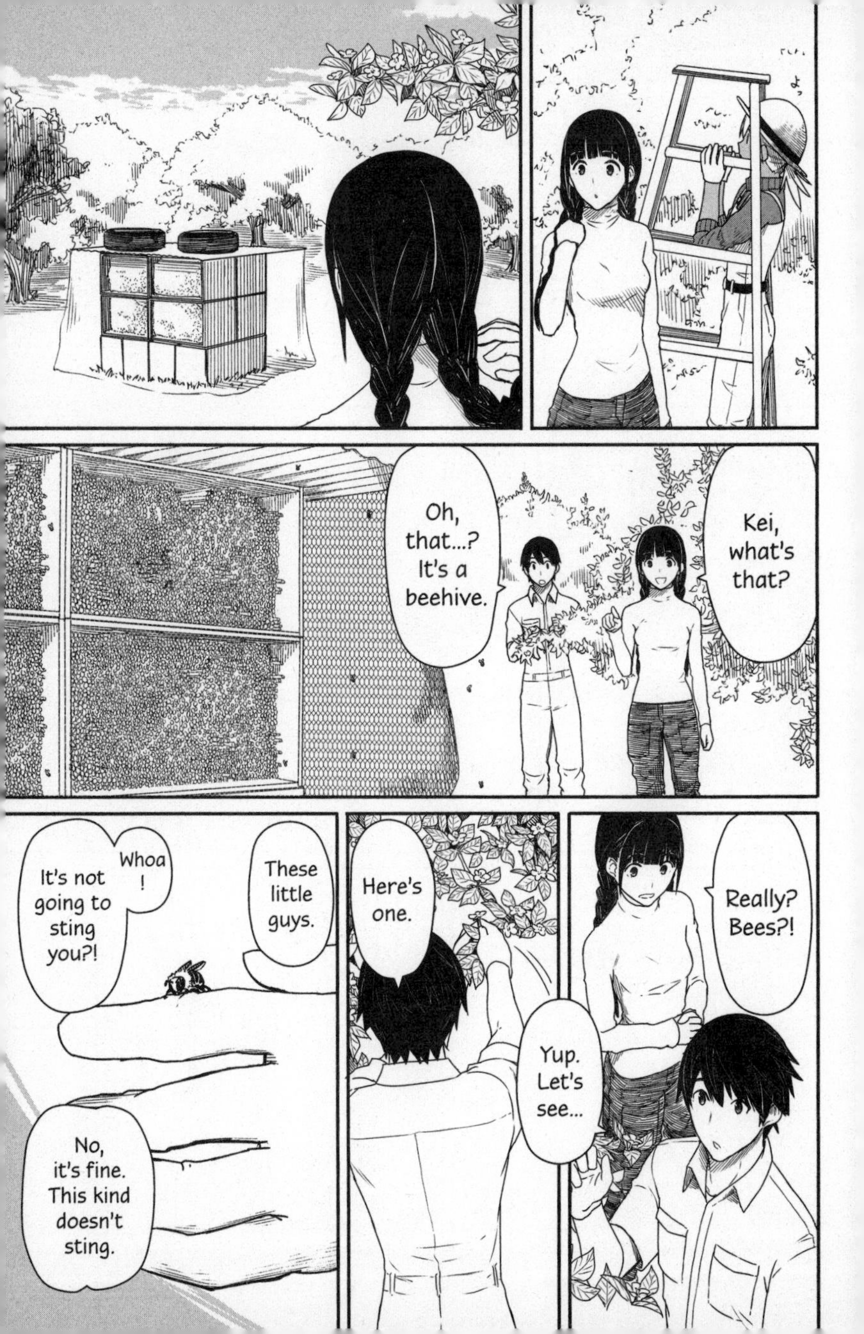
Kei, what's that?
Oh, that...? It's a beehive.
Really? Bees?!
Yup. Let's see...
Here's one.
These little guys.
Whoa!
It's not going to sting you?!
No, it's fine. This kind doesn't sting.

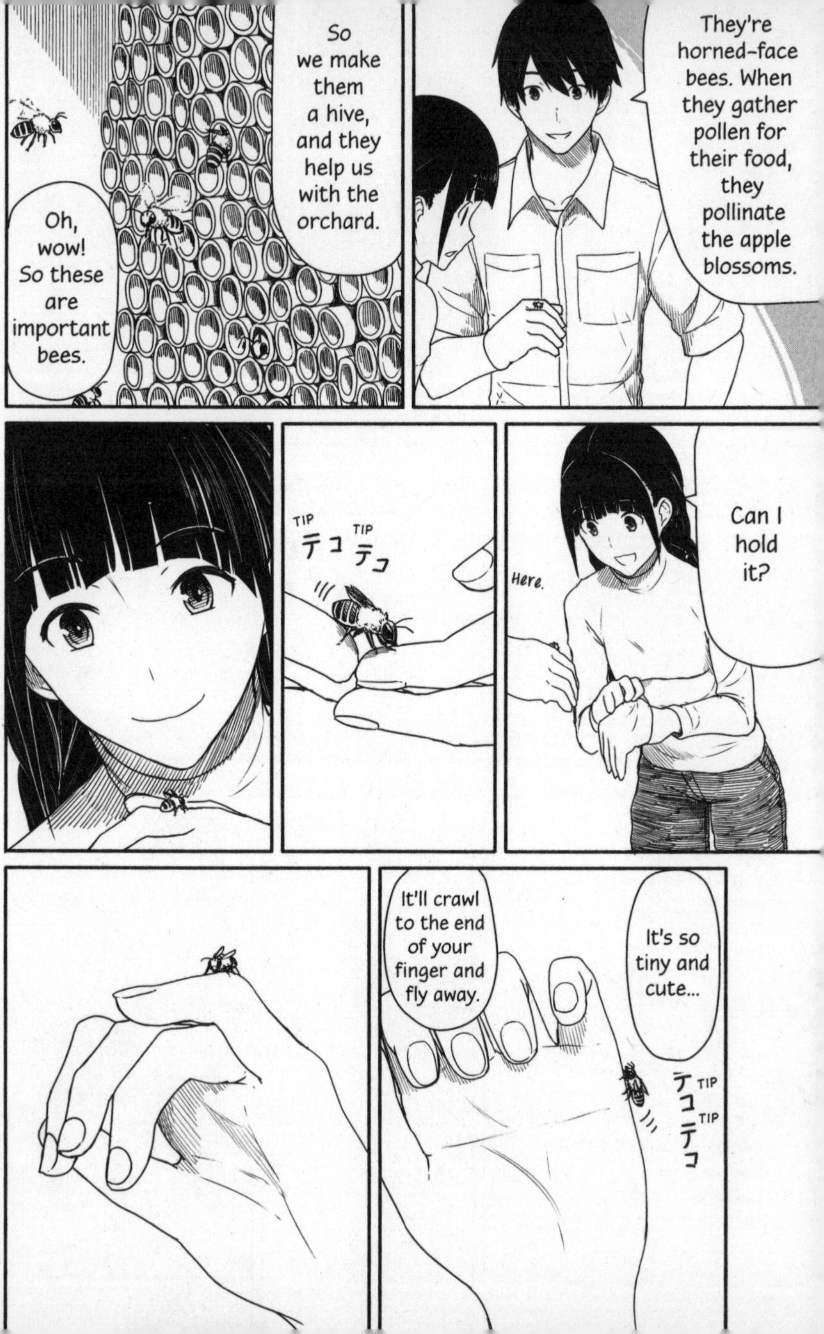
They're horned-face bees. When they gather pollen for their food, they pollinate the apple blossoms.
So we make them a hive, and they help us with the orchard.
Oh, wow! So these are important bees.
Can I hold it?
Here.
TIP テコ TIP テコ
It's so tiny and cute...
It'll crawl to the end of your finger and fly away.
テコ TIP テコ TIP

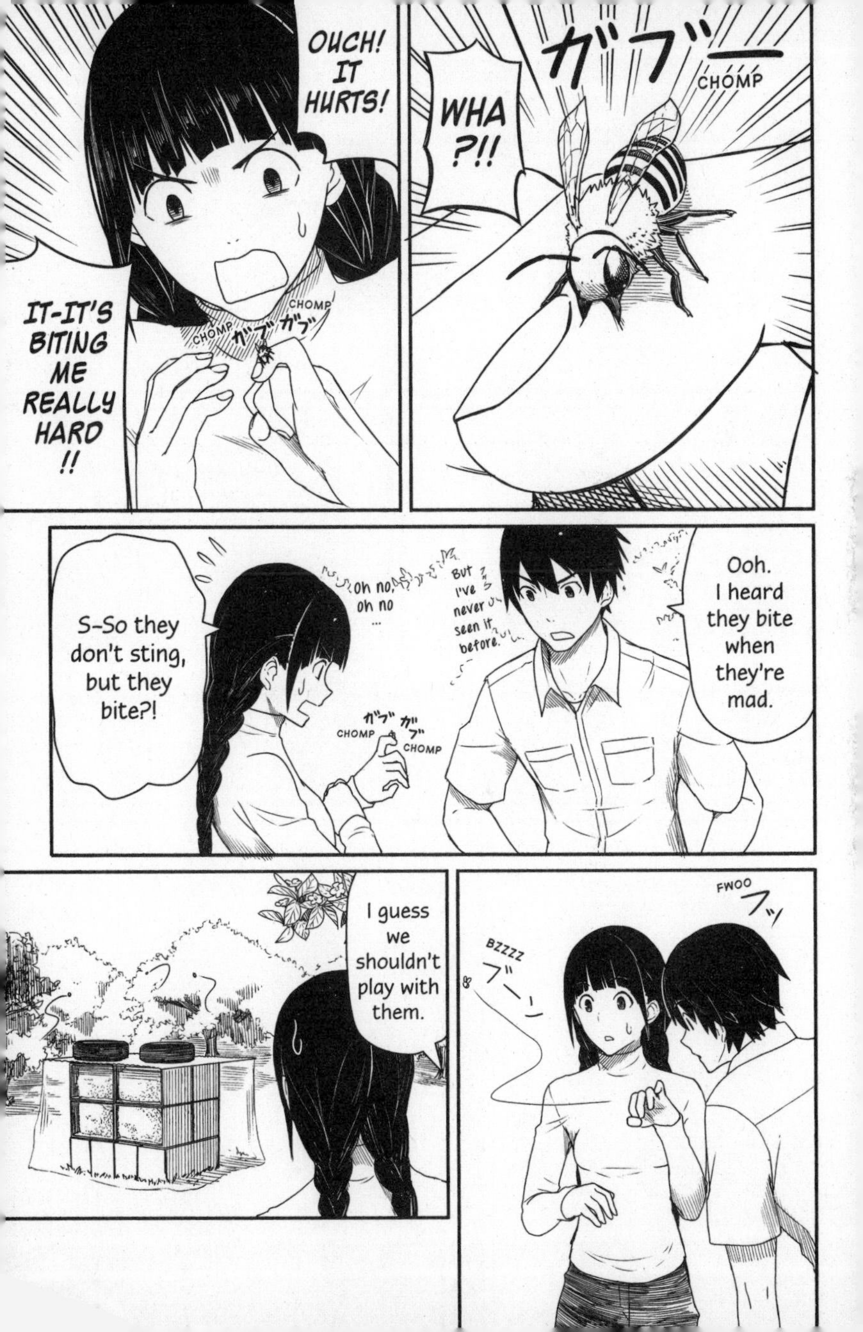
ガブー
CHOMP
WHA ?!!
OUCH! IT HURTS!
IT-IT'S BITING ME REALLY HARD !!
ガブ ガブ
CHOMP CHOMP
Ooh. I heard they bite when they're mad.
But I've never seen it before.
Oh no, oh no ...
S-So they don't sting, but they bite?!
ガブ ガブ
CHOMP CHOMP
FWOO
フッ
BZZZZ
ブーン
I guess we shouldn't play with them.

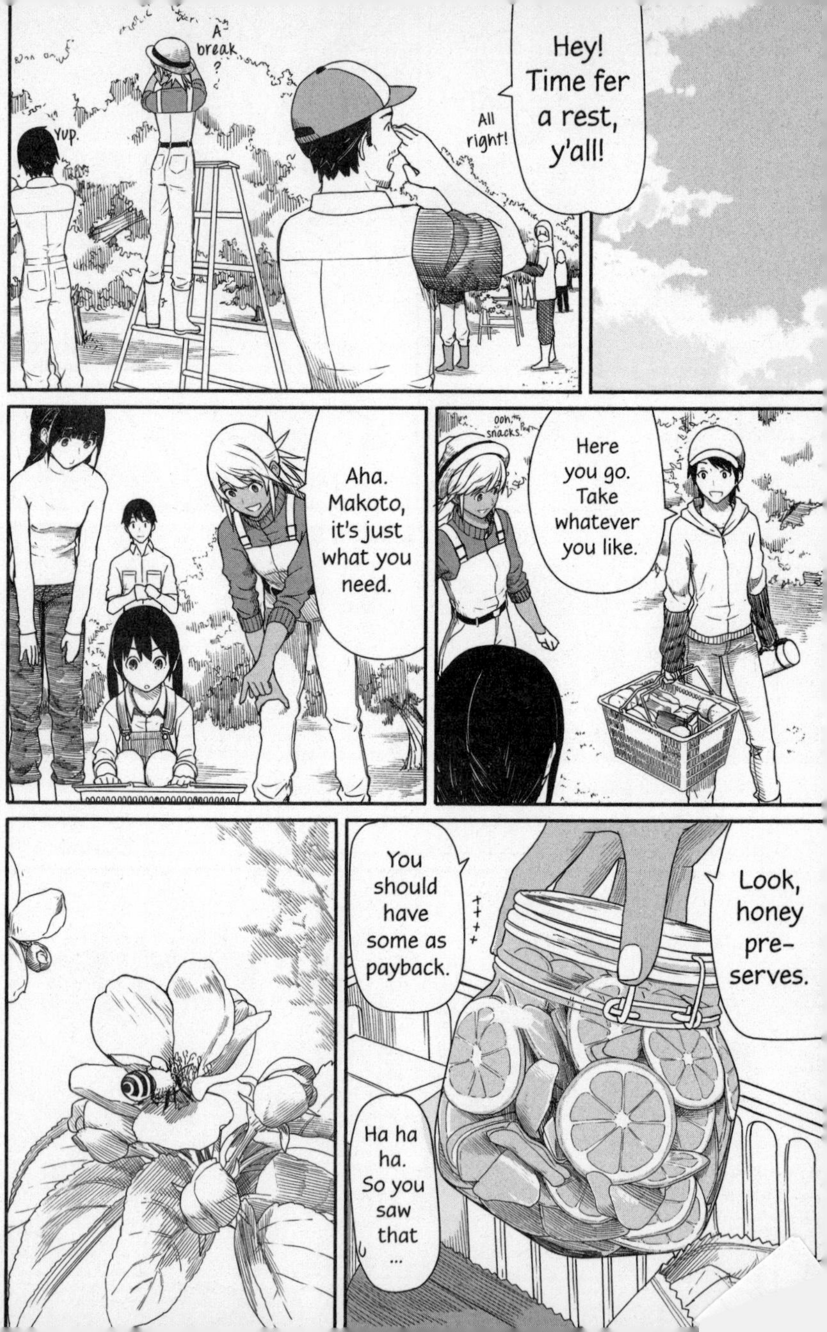
Hey! Time fer a rest, y'all!
All right!
A break?
Yup.
Here you go. Take whatever you like.
ooh, snacks.
Aha. Makoto, it's just what you need.
Look, honey pre- serves.
You should have some as payback.
Ha ha ha. So you saw that ...

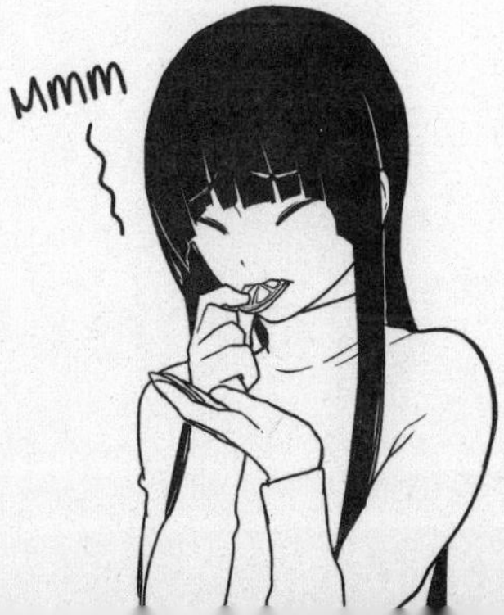
Mmm

Flying
Witch

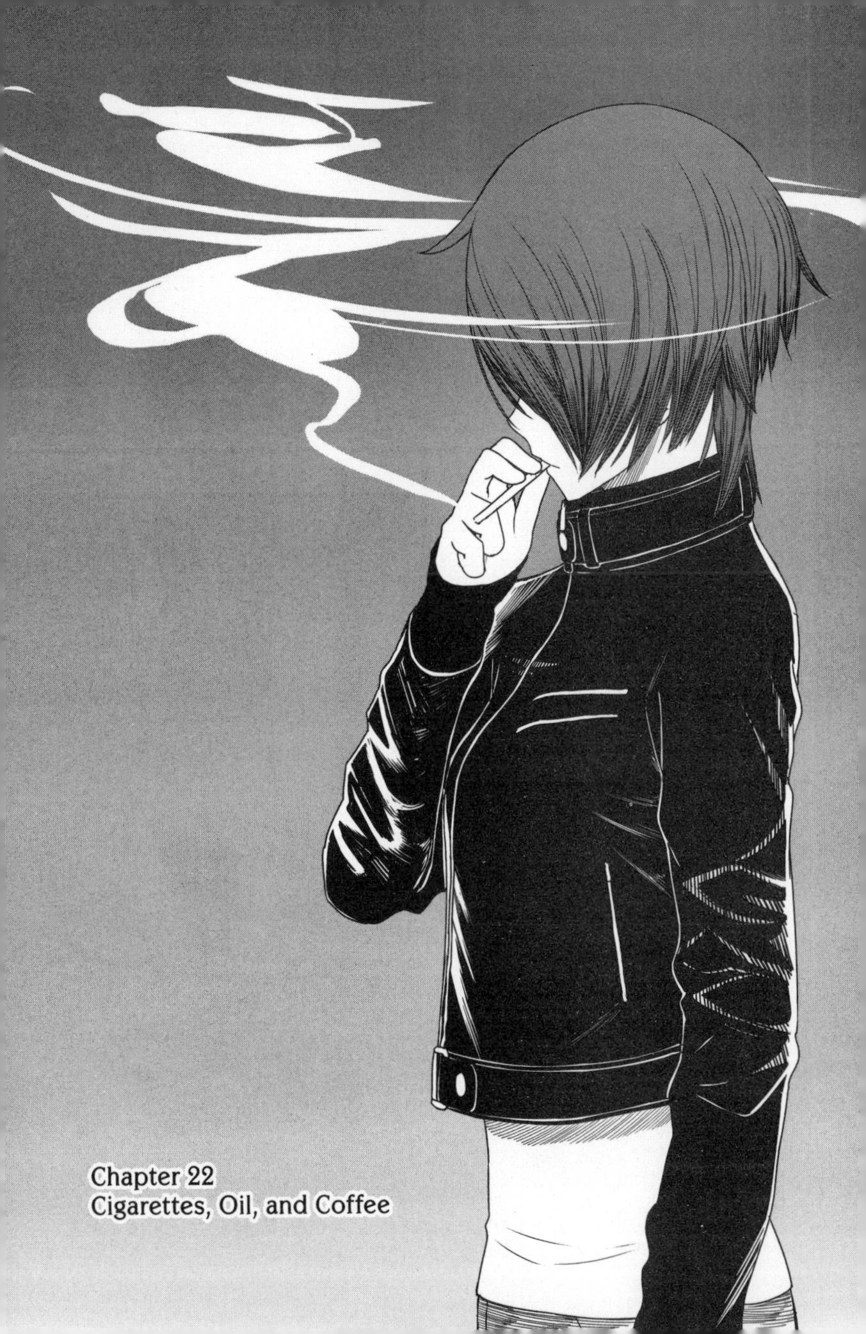

Chapter 22
Cigarettes, Oil, and Coffee

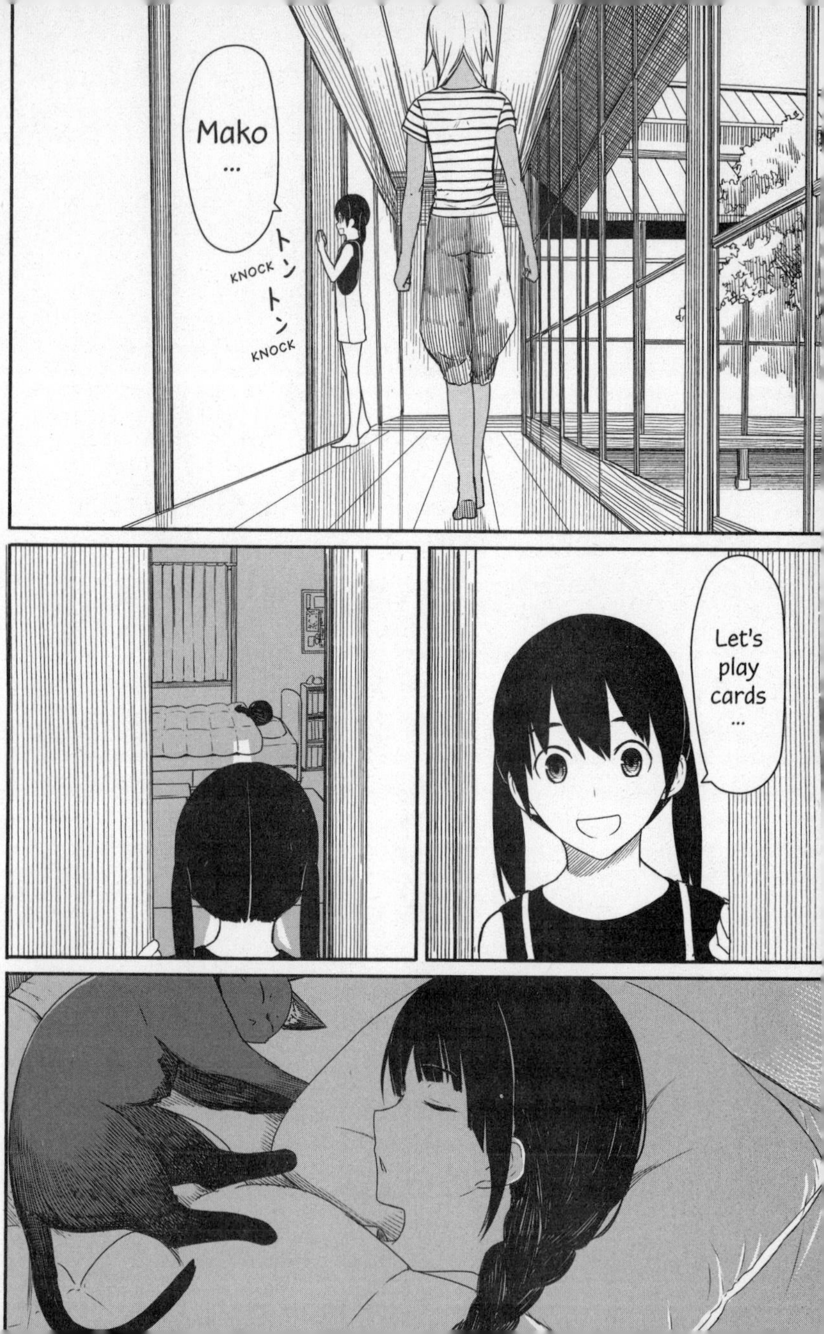
Mako ...
トン KNOCK
トン KNOCK
Let's play cards ...

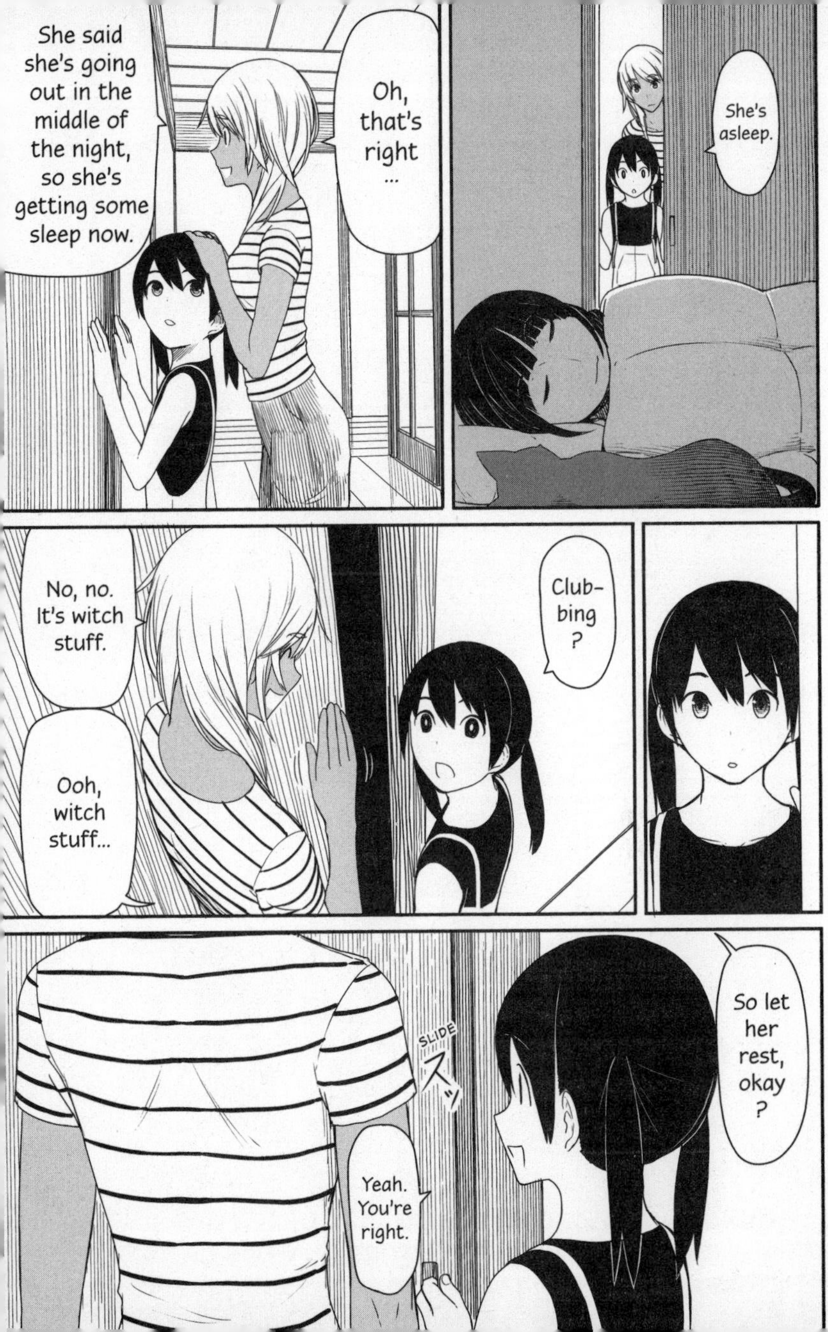
She's asleep.
Oh, that's right ...
She said she's going out in the middle of the night, so she's getting some sleep now.
Club-bing?
No, no. It's witch stuff.
Ooh, witch stuff...
So let her rest, okay?
SLIDE
ズッ
Yeah. You're right.

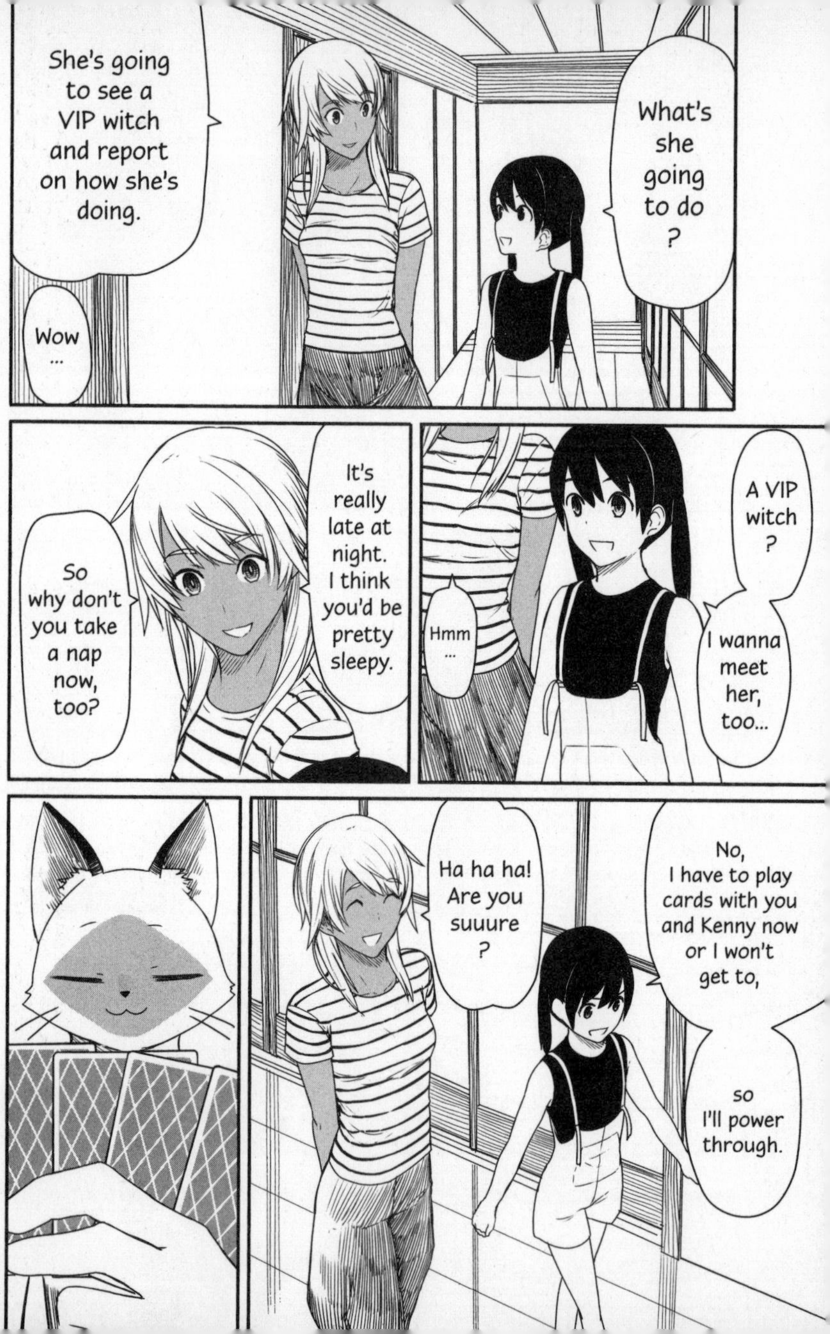
What's she going to do ?
She's going to see a VIP witch and report on how she's doing.
Wow ...
A VIP witch ?
I wanna meet her, too...
Hmm ...
It's really late at night. I think you'd be pretty sleepy.
So why don't you take a nap now, too?
No, I have to play cards with you and Kenny now or I won't get to,
so I'll power through.
Ha ha ha! Are you suuure ?

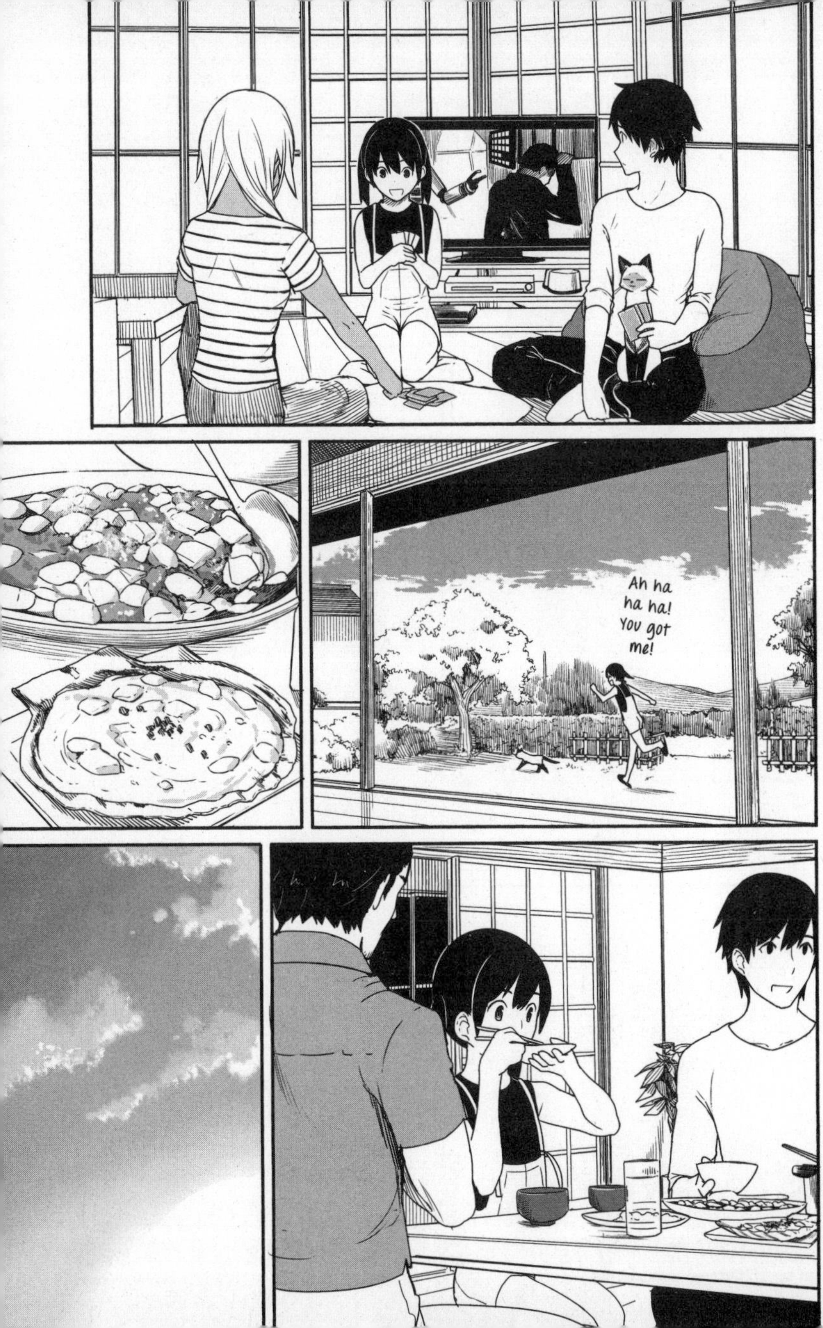
Ah ha ha ha! You got me!

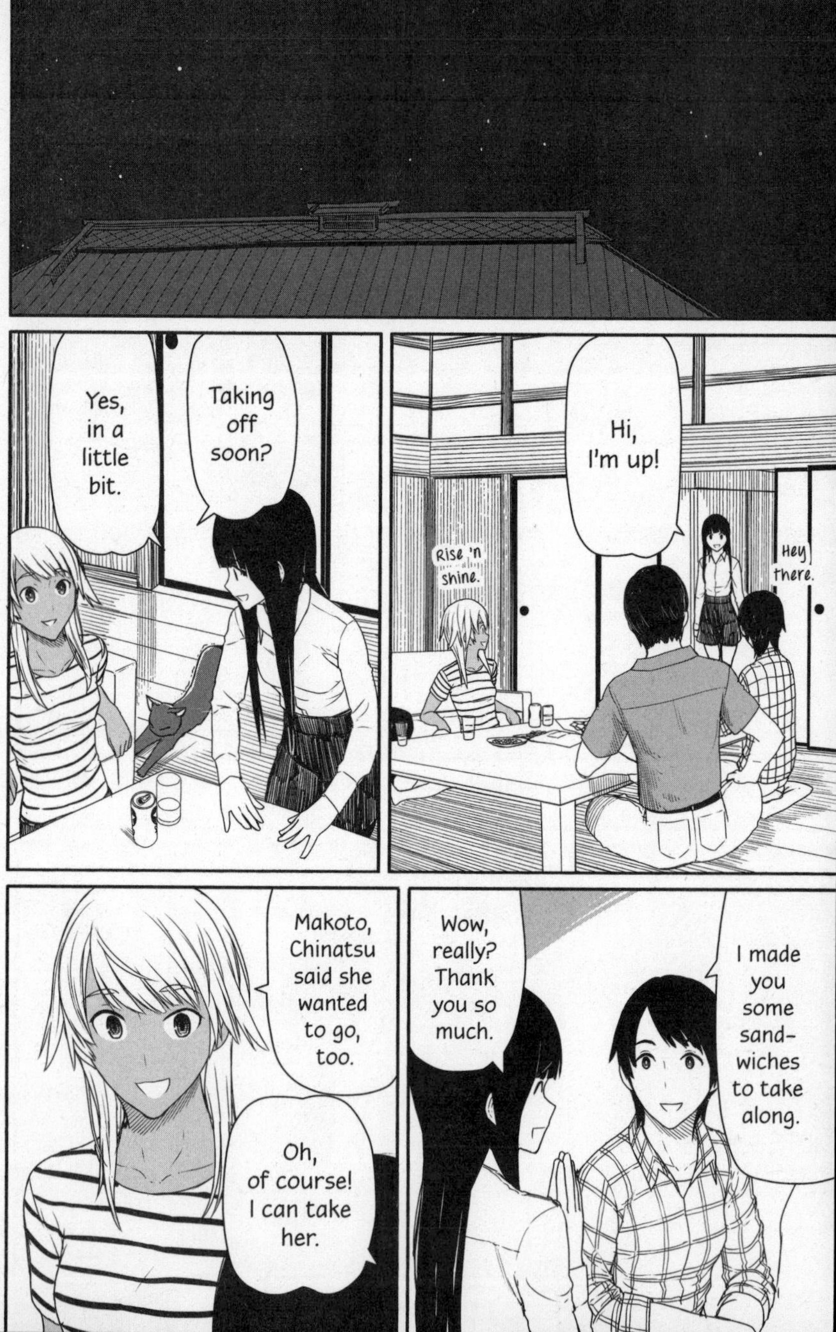
Hi, I'm up!
Hey there.
Rise 'n shine.
Taking off soon?
Yes, in a little bit.
I made you some sand-wiches to take along.
Wow, really? Thank you so much.
Makoto, Chinatsu said she wanted to go, too.
Oh, of course! I can take her.

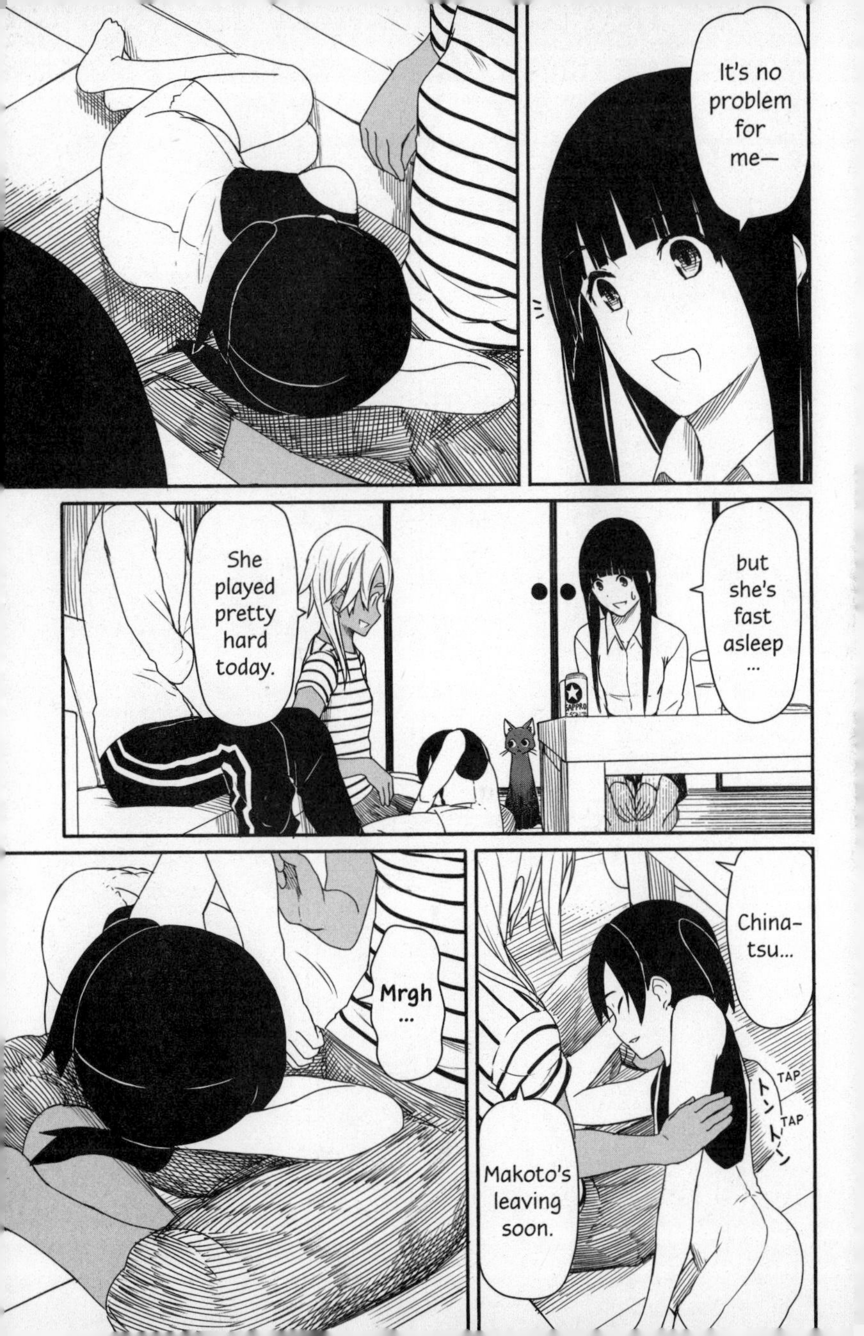
It's no problem for me—
but she's fast asleep ...
She played pretty hard today.
China-tsu...
Makoto's leaving soon.
TAP TAP
Mrgh ...

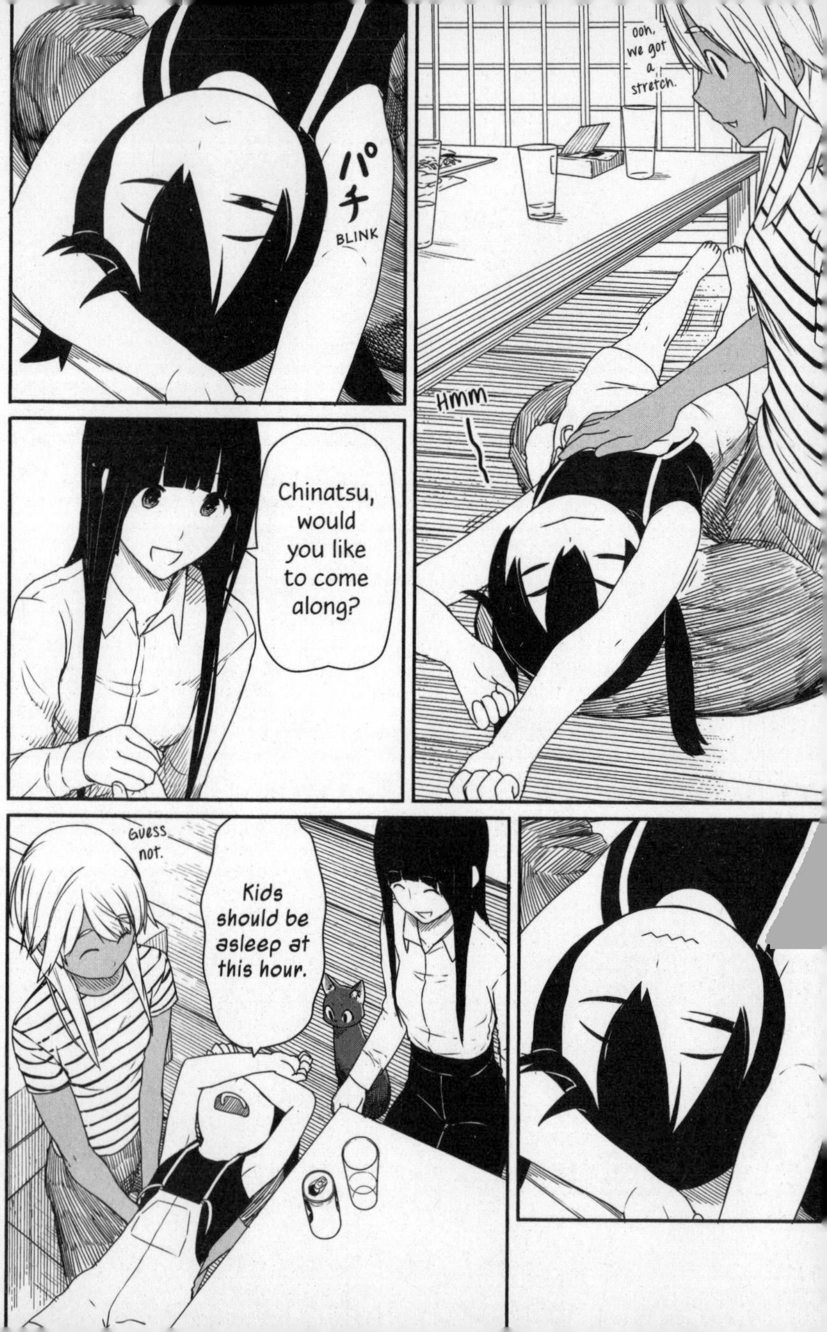

ooh, we got a stretch.
Hmm
パチ
BLINK
Chinatsu, would you like to come along?
Kids should be asleep at this hour.
Guess not.

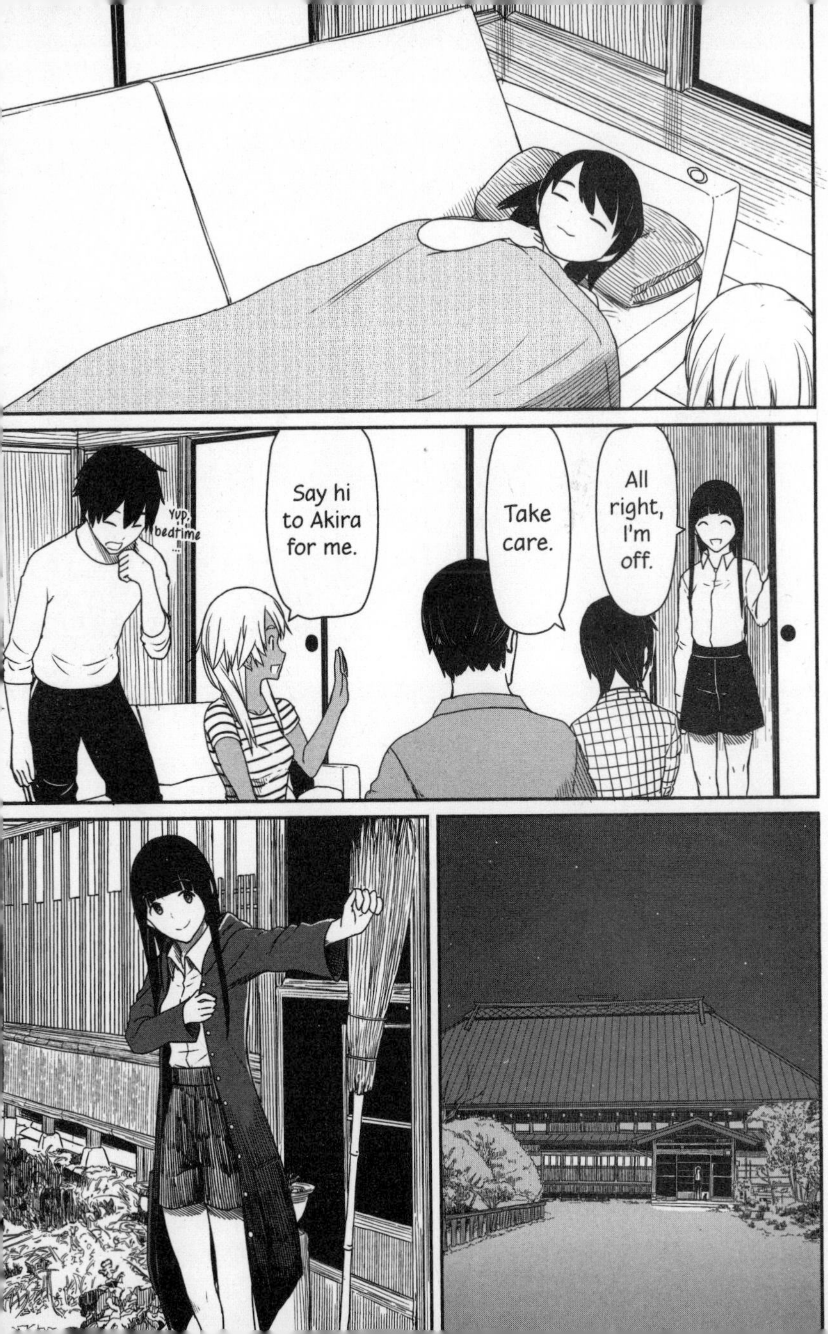
All right, I'm off.
Take care.
Say hi to Akira for me.
Yup, bedtime...

FLUTTER

FLUTTER

Meow.

Yes, it came out nice, didn't it?

Hey, hey! Don't do that! No shredding my robe!!

SWFF

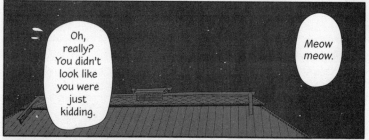

Oh, really? You didn't look like you were just kidding.

Meow meow.

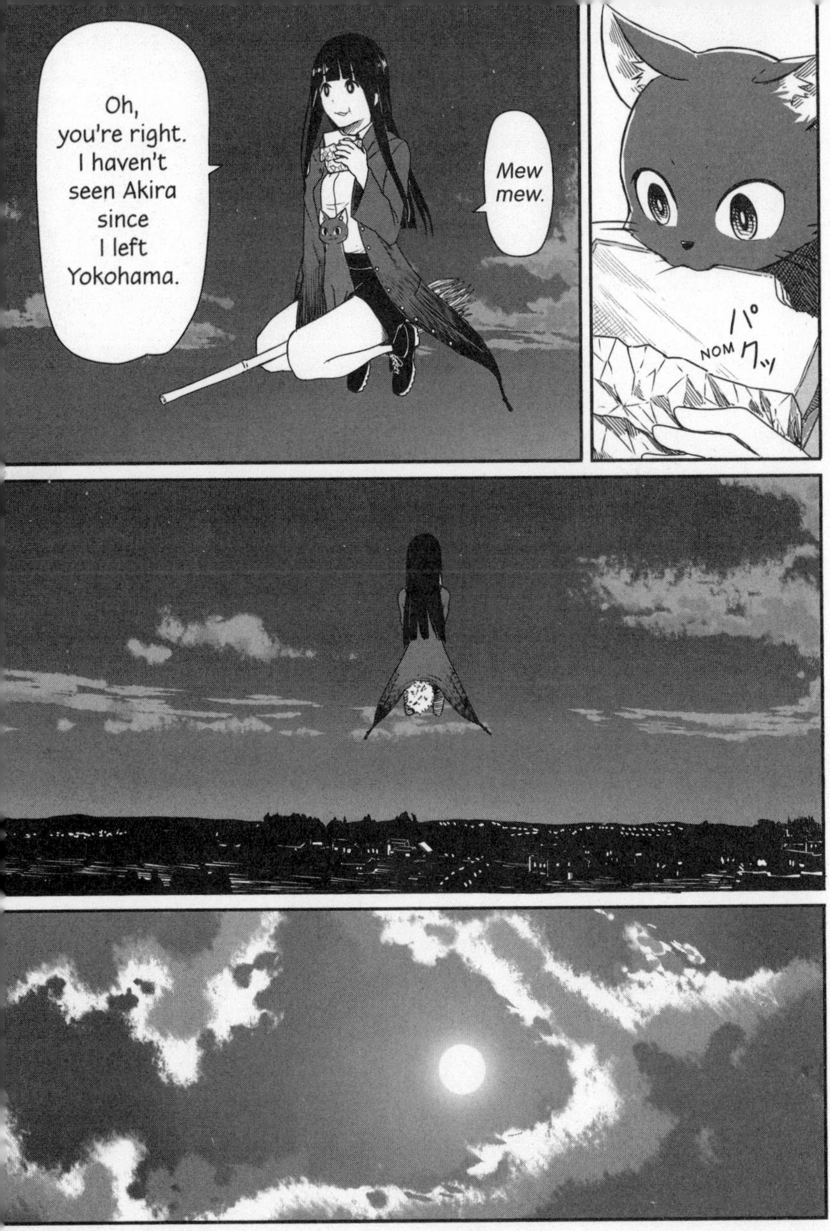
パクッ
NOM
Mew mew.
Oh, you're right. I haven't seen Akira since I left Yokohama.

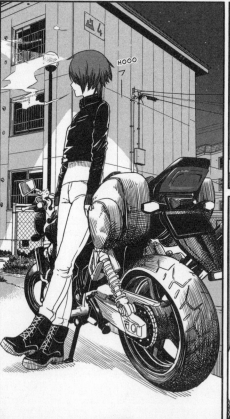

HOOO

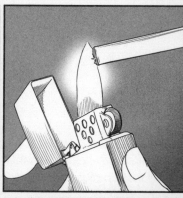

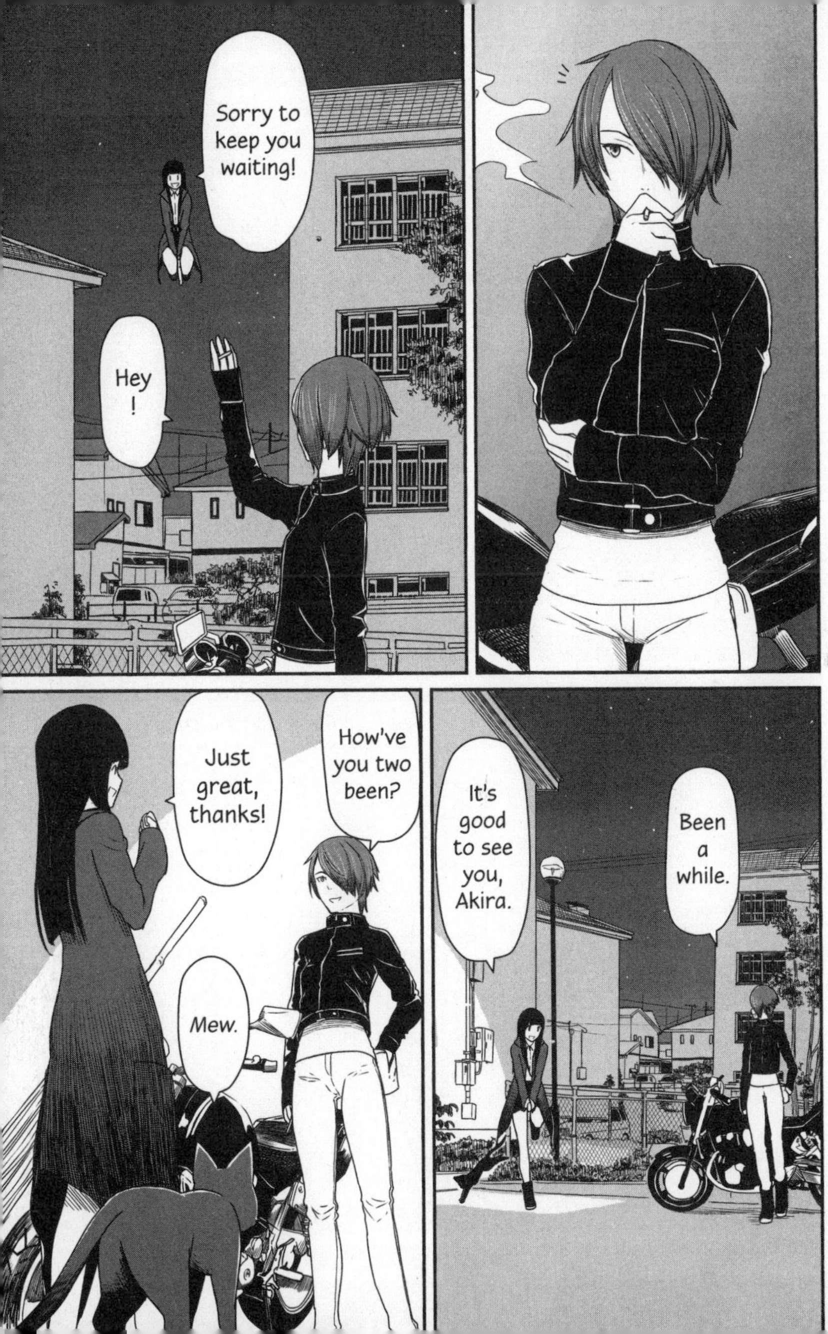
Sorry to keep you waiting!
Hey!
Been a while.
It's good to see you, Akira.
How've you two been?
Just great, thanks!
Mew.

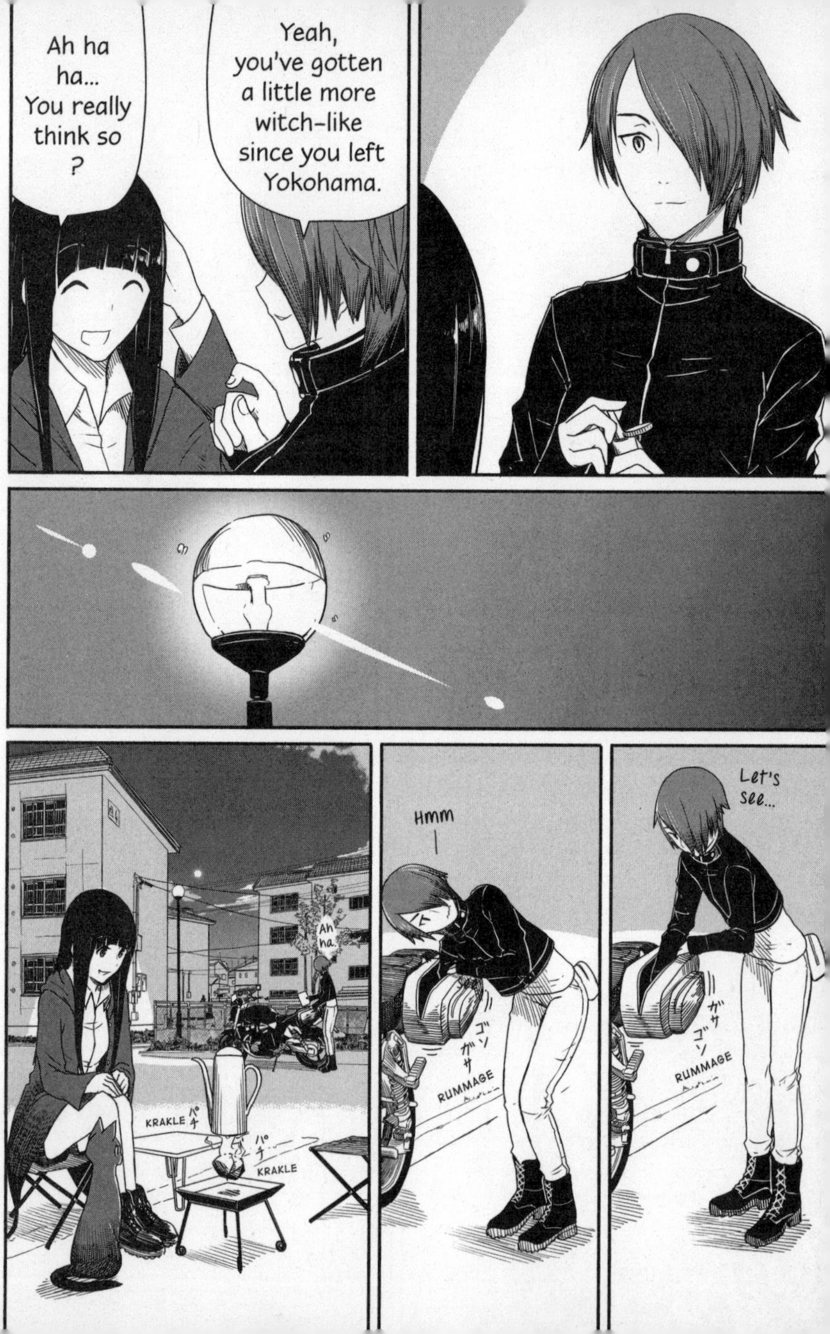
Yeah, you've gotten a little more witch-like since you left Yokohama.
Ah ha ha... You really think so ?
Let's see...
ガサ
ゴソ
RUMMAGE
Hmm
ゴソ
ガサ
RUMMAGE
Ah ha.
KRAKLE
パチ
パチ
KRAKLE

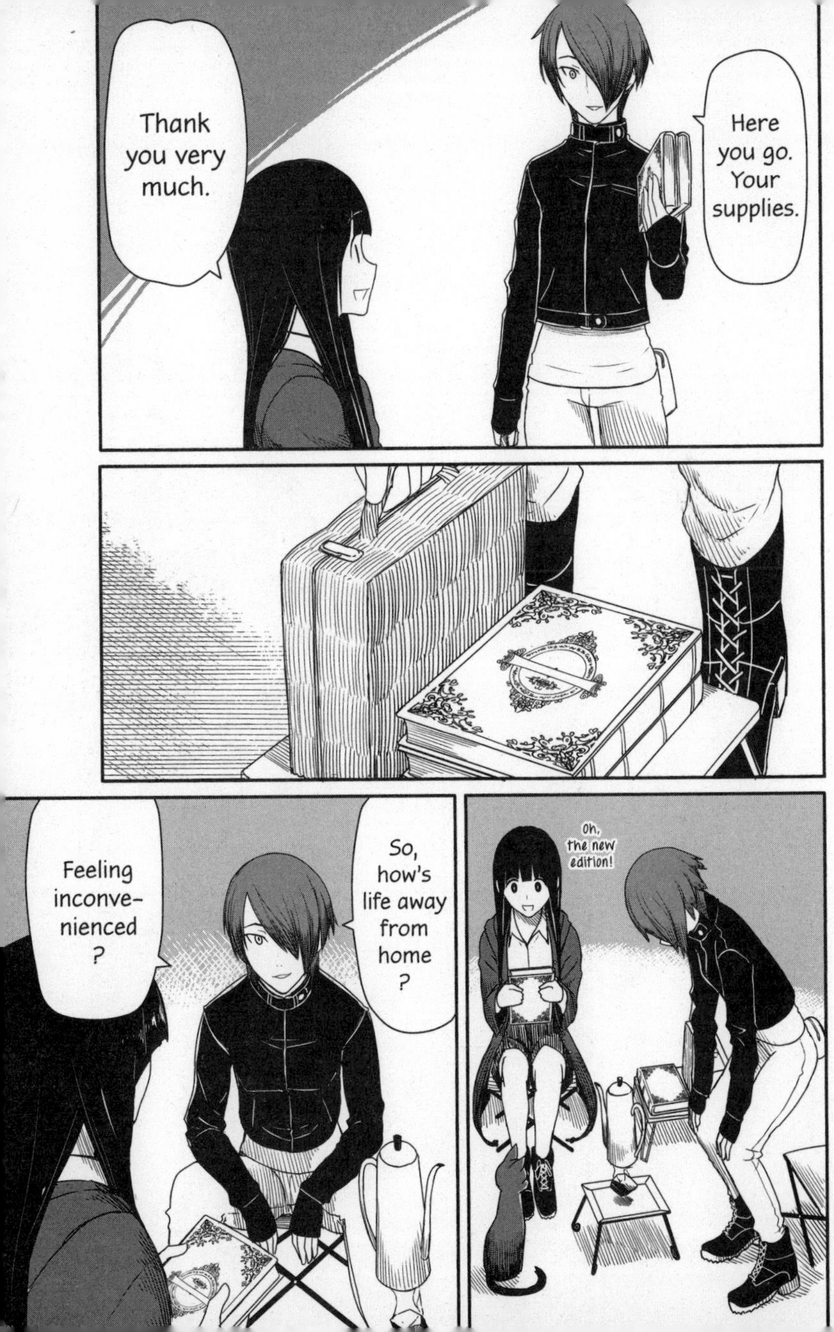
Here you go. Your supplies.
Thank you very much.
Oh, the new edition!
So, how's life away from home?
Feeling inconvenienced?

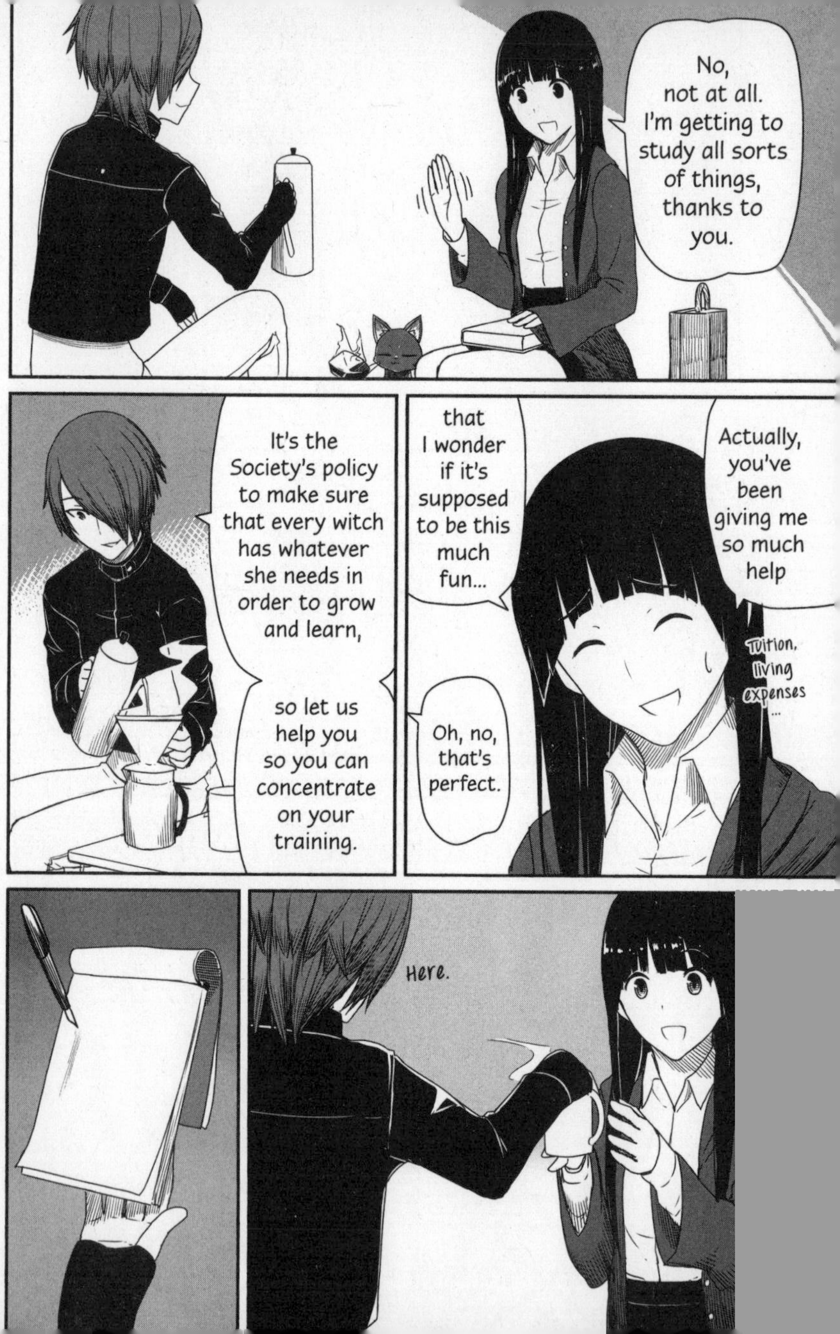
No, not at all. I'm getting to study all sorts of things, thanks to you.
Actually, you've been giving me so much help
that I wonder if it's supposed to be this much fun...
Tuition, living expenses...
Oh, no, that's perfect.
It's the Society's policy to make sure that every witch has whatever she needs in order to grow and learn,
so let us help you so you can concentrate on your training.
Here.

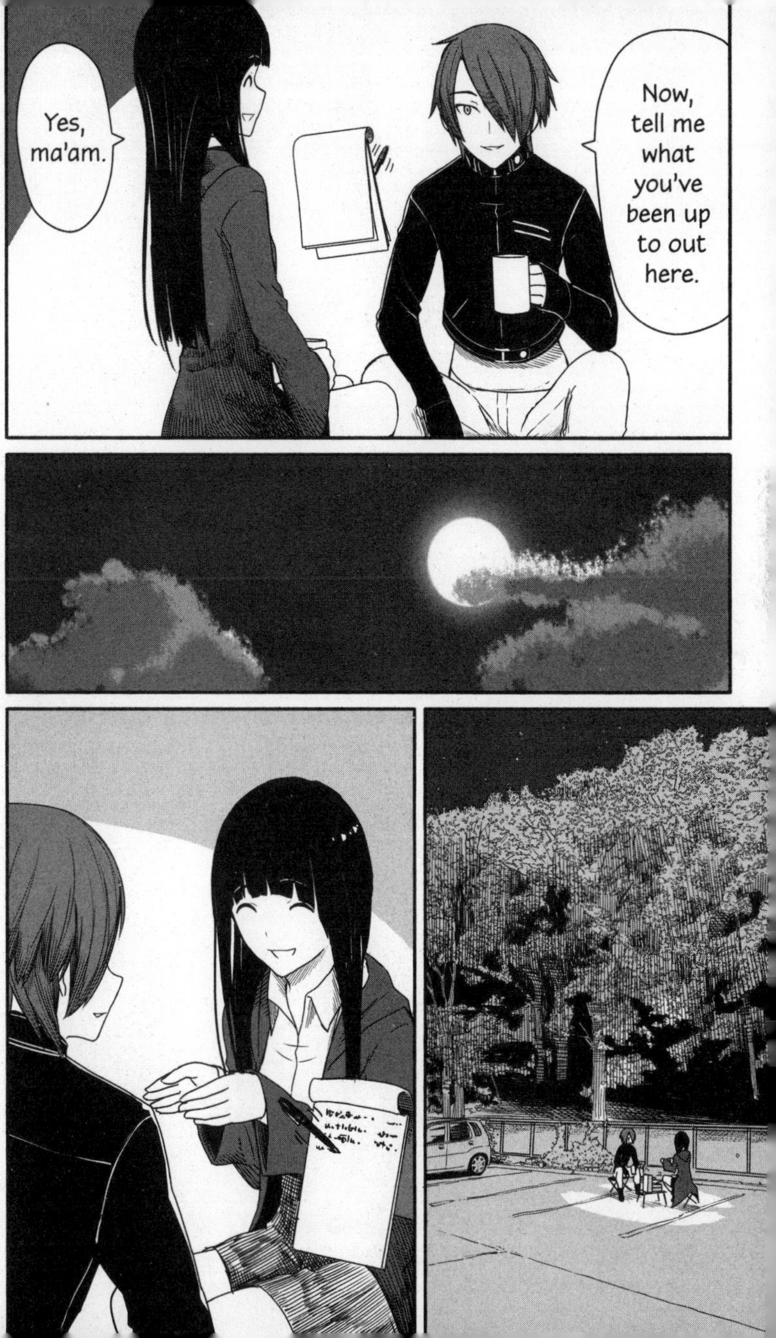
Now, tell me what you've been up to out here.
Yes, ma'am.

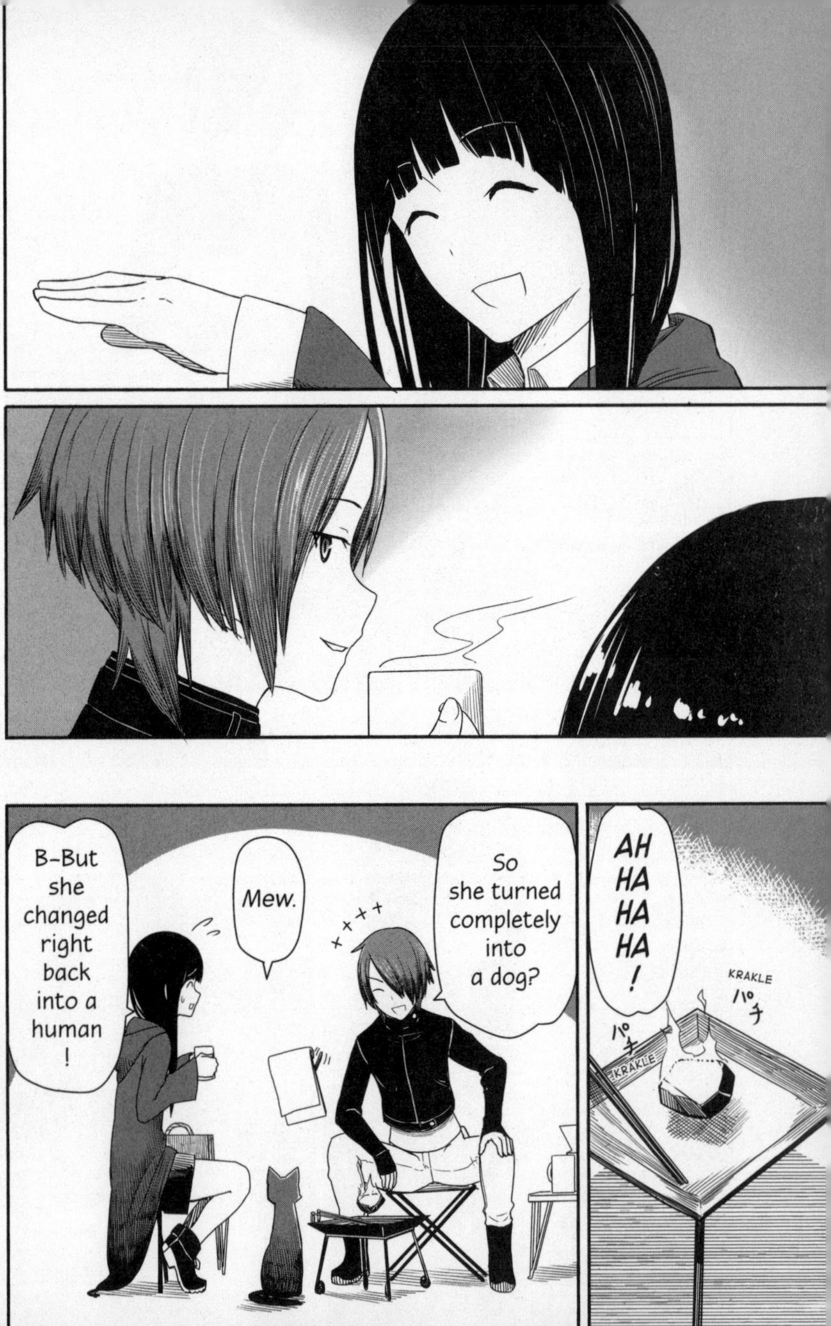
AH HA HA HA!
KRAKLE
パチ
パチ
KRAKLE
So she turned completely into a dog?
Mew.
B-But she changed right back into a human!

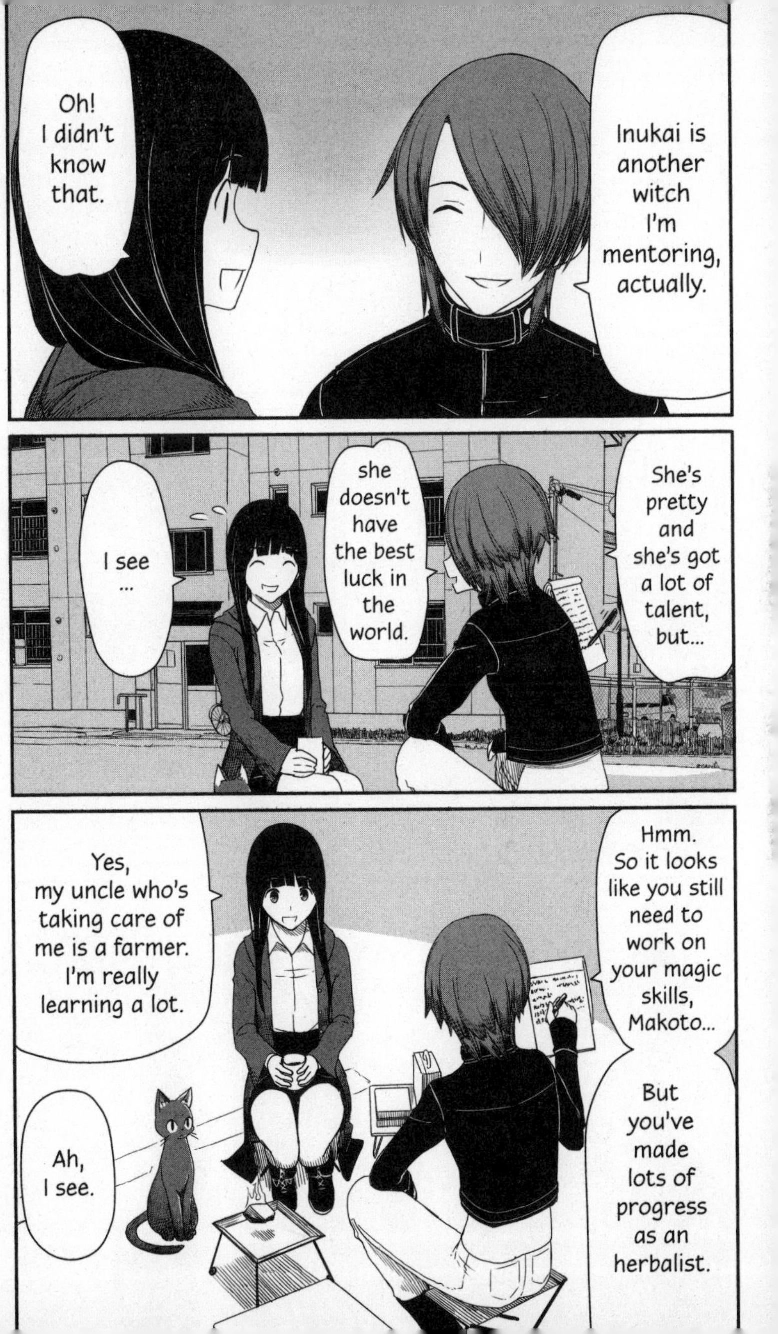
Inukai is another witch I'm mentoring, actually.
Oh! I didn't know that.
She's pretty and she's got a lot of talent, but...
she doesn't have the best luck in the world.
I see ...
Hmm. So it looks like you still need to work on your magic skills, Makoto...
But you've made lots of progress as an herbalist.
Yes, my uncle who's taking care of me is a farmer. I'm really learning a lot.
Ah, I see.

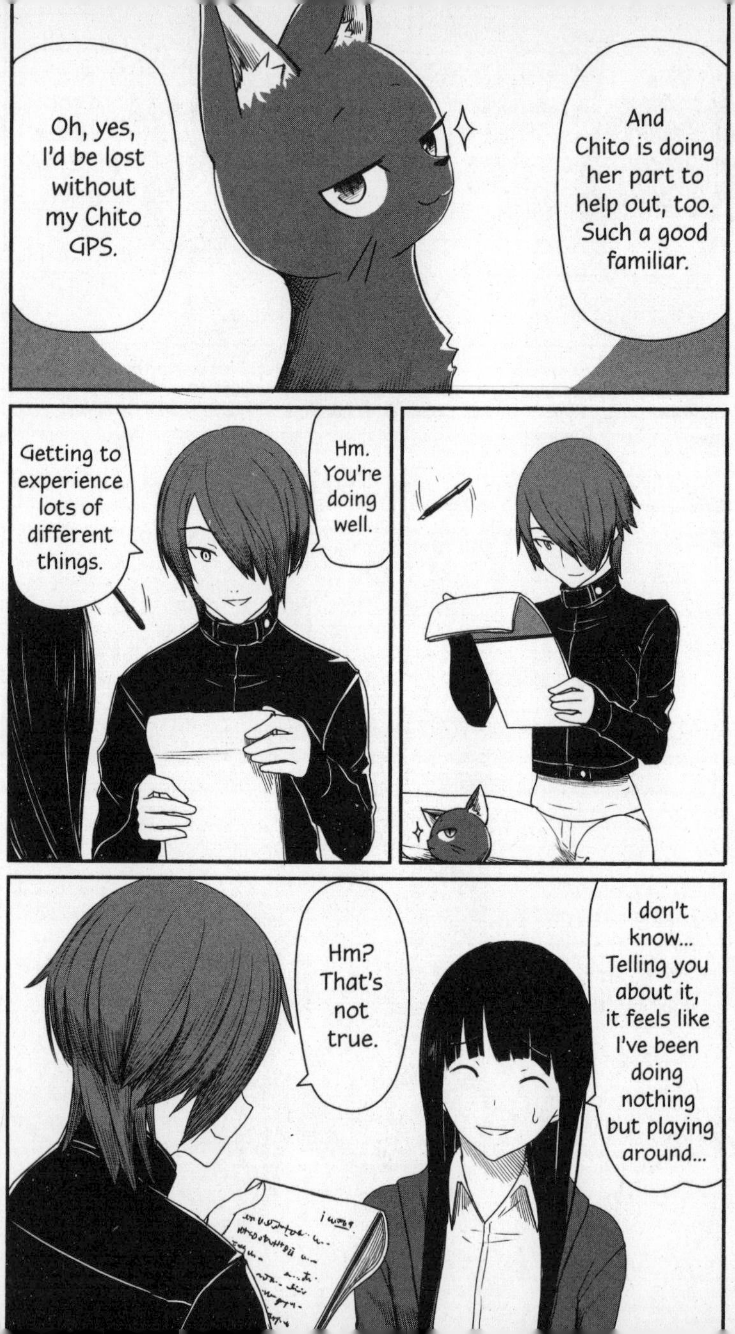
And Chito is doing her part to help out, too. Such a good familiar.
Oh, yes, I'd be lost without my Chito GPS.
Hm. You're doing well.
Getting to experience lots of different things.
I don't know... Telling you about it, it feels like I've been doing nothing but playing around...
Hm? That's not true.

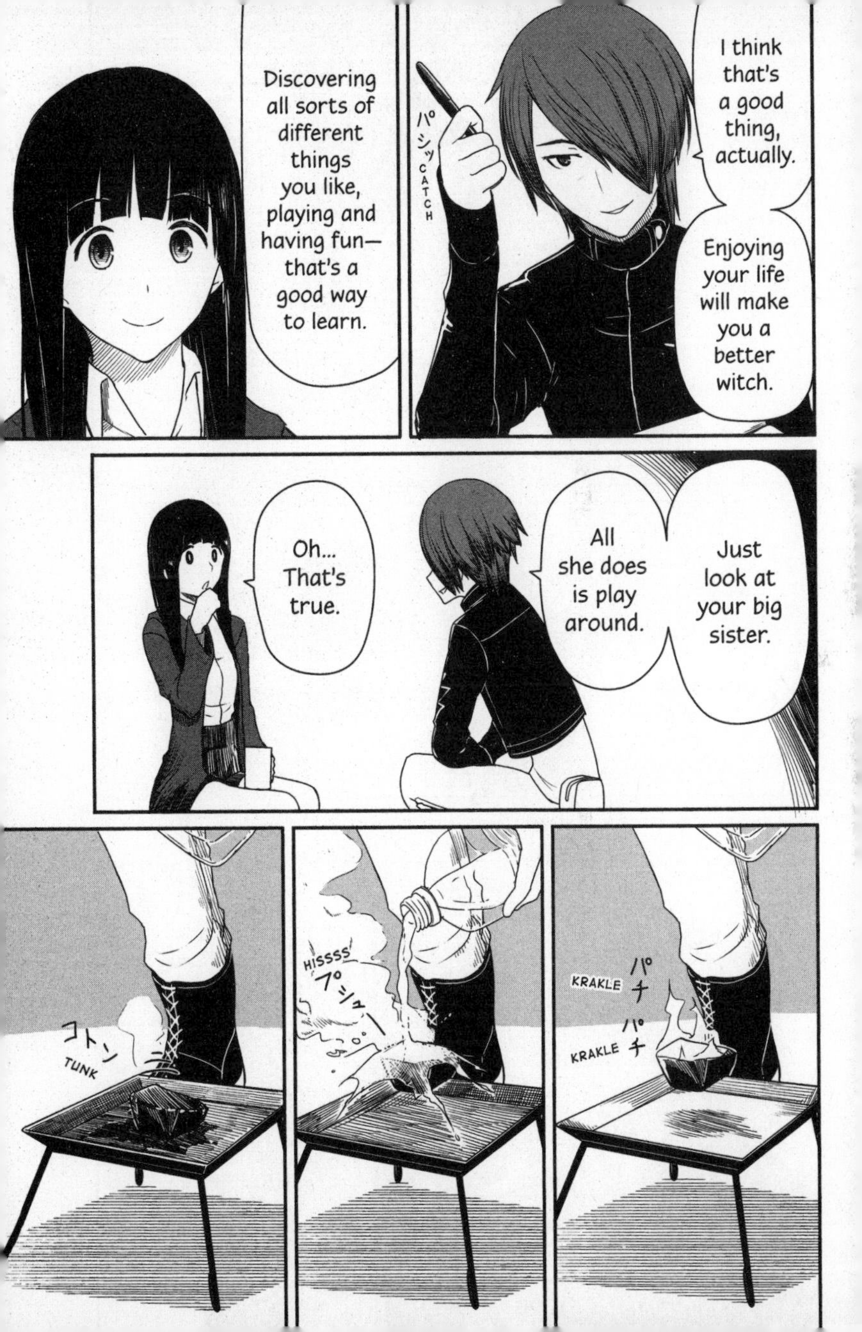
パシッ
CATCH
I think that's a good thing, actually.
Enjoying your life will make you a better witch.
Discovering all sorts of different things you like, playing and having fun—that's a good way to learn.
Just look at your big sister.
All she does is play around.
Oh... That's true.
パチ
KRAKLE
パチ
KRAKLE
HISSSS
コトン
TUNK

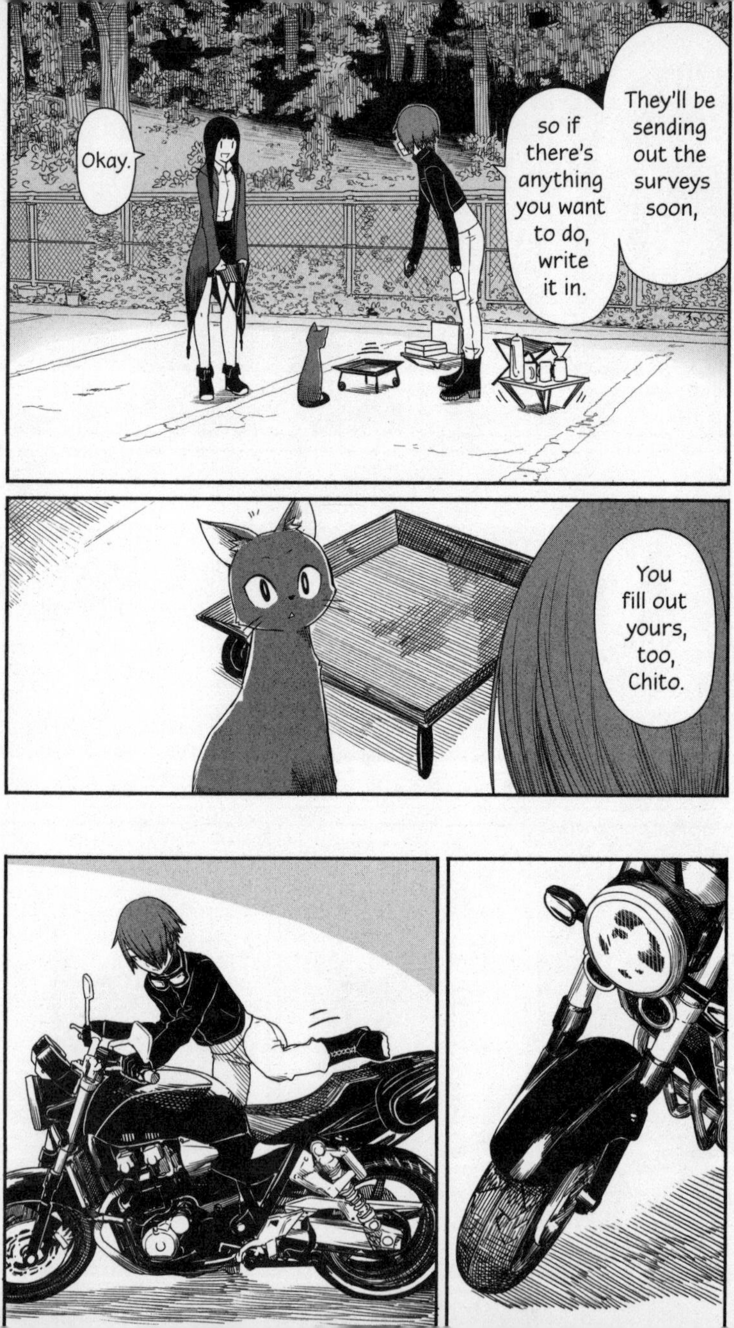
They'll be sending out the surveys soon,
so if there's anything you want to do, write it in.
Okay.
You fill out yours, too, Chito.

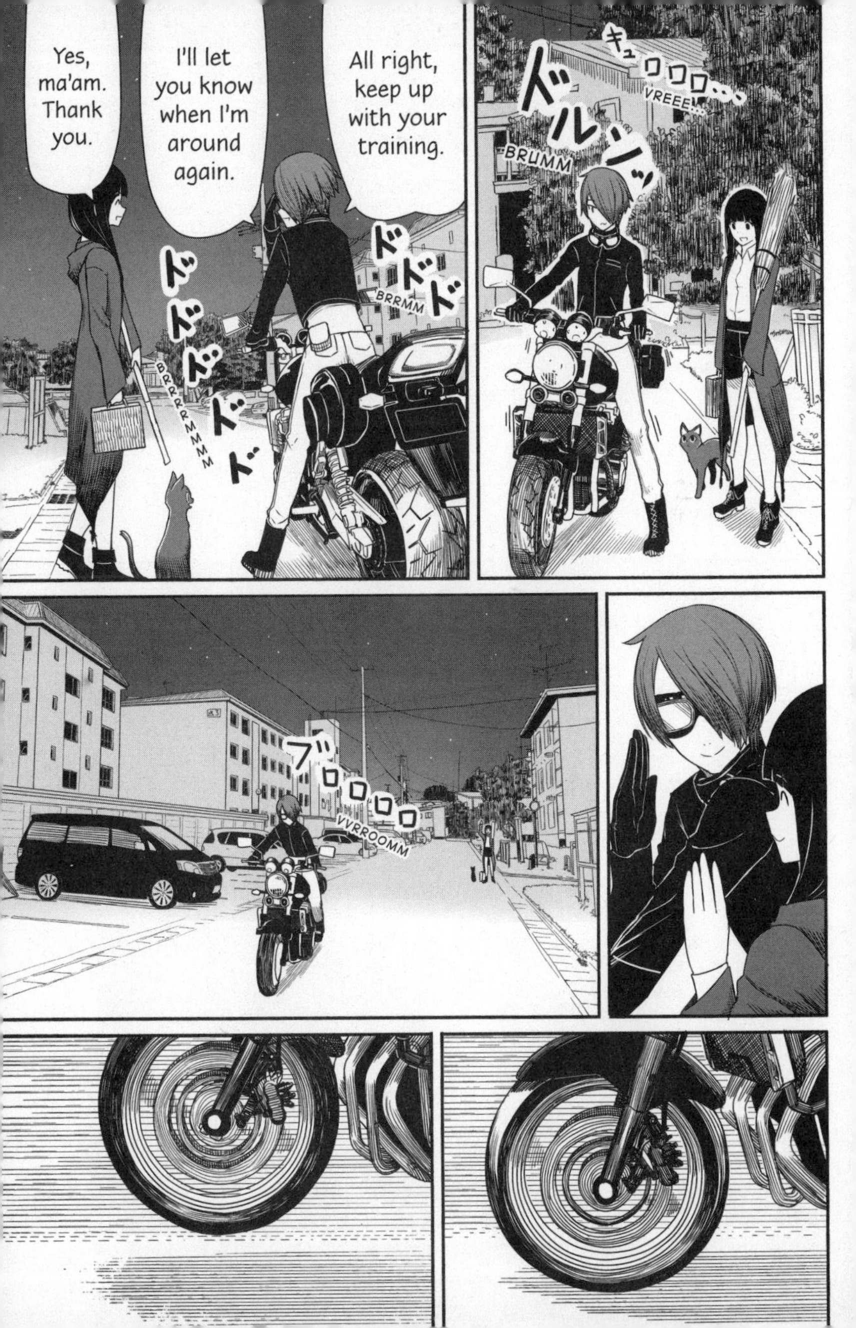
キュワワワ…
VREEE…
ドルンッ
BRUMM
All right, keep up with your training.
I'll let you know when I'm around again.
Yes, ma'am. Thank you.
ドドド
BRRMM
ドドドドド
BRRRRMMM
ブロロロロ
VVRROOMM

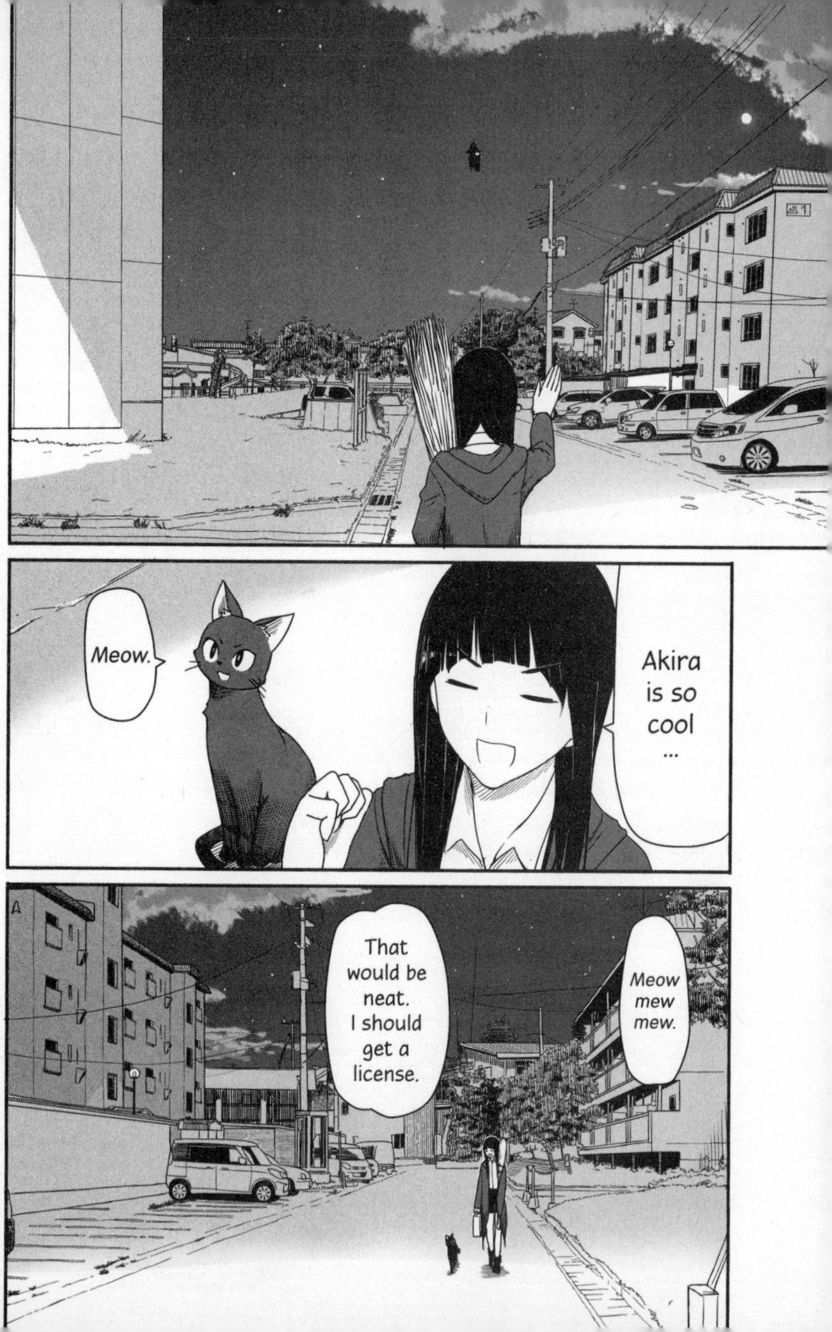
Akira is so cool ...
Meow.
Meow mew mew.
That would be neat. I should get a license.

Flying
Witch

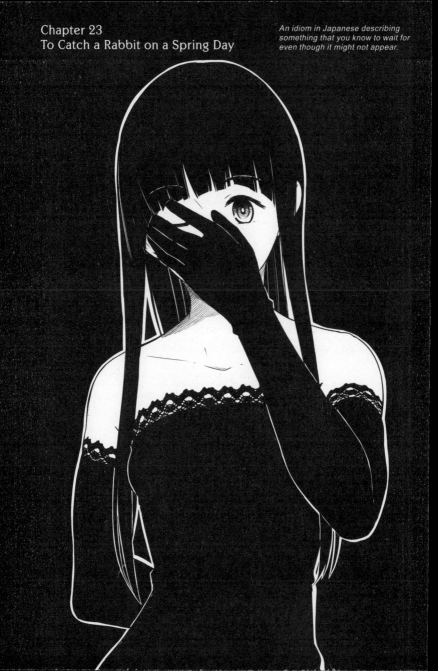

Chapter 23
To Catch a Rabbit on a Spring Day

An idiom in Japanese describing something that you know to wait for even though it might not appear.

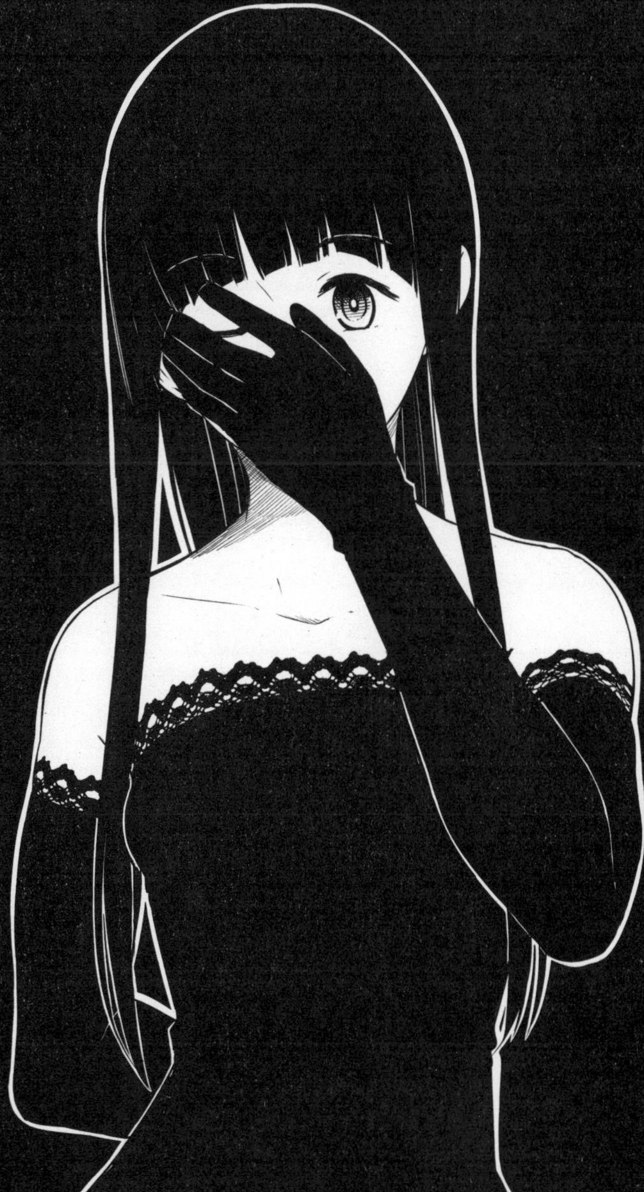

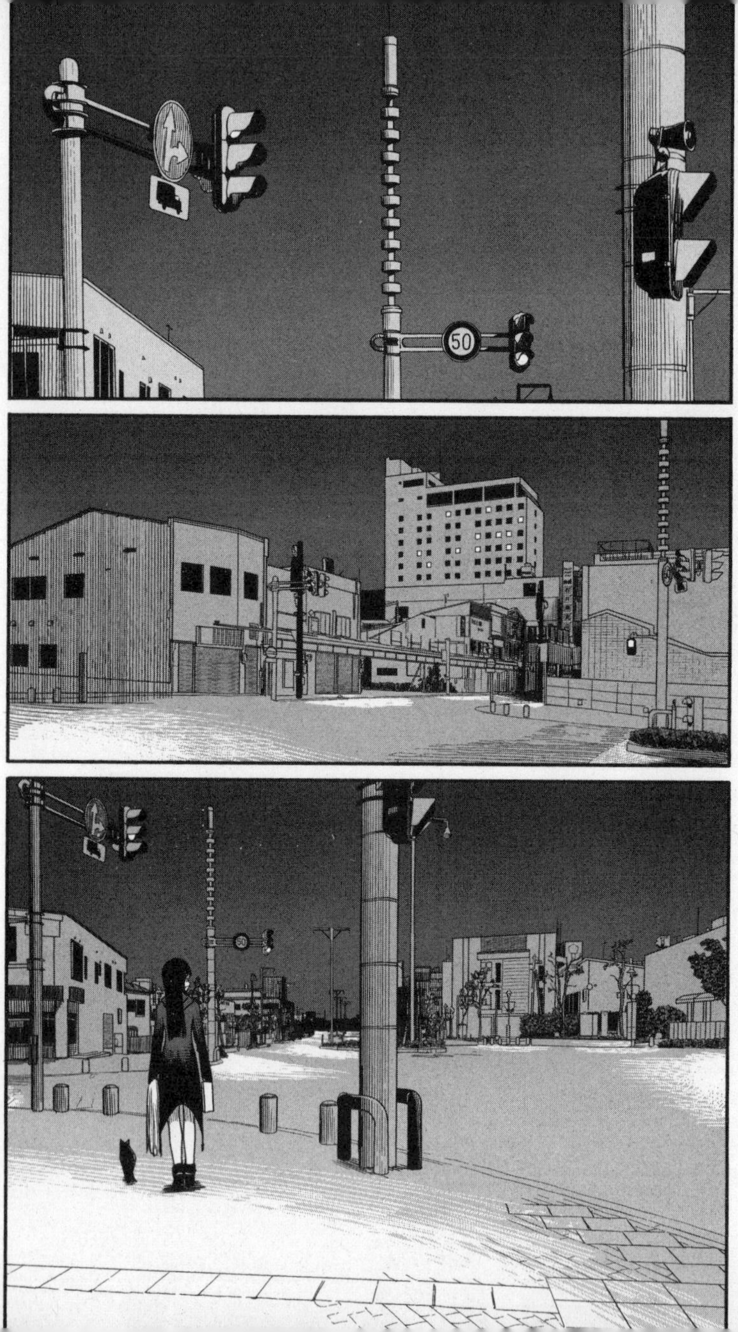
50

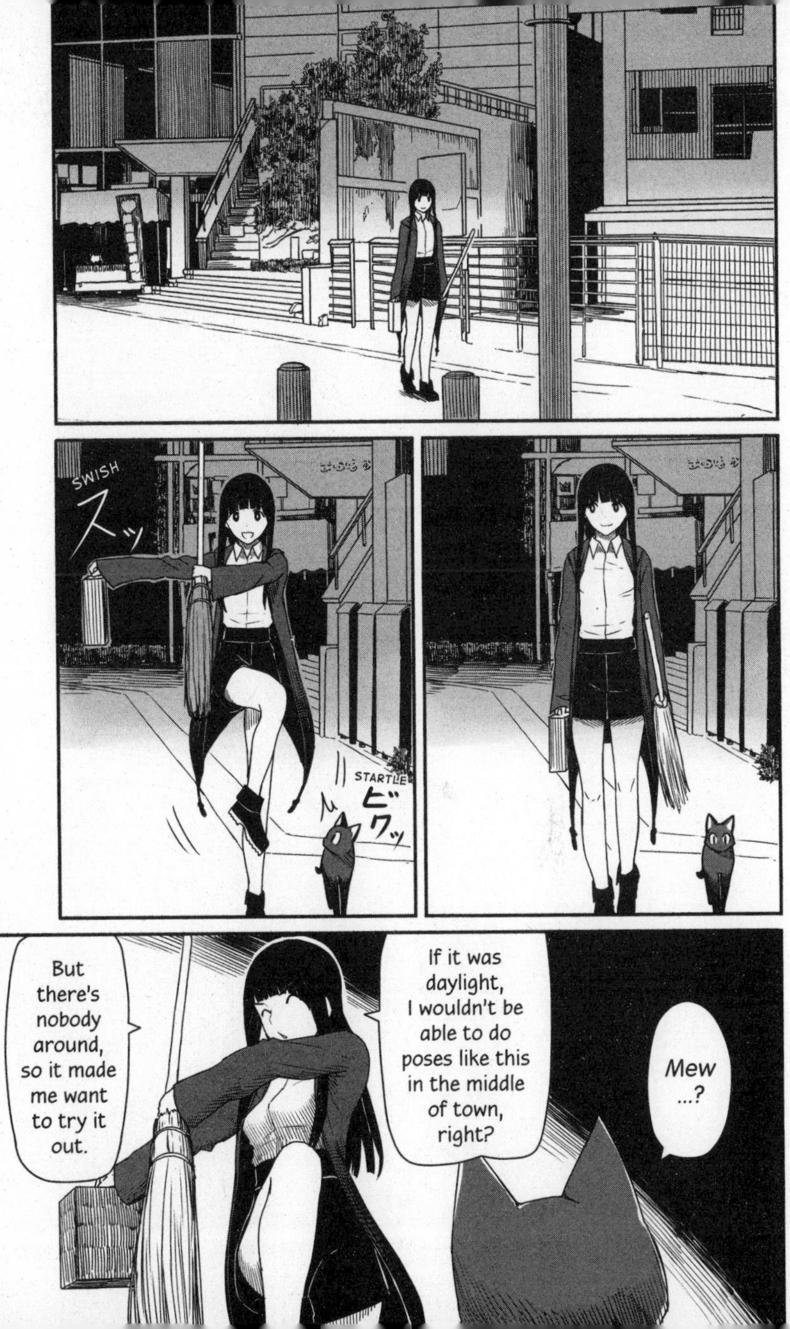
SWISH
スッ
STARTLE
ビクッ
Mew ...?
If it was daylight, I wouldn't be able to do poses like this in the middle of town, right?
But there's nobody around, so it made me want to try it out.

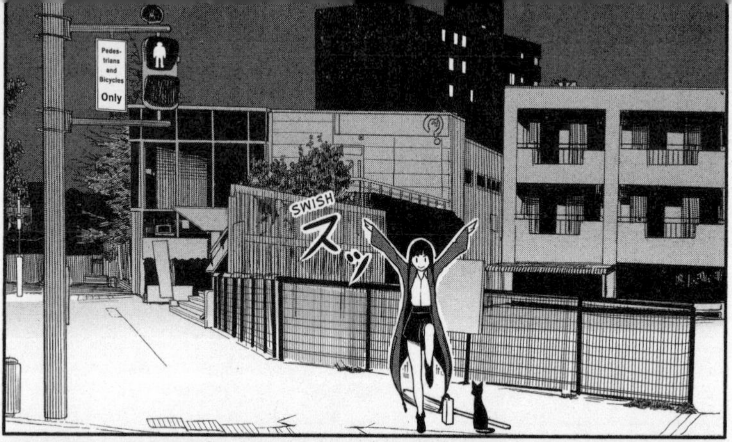
Pedes-
trians
and
Bicycles
Only
SWISH
スッ
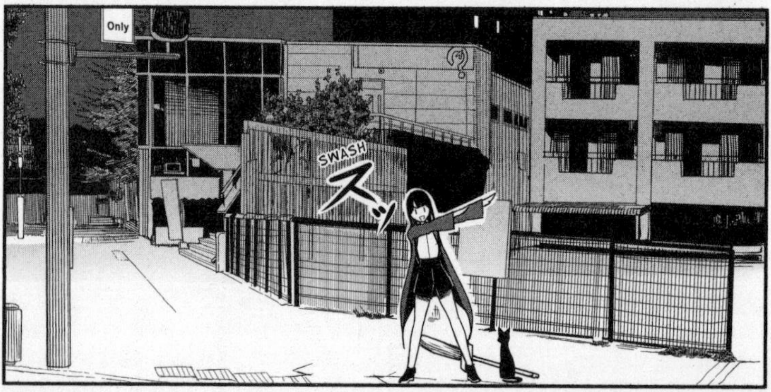
Only
SWASH
スッ
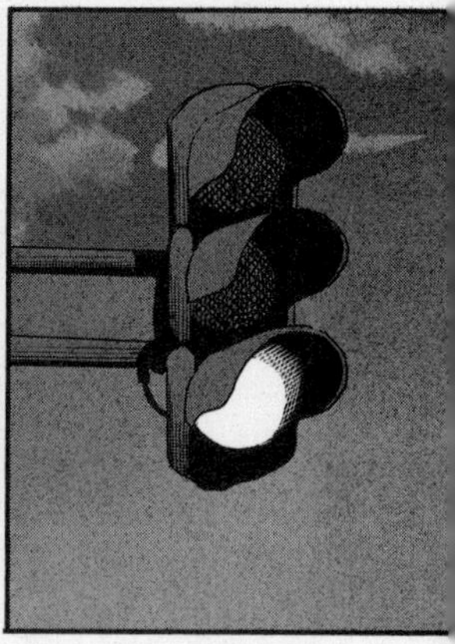
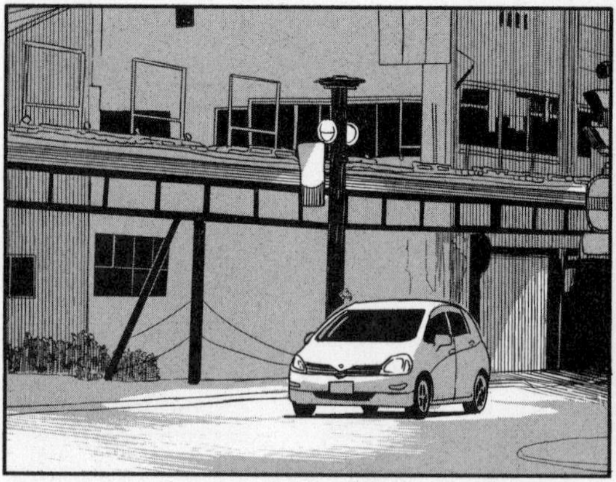

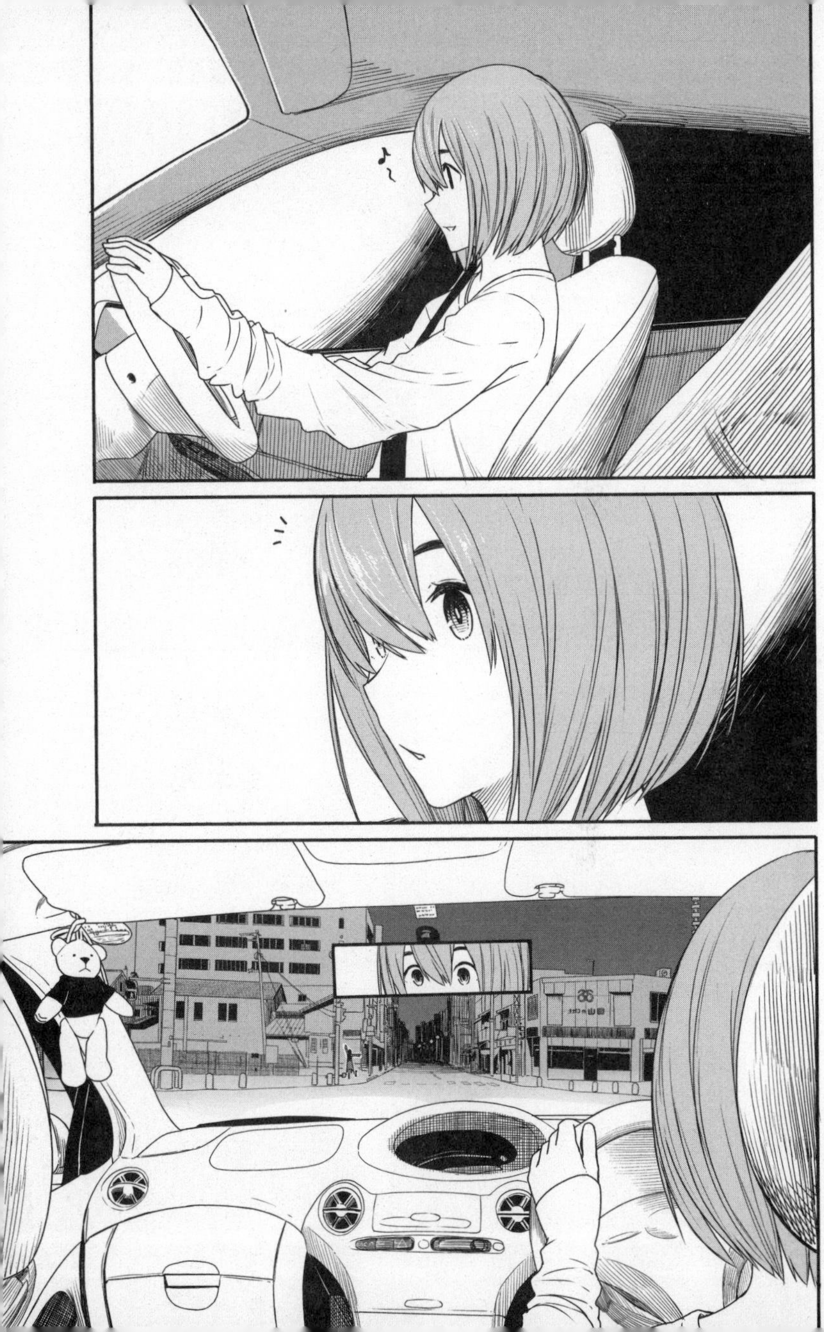

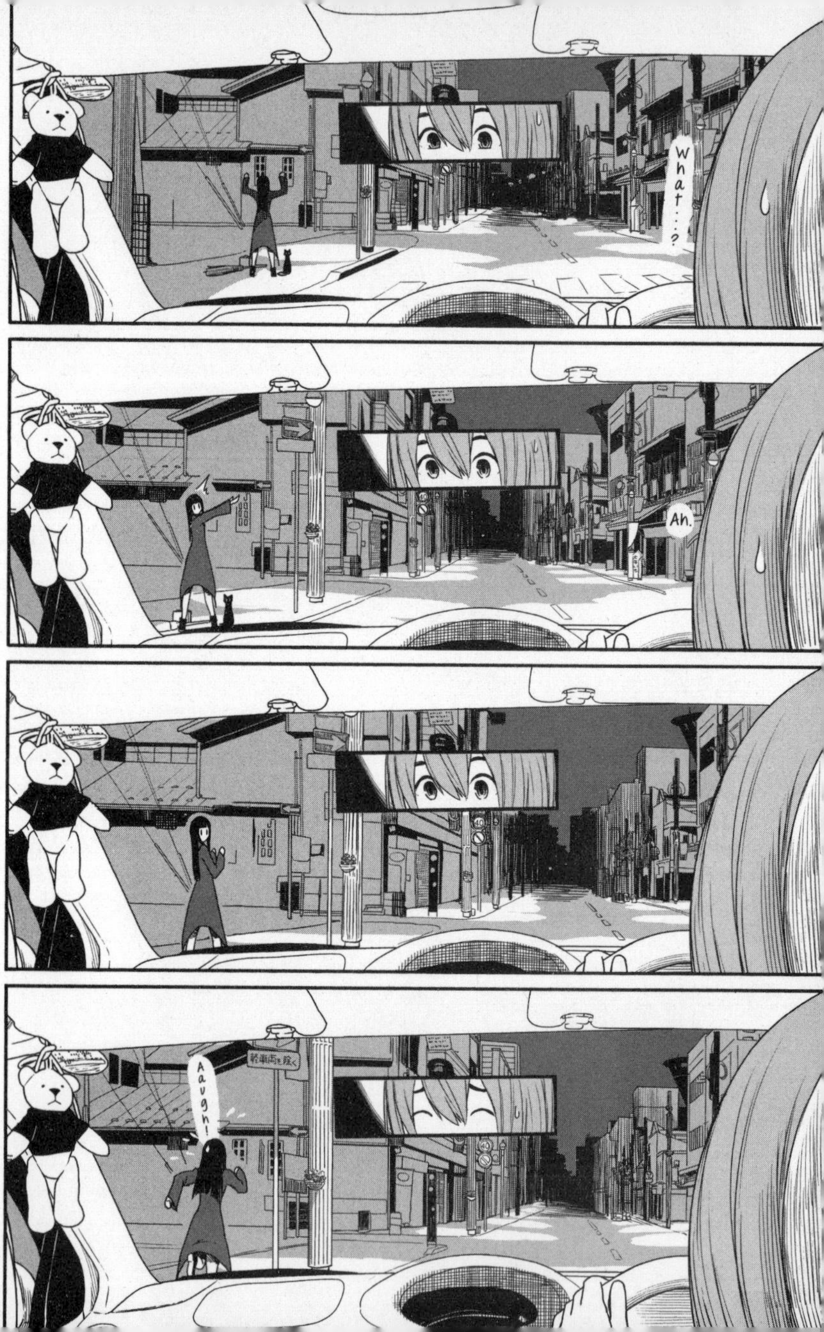
What...?
Ah.
Aaugh!

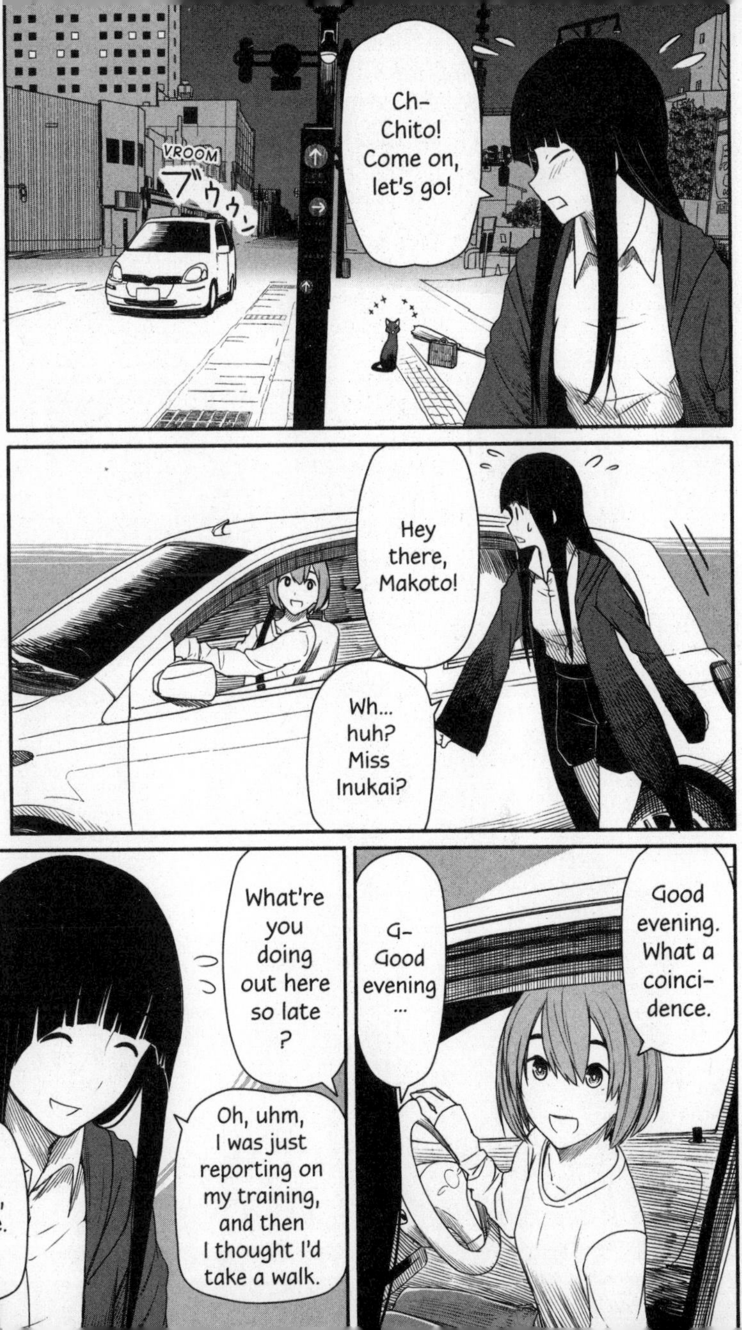
Ch- Chito! Come on, let's go!
VROOM
ブウゥン
Hey there, Makoto!
Wh... huh? Miss Inukai?
Good evening. What a coinci- dence.
G- Good evening ...
What're you doing out here so late ?
Oh, uhm, I was just reporting on my training, and then I thought I'd take a walk.
Ooh, I see.

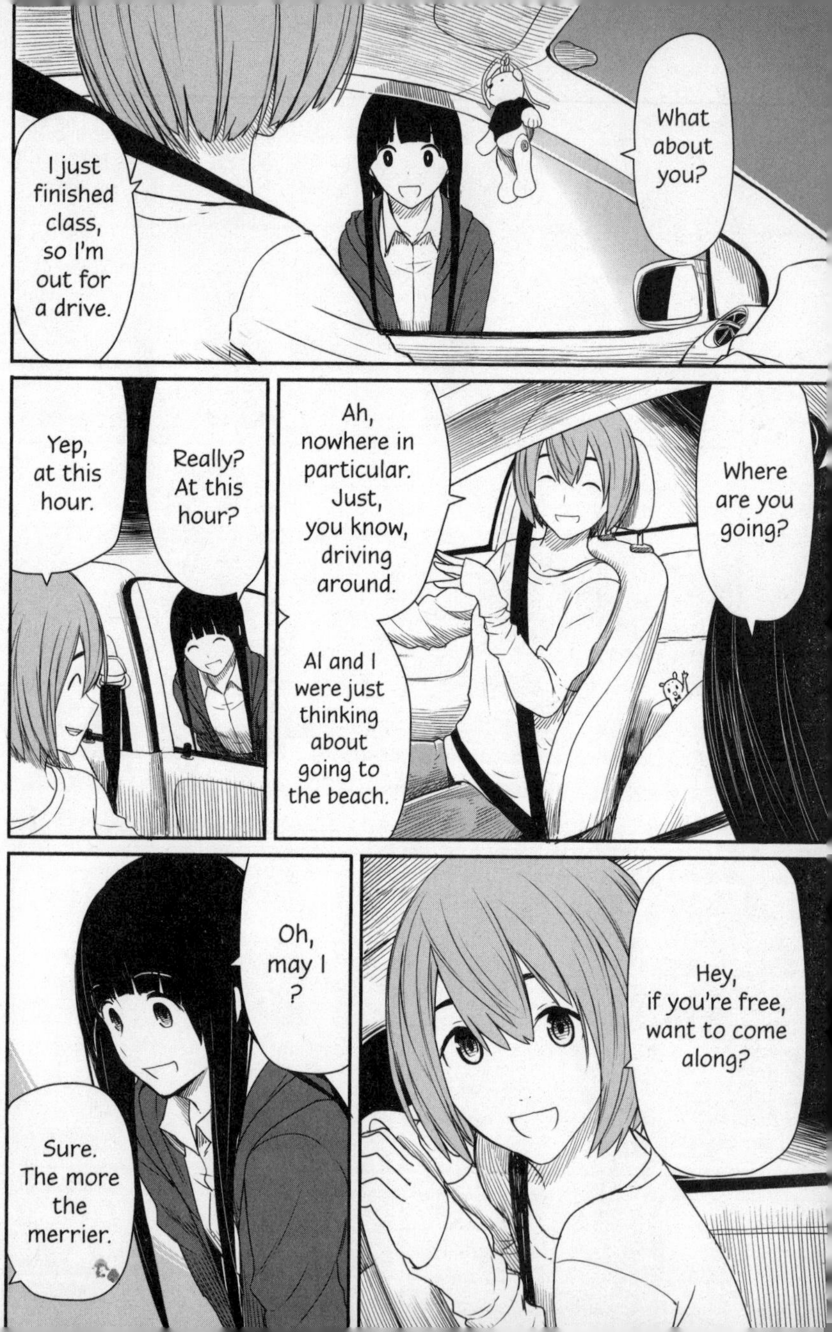
What about you?
I just finished class, so I'm out for a drive.
Where are you going?
Ah, nowhere in particular. Just, you know, driving around.
Al and I were just thinking about going to the beach.
Really? At this hour?
Yep, at this hour.
Hey, if you're free, want to come along?
Oh, may I ?
Sure. The more the merrier.

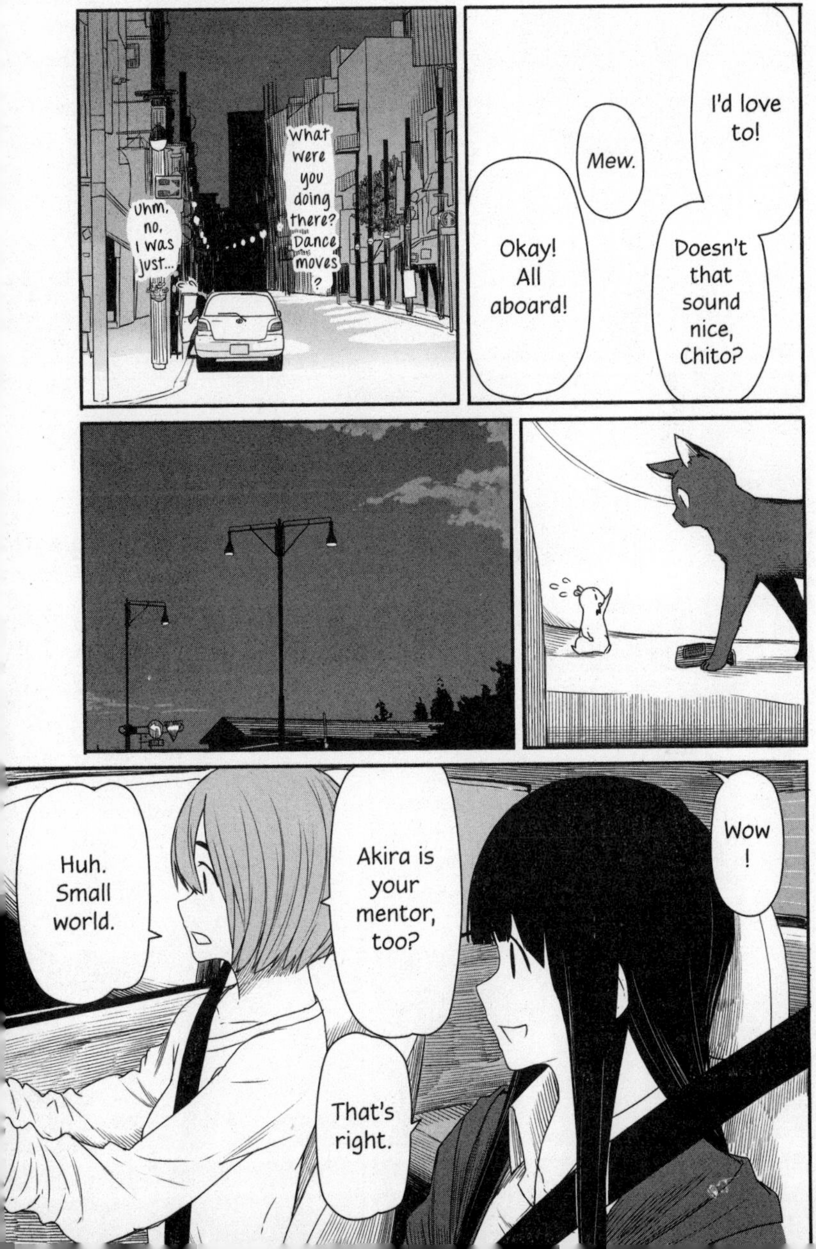
I'd love to!
Doesn't that sound nice, Chito?
Mew.
Okay! All aboard!
What were you doing there? Dance moves?
Uhm, no. I was just...
Wow!
Akira is your mentor, too?
That's right.
Huh. Small world.

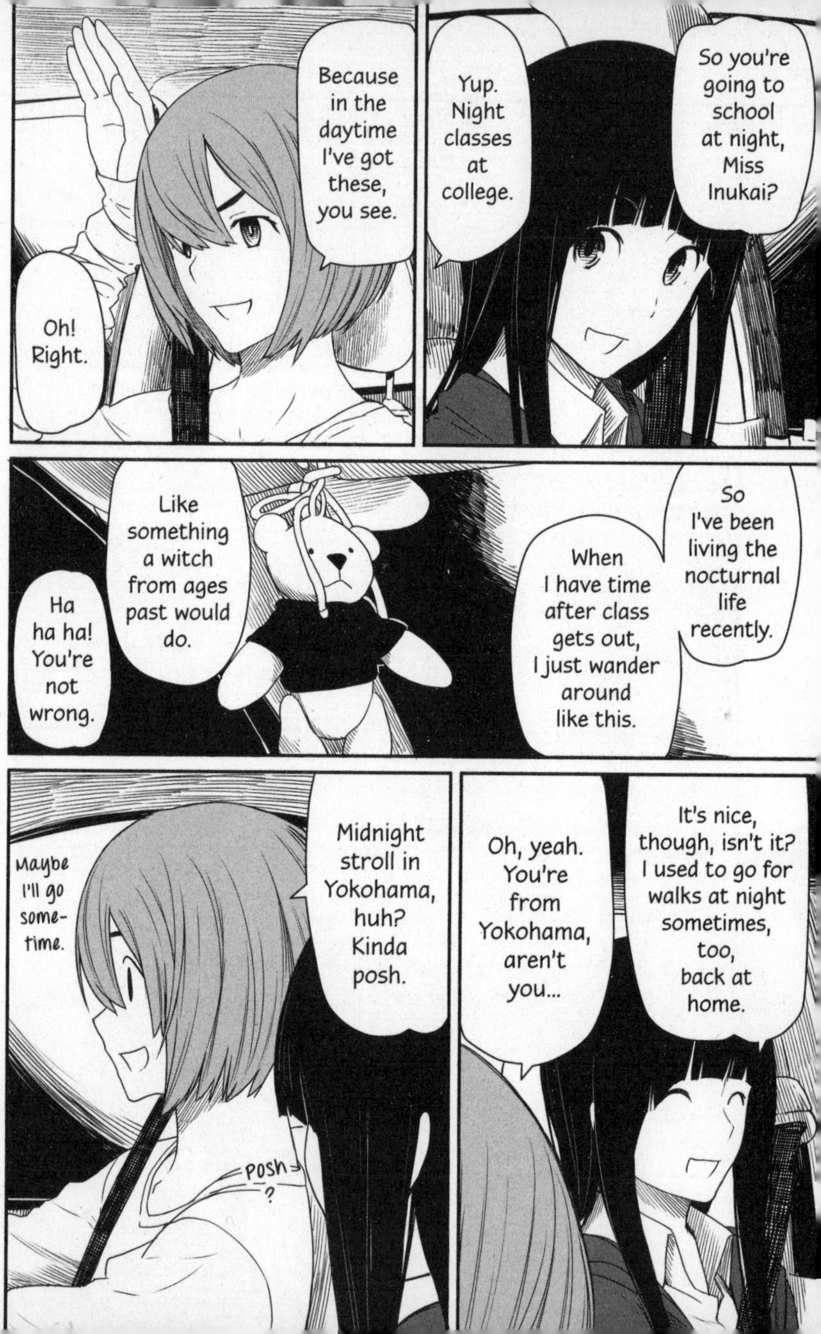
So you're going to school at night, Miss Inukai?
Yup. Night classes at college.
Because in the daytime I've got these, you see.
Oh! Right.
So I've been living the nocturnal life recently.
When I have time after class gets out, I just wander around like this.
Like something a witch from ages past would do.
Ha ha ha! You're not wrong.
It's nice, though, isn't it? I used to go for walks at night sometimes, too, back at home.
Oh, yeah. You're from Yokohama, aren't you...
Midnight stroll in Yokohama, huh? Kinda posh.
Maybe I'll go sometime.
Posh?

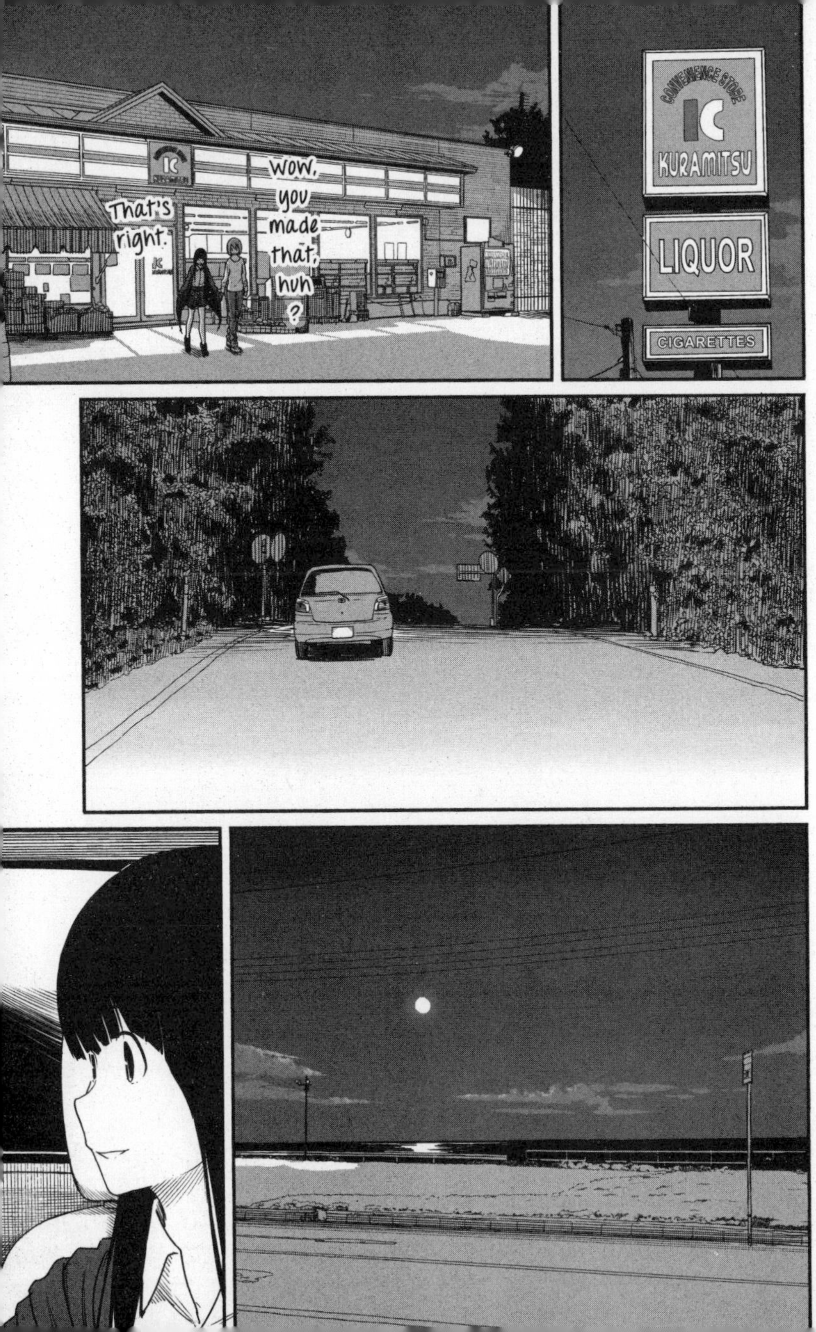
CONVENIENCE STORE
IC
KURAMITSU
LIQUOR
CIGARETTES
Wow, you made that, huh?
That's right.

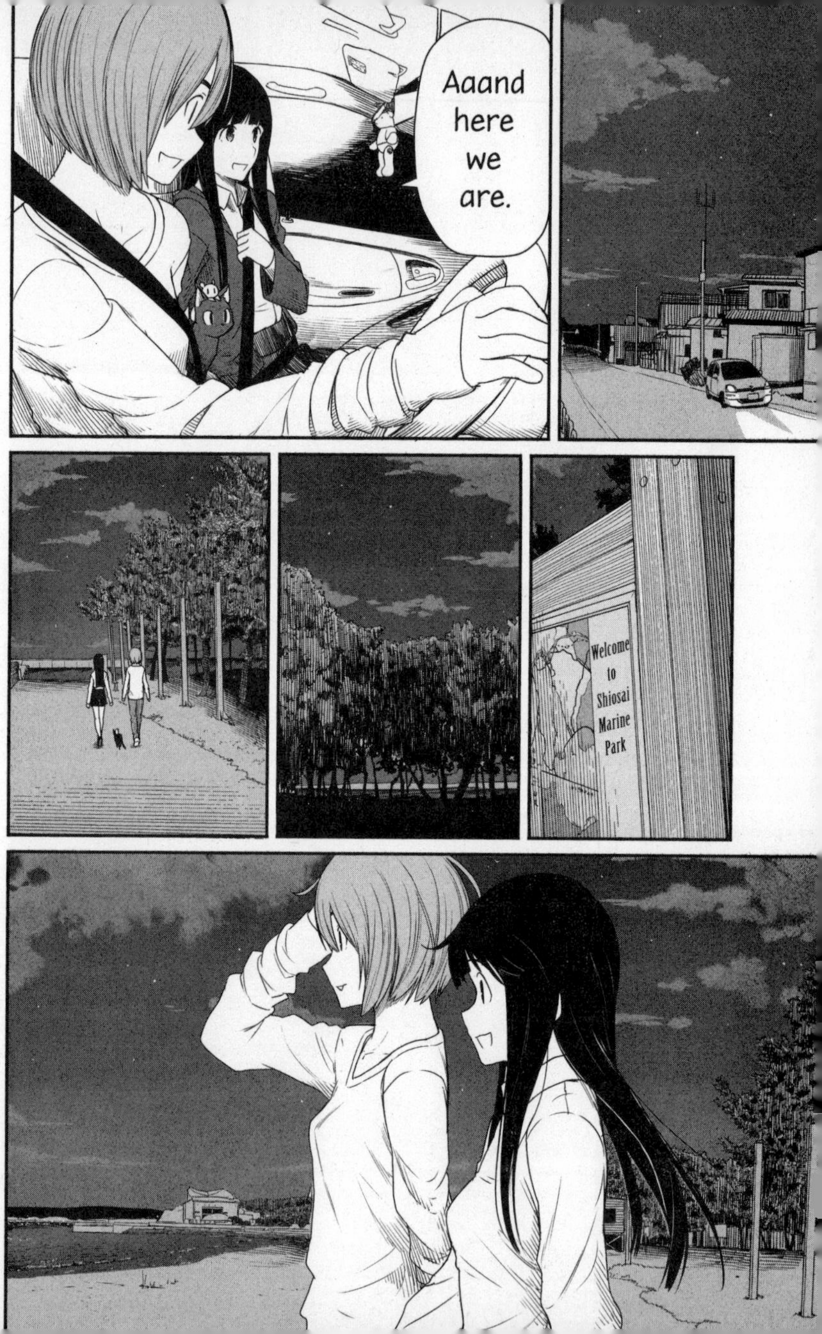
Aaand here we are.
Welcome to Shiosai Marine Park

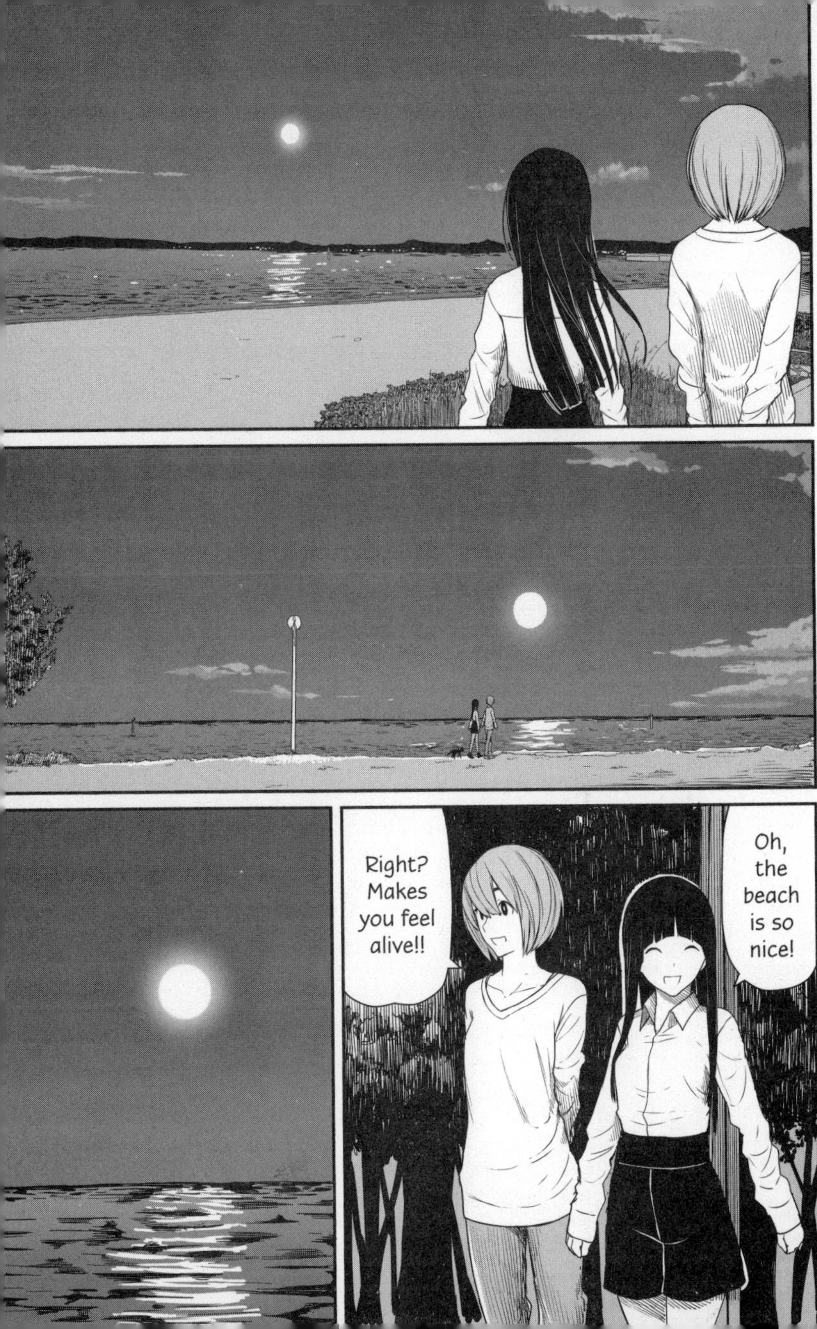
Oh, the beach is so nice!
Right? Makes you feel alive!!

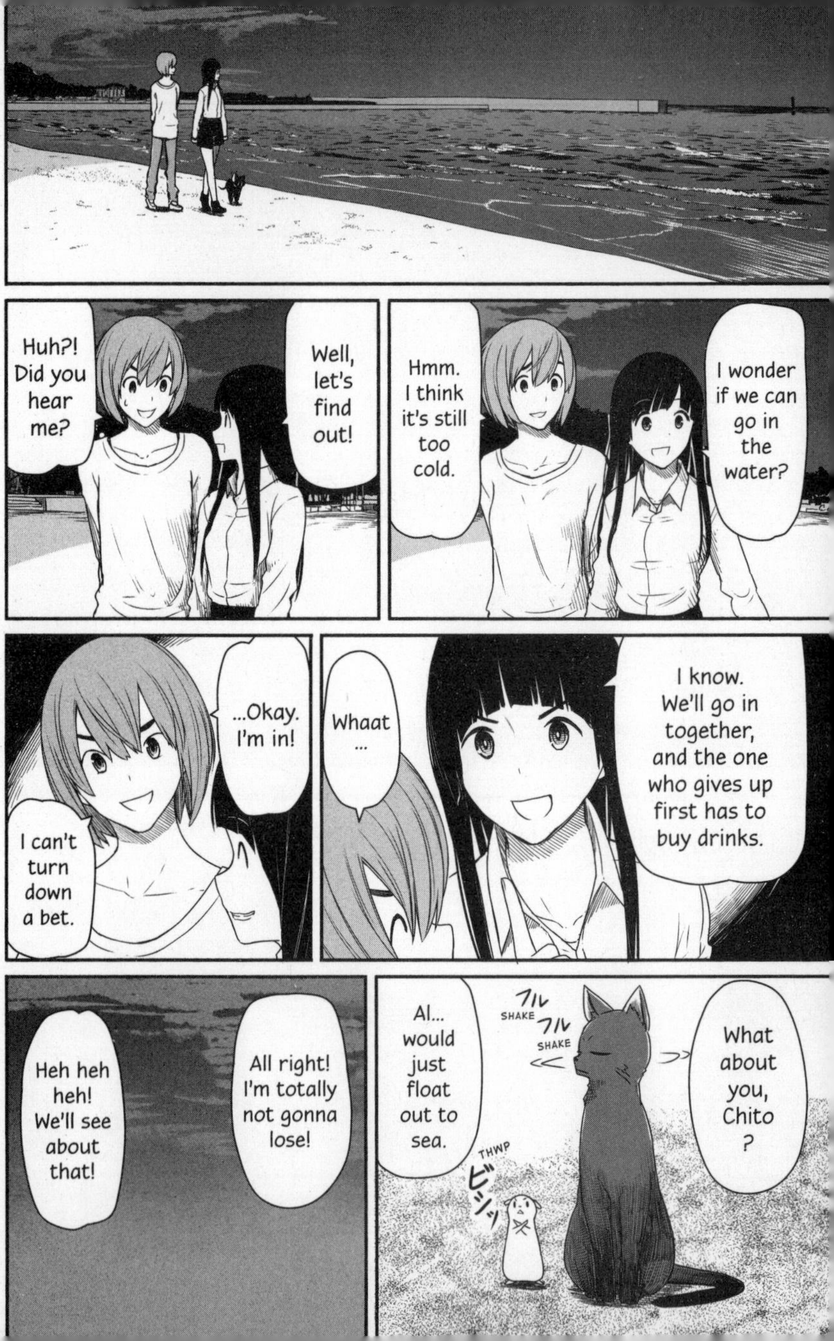

I wonder if we can go in the water?
Hmm. I think it's still too cold.
Well, let's find out!
Huh?! Did you hear me?
I know. We'll go in together, and the one who gives up first has to buy drinks.
Whaat ...
...Okay. I'm in!
I can't turn down a bet.
What about you, Chito?
フル SHAKE フル SHAKE
Al... would just float out to sea.
ビシッ THWP
All right! I'm totally not gonna lose!
Heh heh heh! We'll see about that!

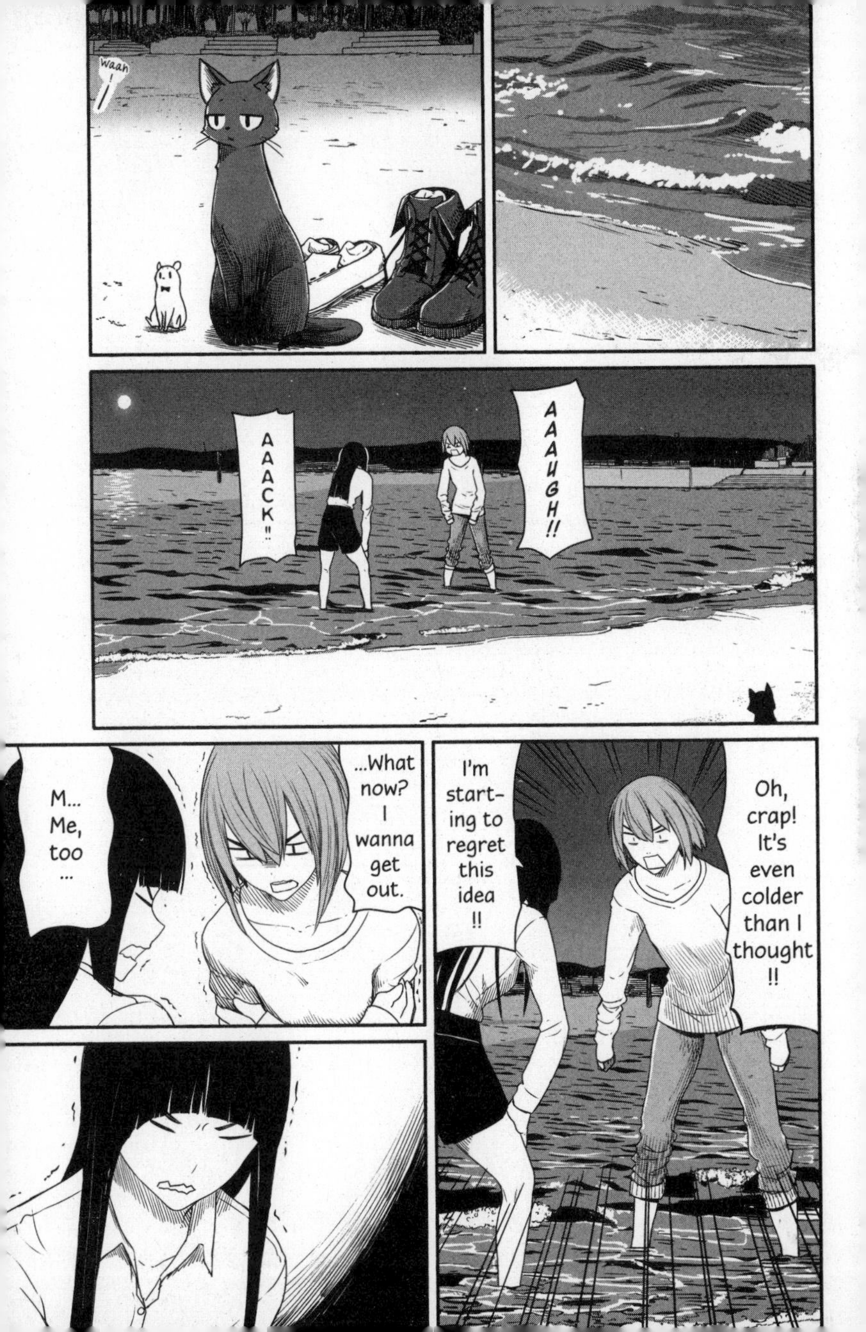
waan!
AAAUGH!!
AAACK!!
Oh, crap! It's even colder than I thought!!
I'm start-ing to regret this idea!!
...What now? I wanna get out.
M... Me, too...

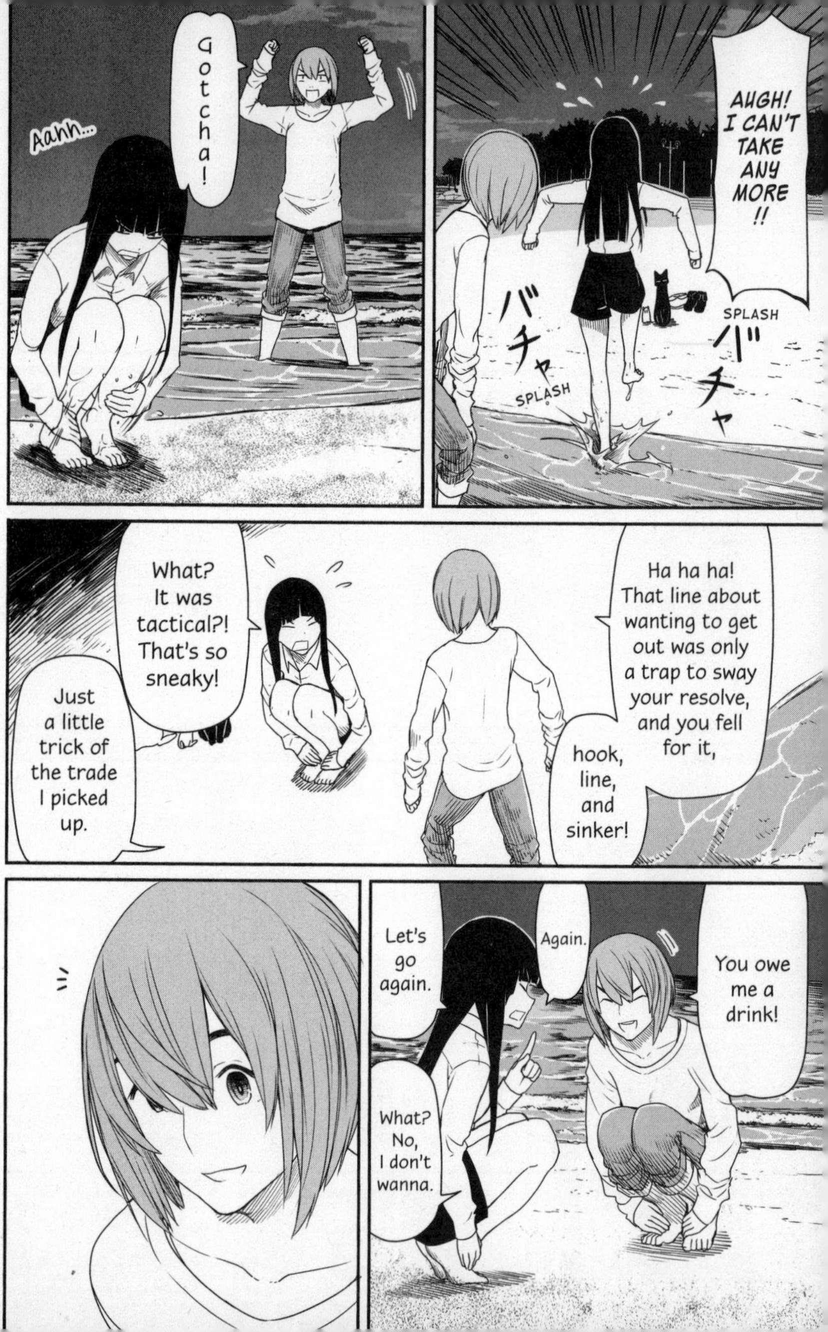
AUGH! I CAN'T TAKE ANY MORE !!
バチャ
SPLASH
バチャ
SPLASH
Gotcha!
Aahh...
Ha ha ha! That line about wanting to get out was only a trap to sway your resolve, and you fell for it,
hook, line, and sinker!
What? It was tactical?! That's so sneaky!
Just a little trick of the trade I picked up.
You owe me a drink!
Again.
Let's go again.
What? No, I don't wanna.

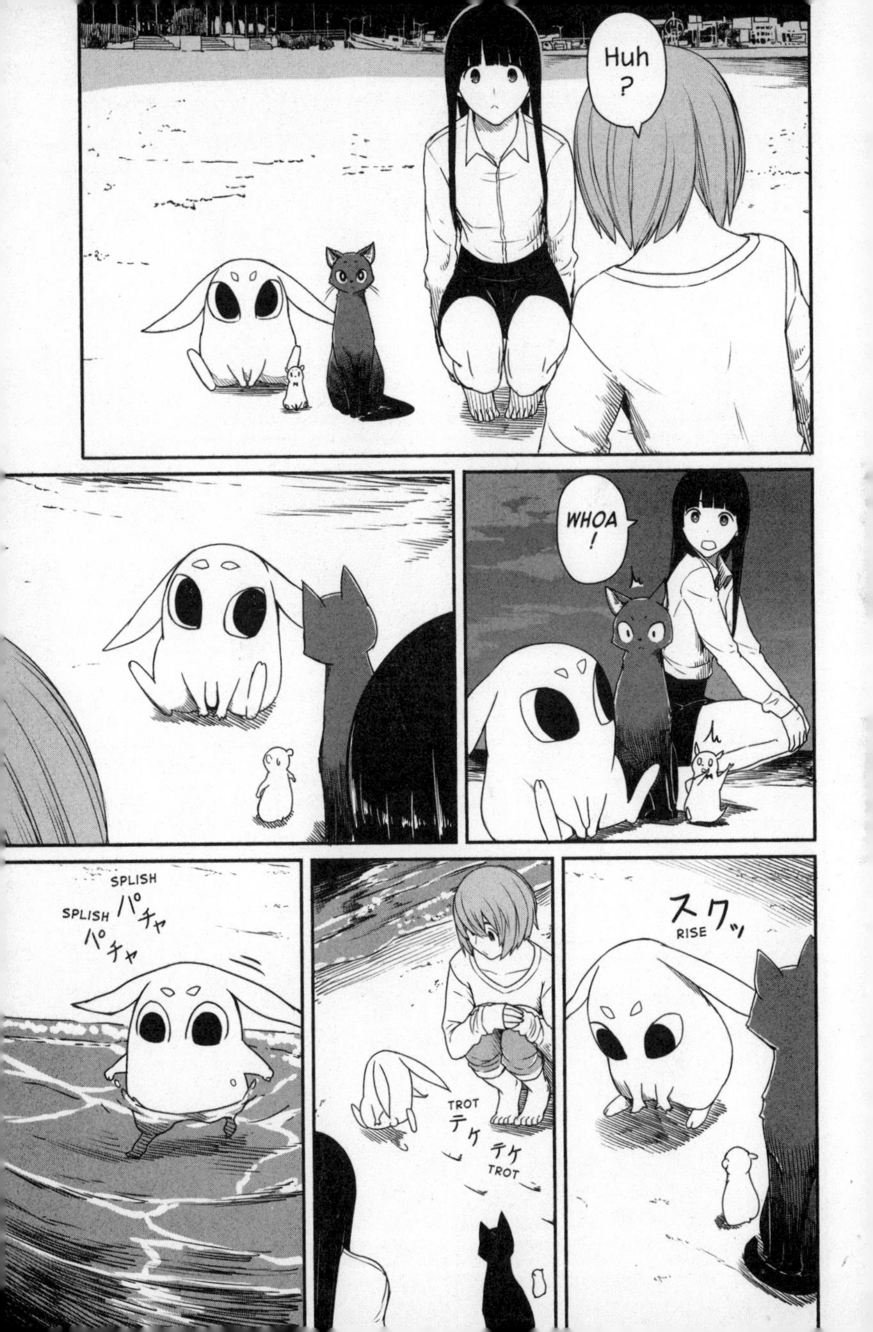
Huh ?
WHOA !
スワッ
RISE
TROT
テケ
テケ
TROT
SPLISH
パチャ
SPLISH
パチャ

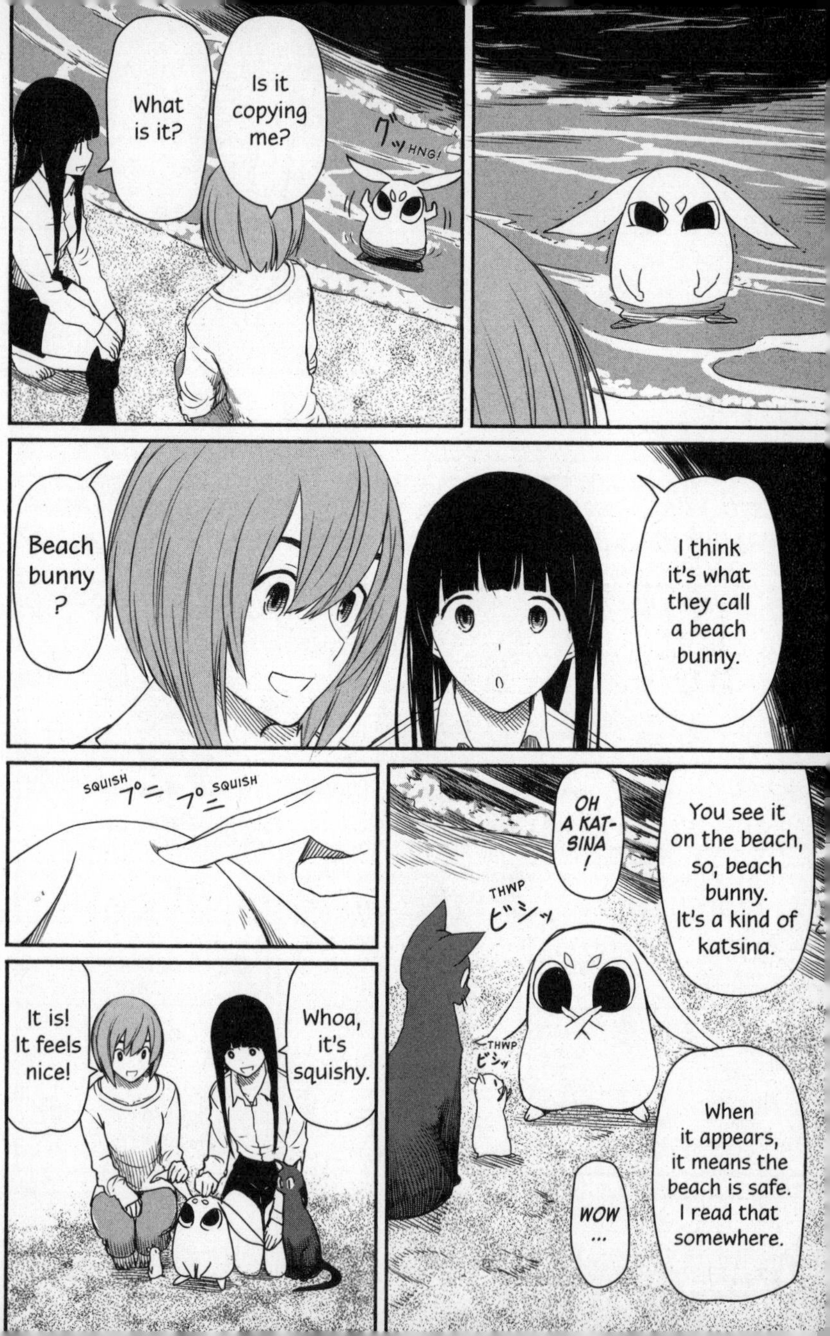

Is it copying me?
What is it?
グッ HNG!
I think it's what they call a beach bunny.
Beach bunny?
You see it on the beach, so, beach bunny. It's a kind of katsina.
OH A KAT-SINA!
THWP ビシッ
THWP ビシッ
When it appears, it means the beach is safe. I read that somewhere.
WOW ...
SQUISH プニ
プニ SQUISH
Whoa, it's squishy.
It is! It feels nice!

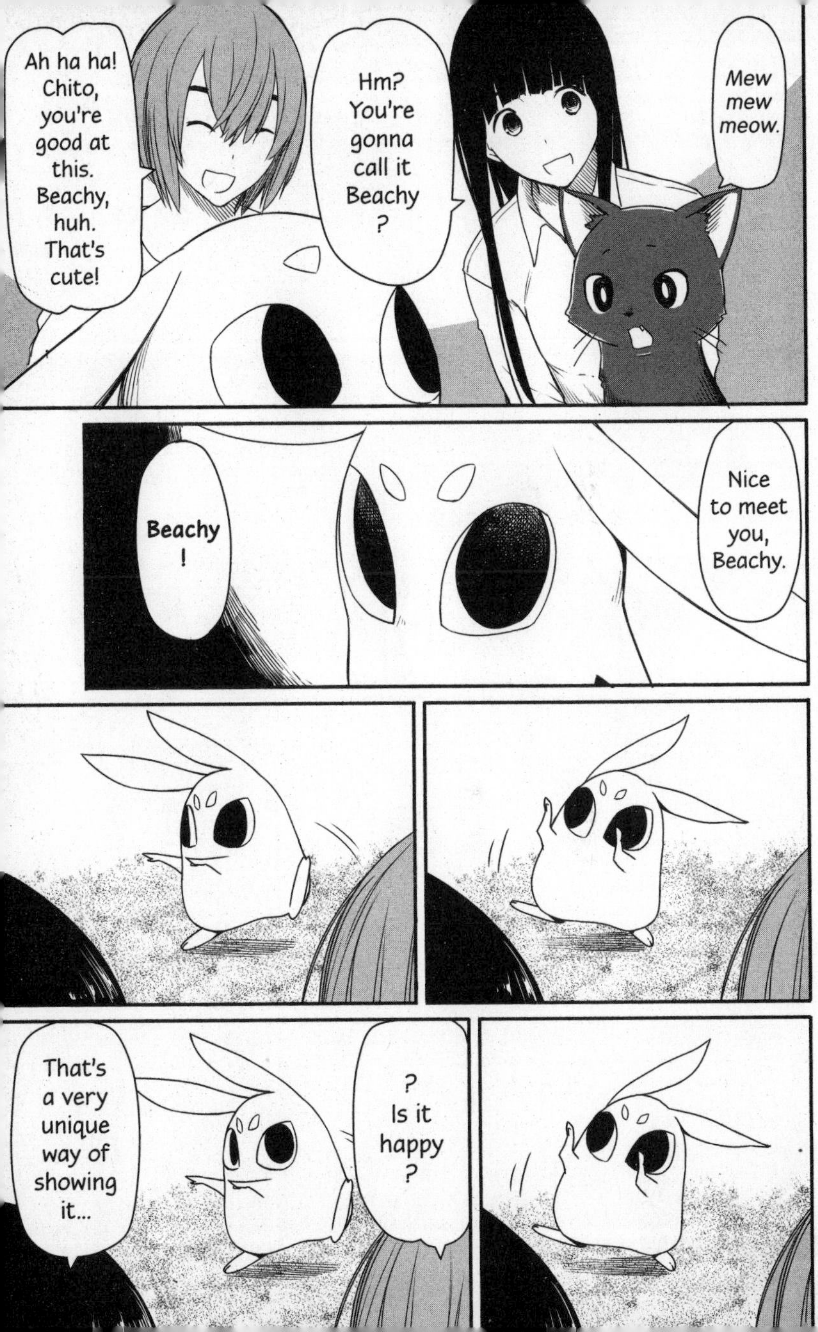
Mew mew meow.
Hm? You're gonna call it Beachy?
Ah ha ha! Chito, you're good at this. Beachy, huh. That's cute!
Nice to meet you, Beachy.
Beachy!
? Is it happy?
That's a very unique way of showing it...

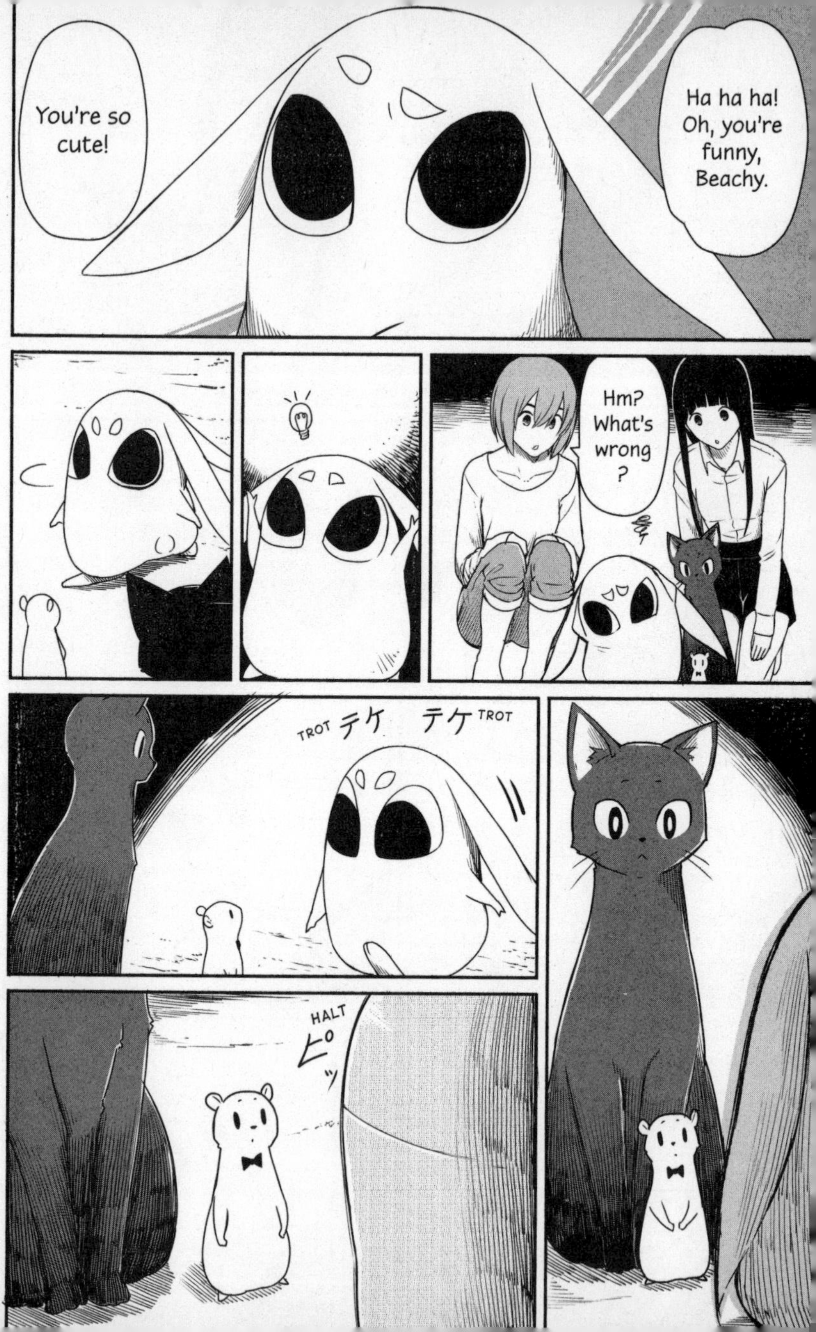
Ha ha ha! Oh, you're funny, Beachy.
You're so cute!
Hm? What's wrong ?
テケ TROT
TROT テケ
HALT ピッ

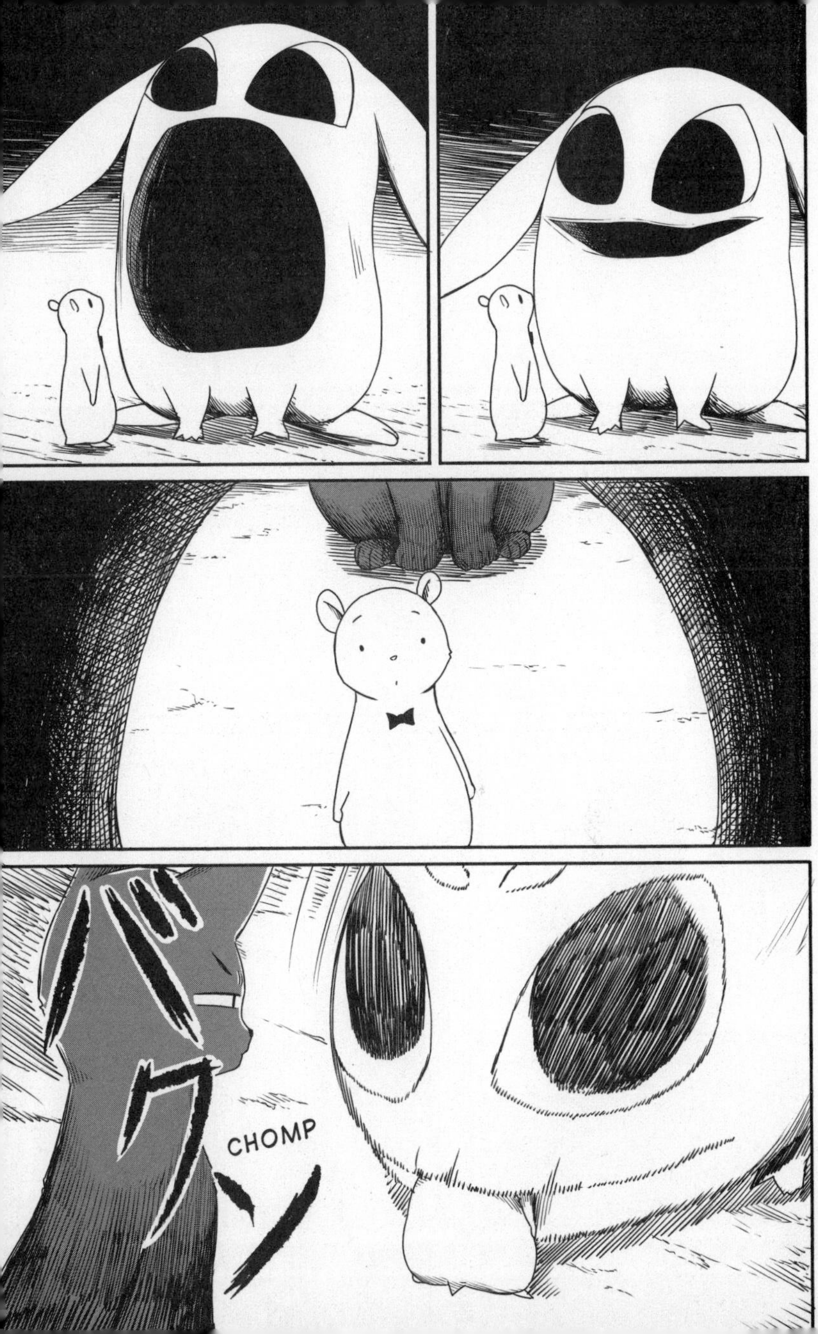
CHOMP

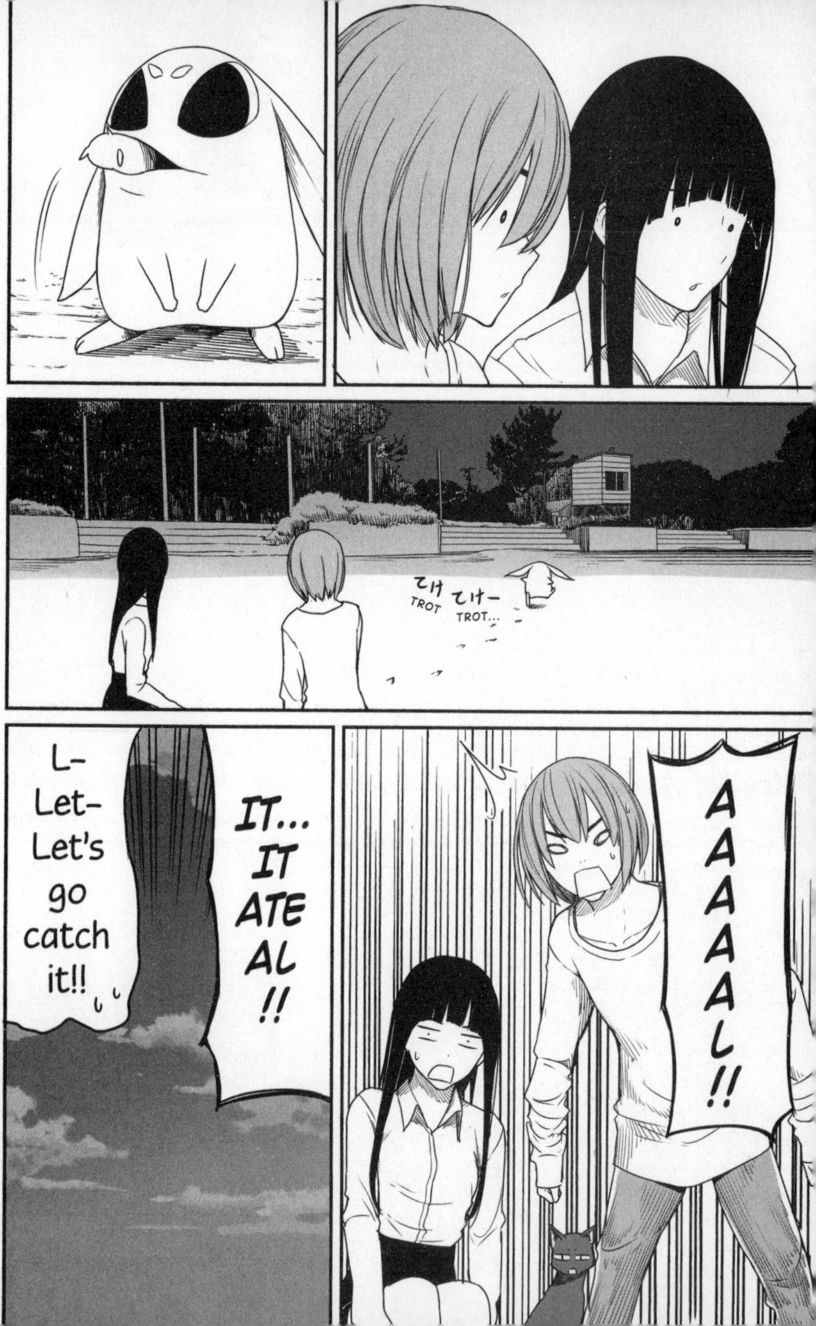
てけ TROT
てけー TROT...
AAAAAL!!
IT... IT ATE AL!!
L-Let-Let's go catch it!!

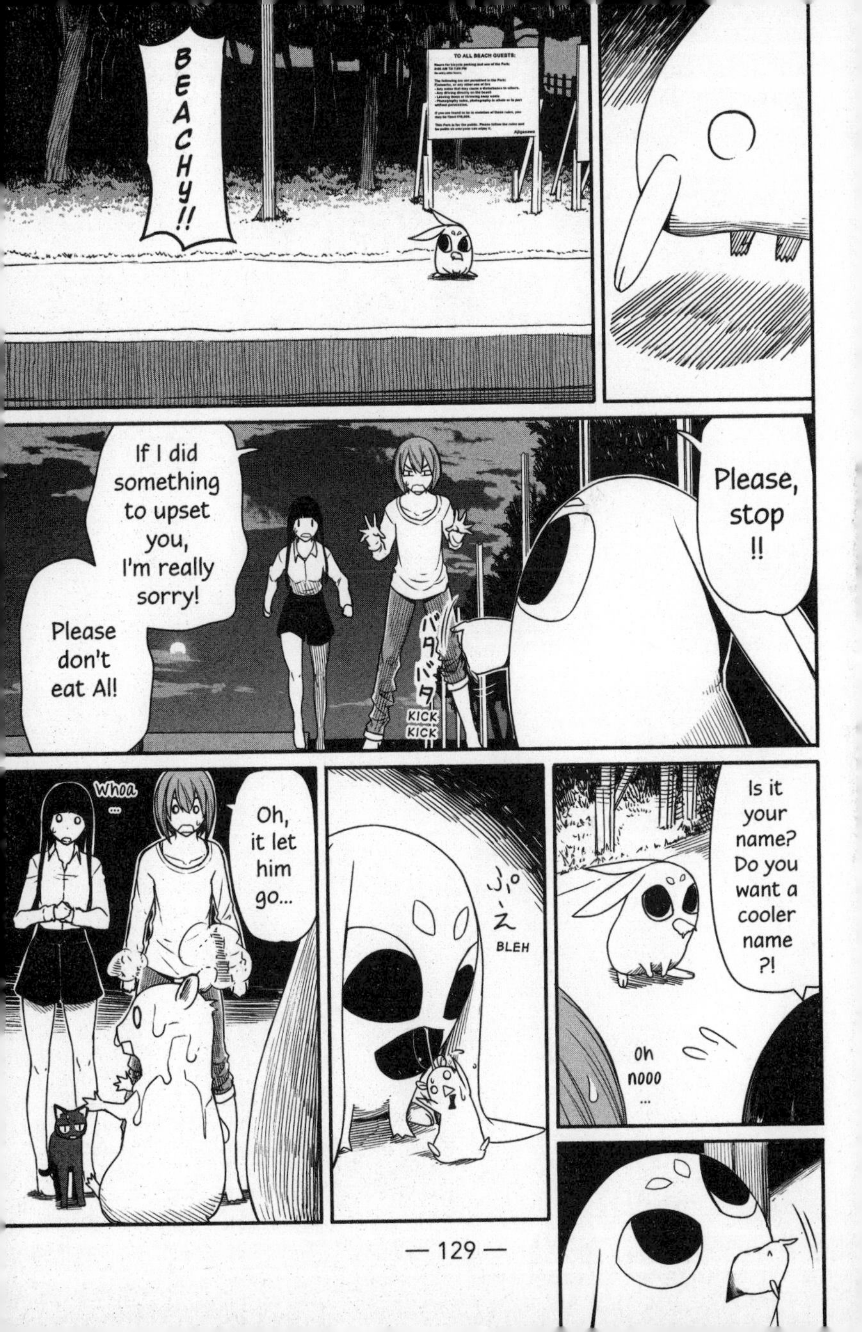
BEACHY!!
TO ALL BEACH GUESTS:
Please, stop!!
バタバタ
KICK KICK
If I did something to upset you, I'm really sorry!
Please don't eat Al!
Is it your name? Do you want a cooler name?!
Oh nooo ...
ぷえ
BLEH
Oh, it let him go...
Whoa ...

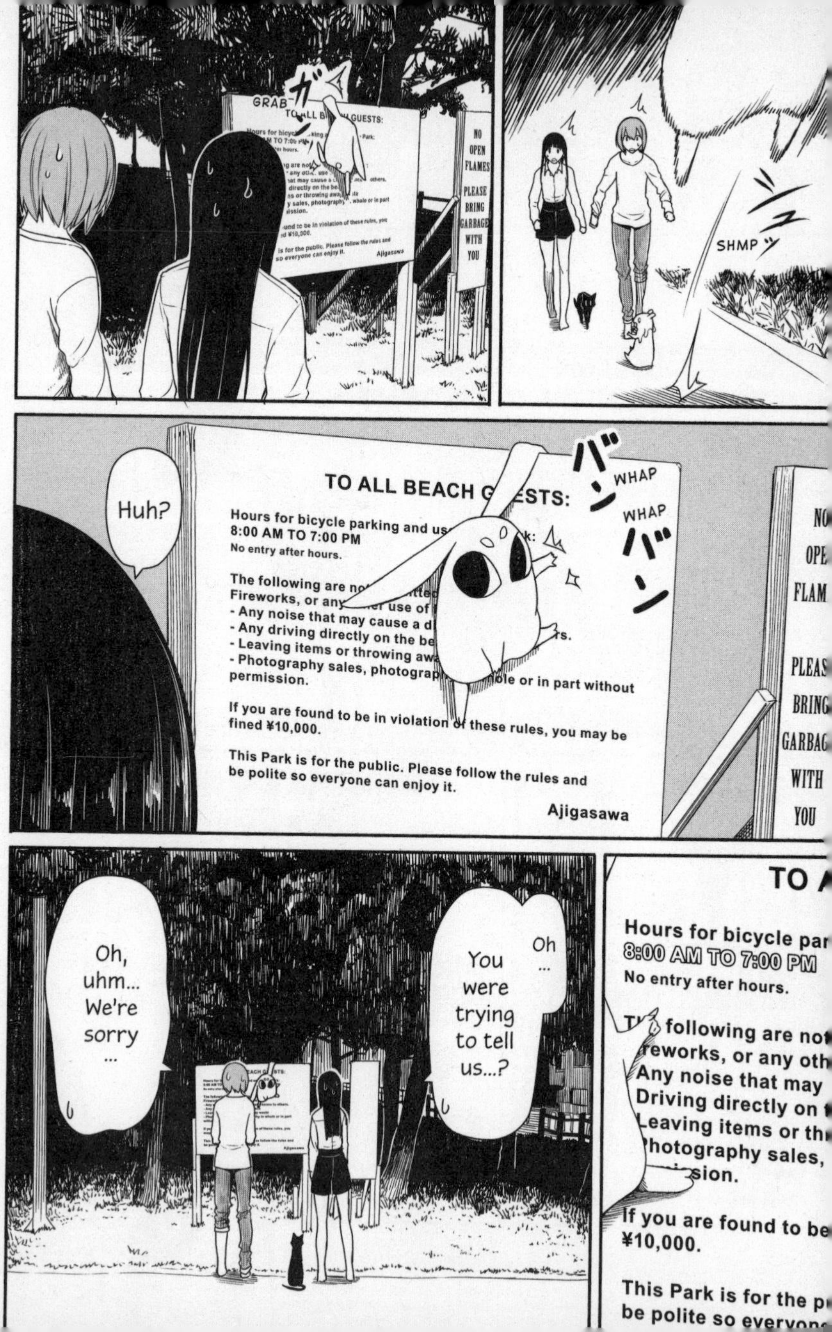
SHMP
GRAB
TO ALL BEACH GUESTS:
NO OPEN FLAMES
PLEASE BRING GARBAGE WITH YOU
Huh?
TO ALL BEACH G ESTS:
Hours for bicycle parking and us
8:00 AM TO 7:00 PM
No entry after hours.
If you are found to be in violation of these rules, you may be
fined ¥10,000.
This Park is for the public. Please follow the rules and
be polite so everyone can enjoy it.
Ajigasawa
WHAP
WHAP
TO A
Hours for bicycle par
8:00 AM TO 7:00 PM
No entry after hours.
If you are found to be
¥10,000.
This Park is for the p
Oh ...
You were trying to tell us...?
Oh, uhm... We're sorry ...

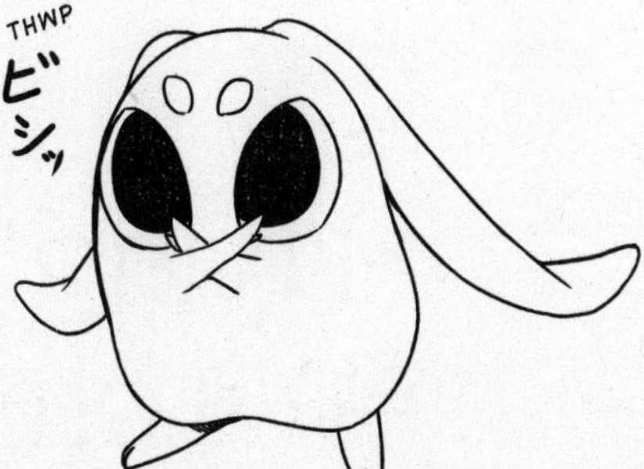
THWP
ビシッ

Flying
Witch

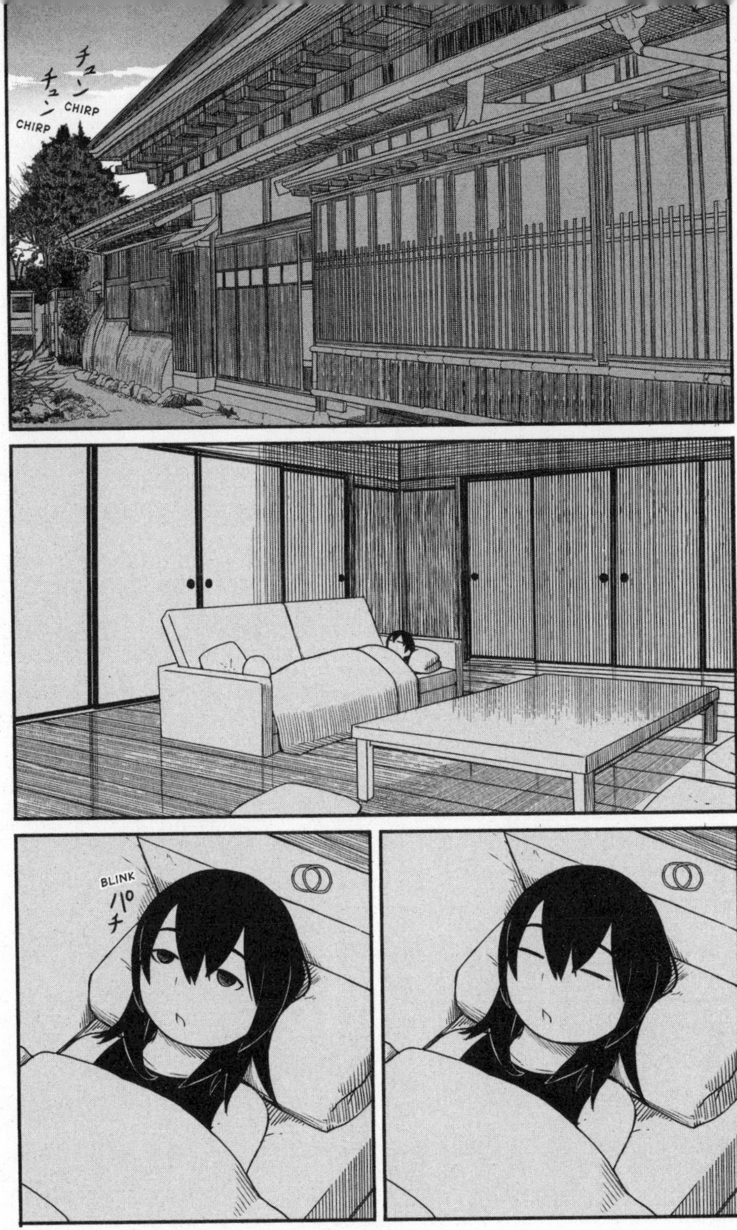
チュン
CHIRP
チュン
CHIRP
BLINK
パチ

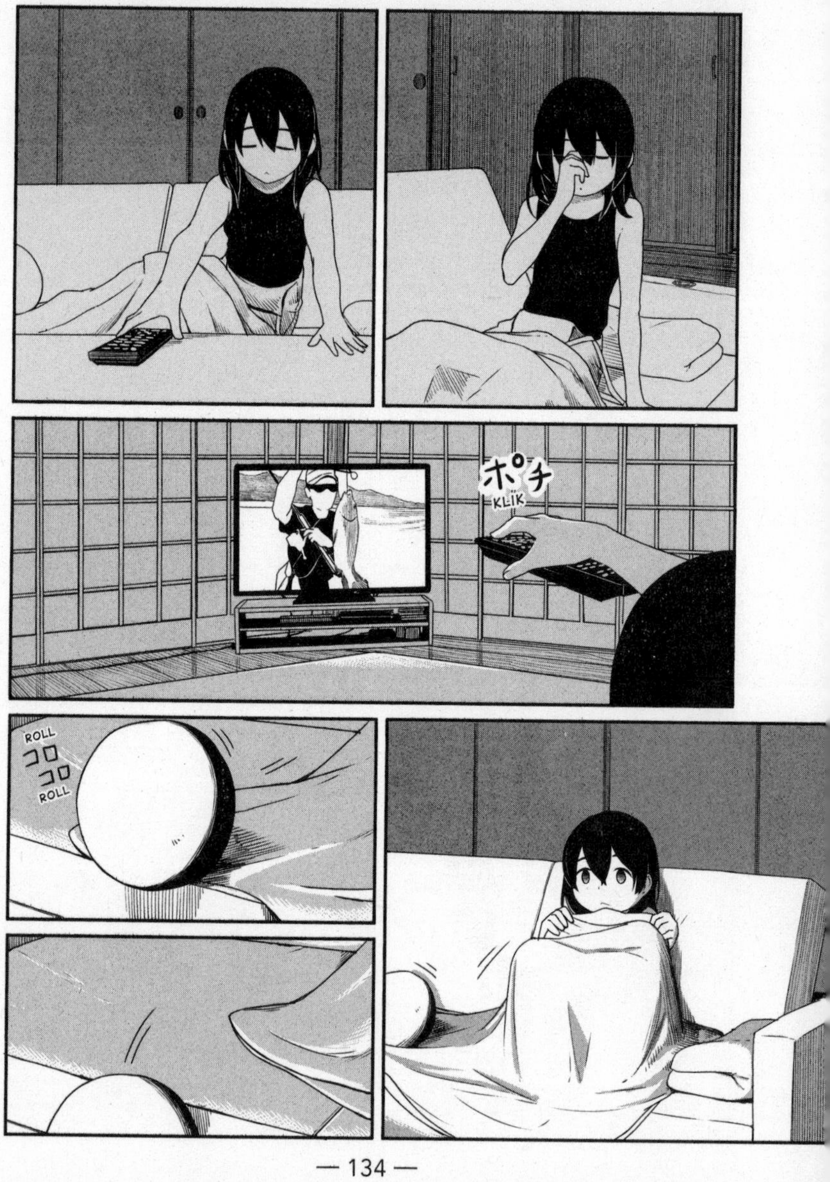
ポチ
KLIK
ROLL
コロ
コロ
ROLL

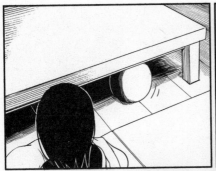

BOUNCE
ボボン

A ball ...?

BOUNCE
ボーン
ボーン
BOUNCE
BOUNCE
〈ボーン
BOUNCE

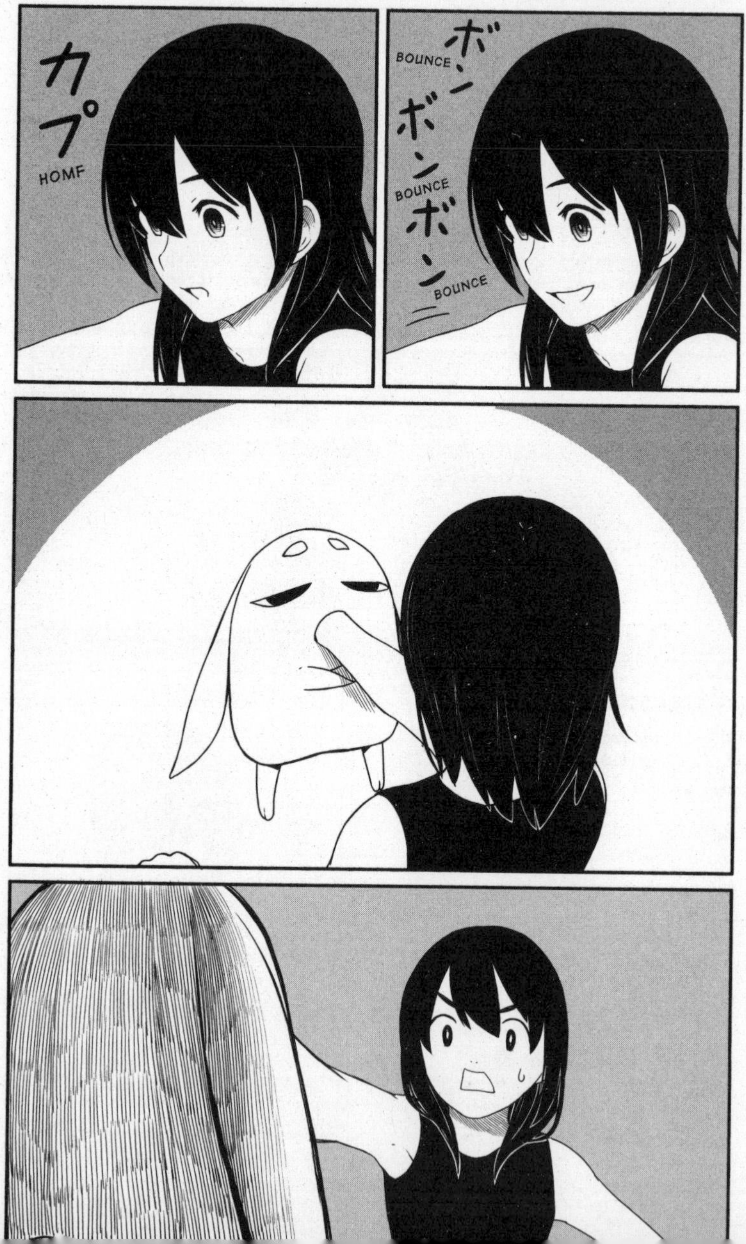
ボン
BOUNCE
ボン
BOUNCE
ボン
BOUNCE
カプ
HOMF

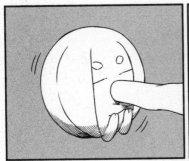

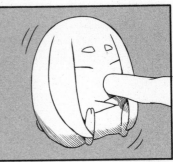

FLAIL FLAIL

Am... Am I still dreaming?!

Huh?

Chapter 24
The Rabbit's Headstand

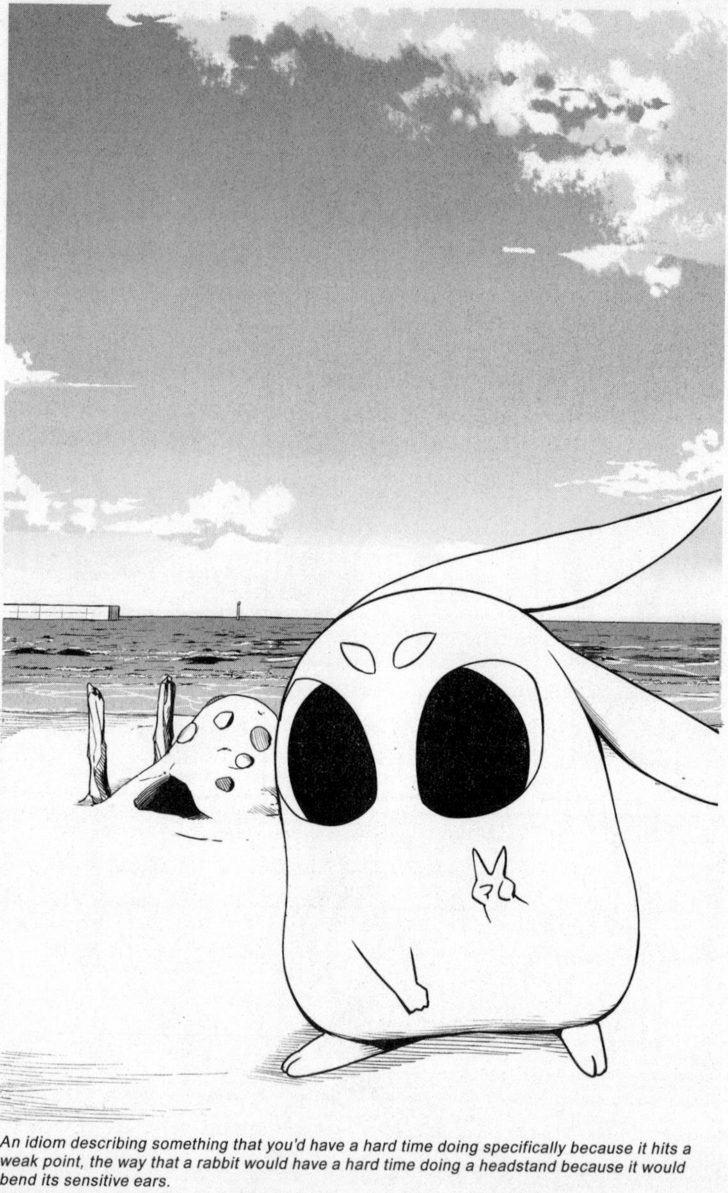

An idiom describing something that you'd have a hard time doing specifically because it hits a weak point, the way that a rabbit would have a hard time doing a headstand because it would bend its sensitive ears.

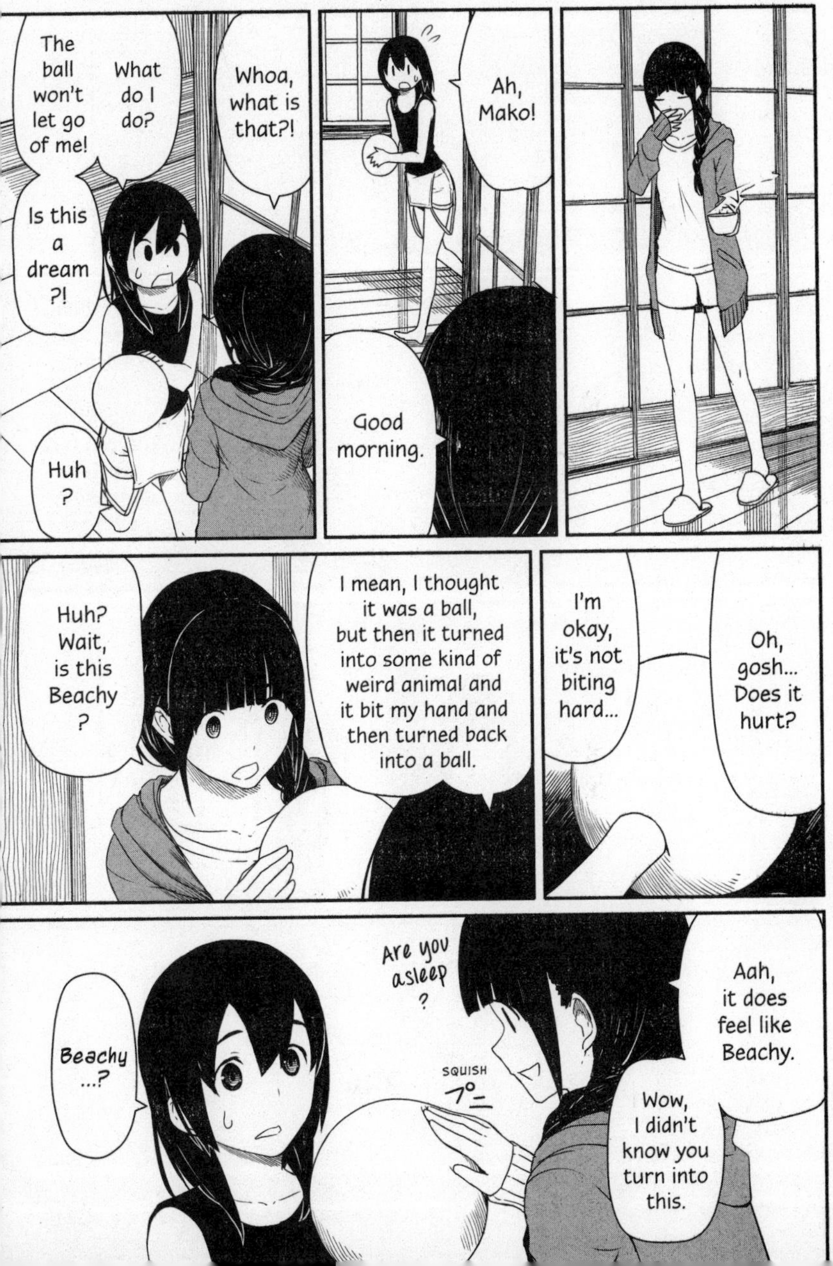
Ah, Mako!
Good morning.
Whoa, what is that?!
What do I do?
The ball won't let go of me!
Is this a dream ?!
Huh ?
Oh, gosh... Does it hurt?
I'm okay, it's not biting hard...
I mean, I thought it was a ball, but then it turned into some kind of weird animal and it bit my hand and then turned back into a ball.
Huh? Wait, is this Beachy ?
Aah, it does feel like Beachy.
Are you asleep ?
SQUISH
Wow, I didn't know you turn into this.
Beachy ...?

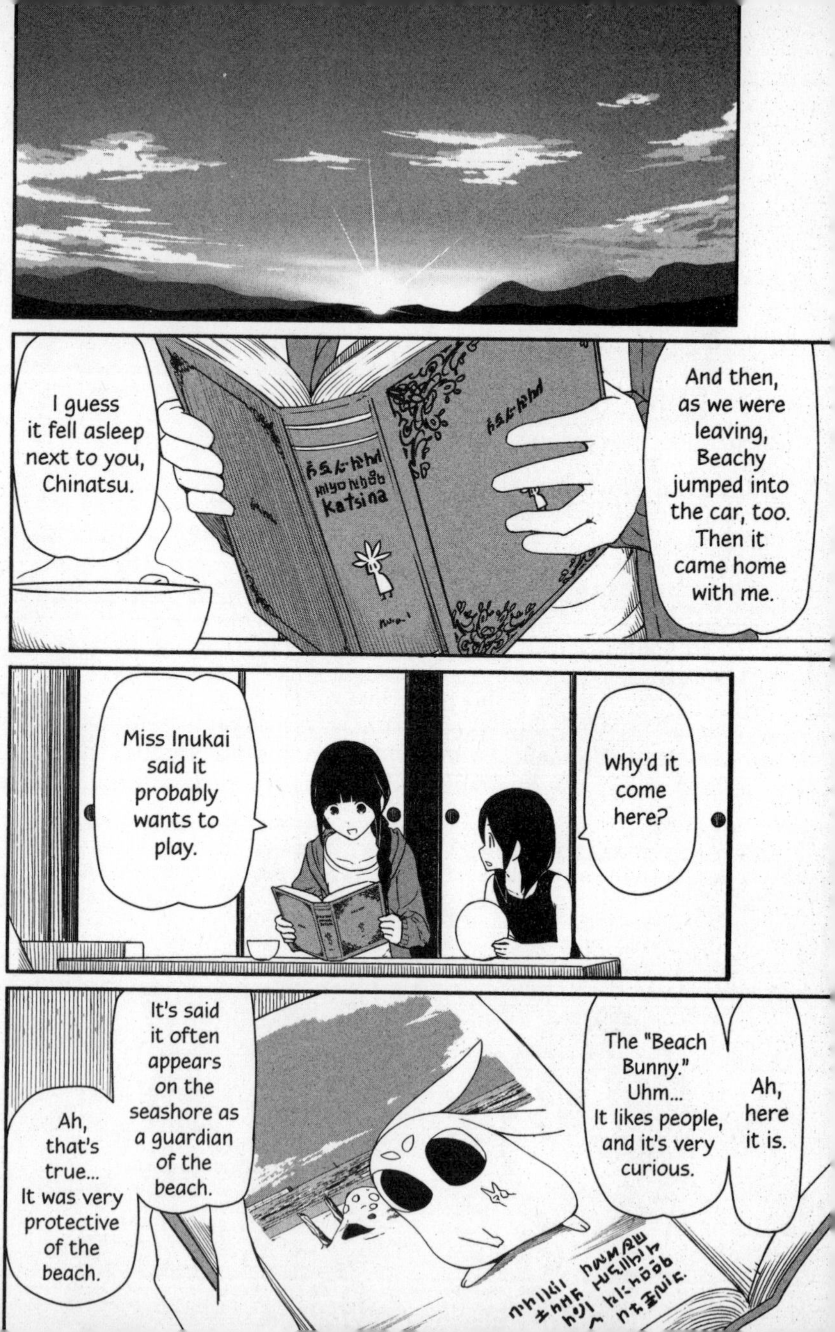
And then, as we were leaving, Beachy jumped into the car, too. Then it came home with me.
I guess it fell asleep next to you, Chinatsu.
Katsina
Why'd it come here?
Miss Inukai said it probably wants to play.
Ah, here it is.
The "Beach Bunny." Uhm... It likes people, and it's very curious.
It's said it often appears on the seashore as a guardian of the beach.
Ah, that's true... It was very protective of the beach.

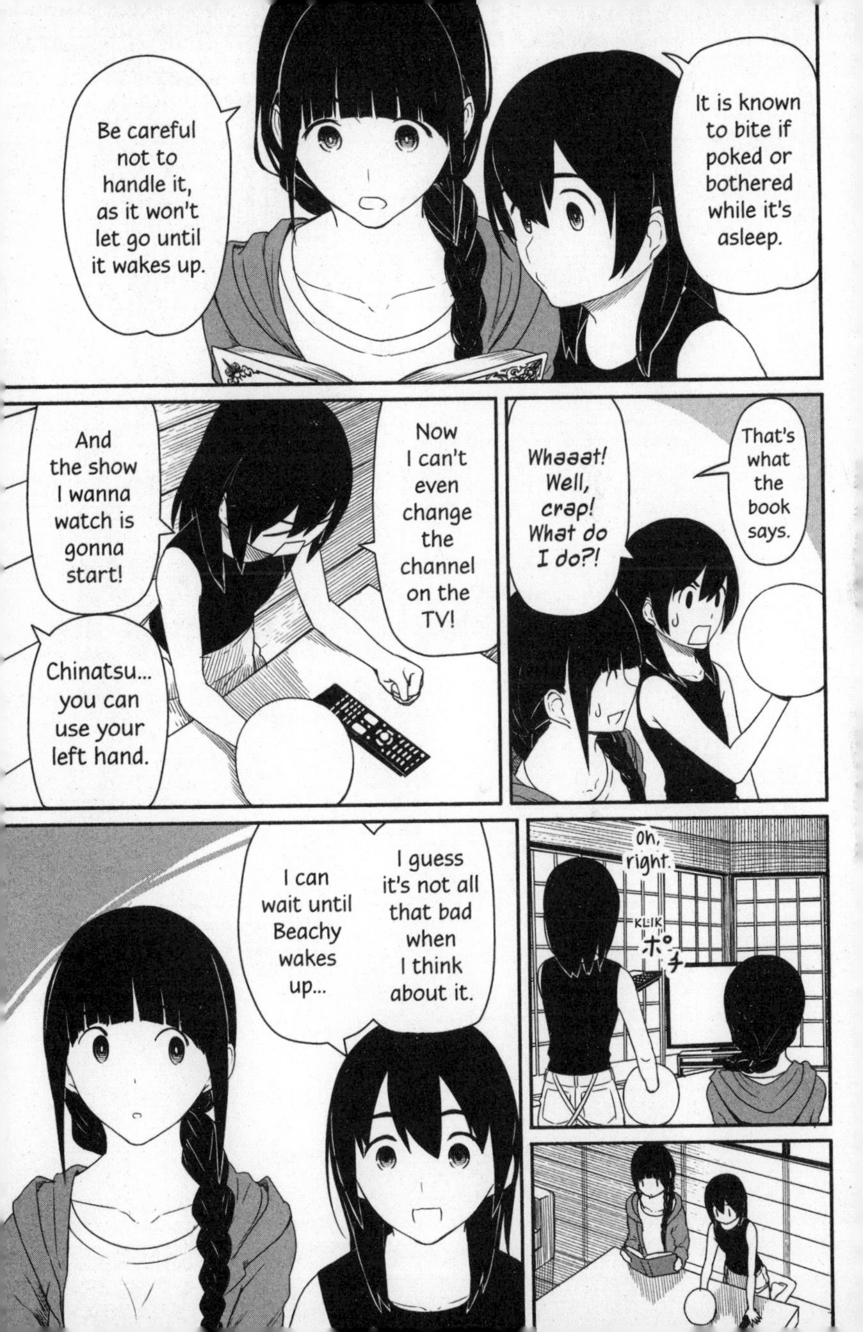
It is known to bite if poked or bothered while it's asleep.
Be careful not to handle it, as it won't let go until it wakes up.
That's what the book says.
Whaaat! Well, crap! What do I do?!
Now I can't even change the channel on the TV!
And the show I wanna watch is gonna start!
Chinatsu... you can use your left hand.
Oh, right.
KLIK
ポチ
I guess it's not all that bad when I think about it.
I can wait until Beachy wakes up...

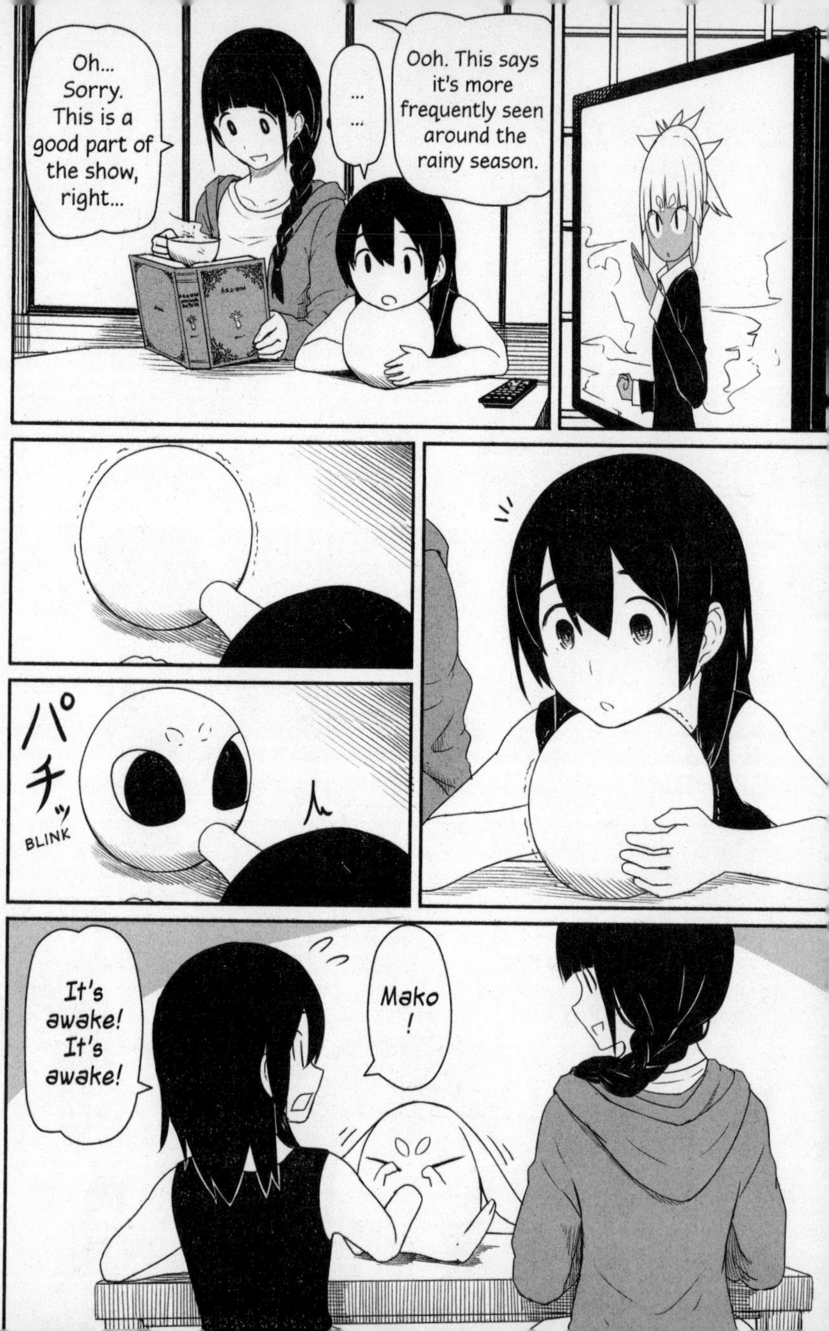
Ooh. This says it's more frequently seen around the rainy season.
... ...
Oh... Sorry. This is a good part of the show, right...
パチッ
BLINK
Mako!
It's awake! It's awake!

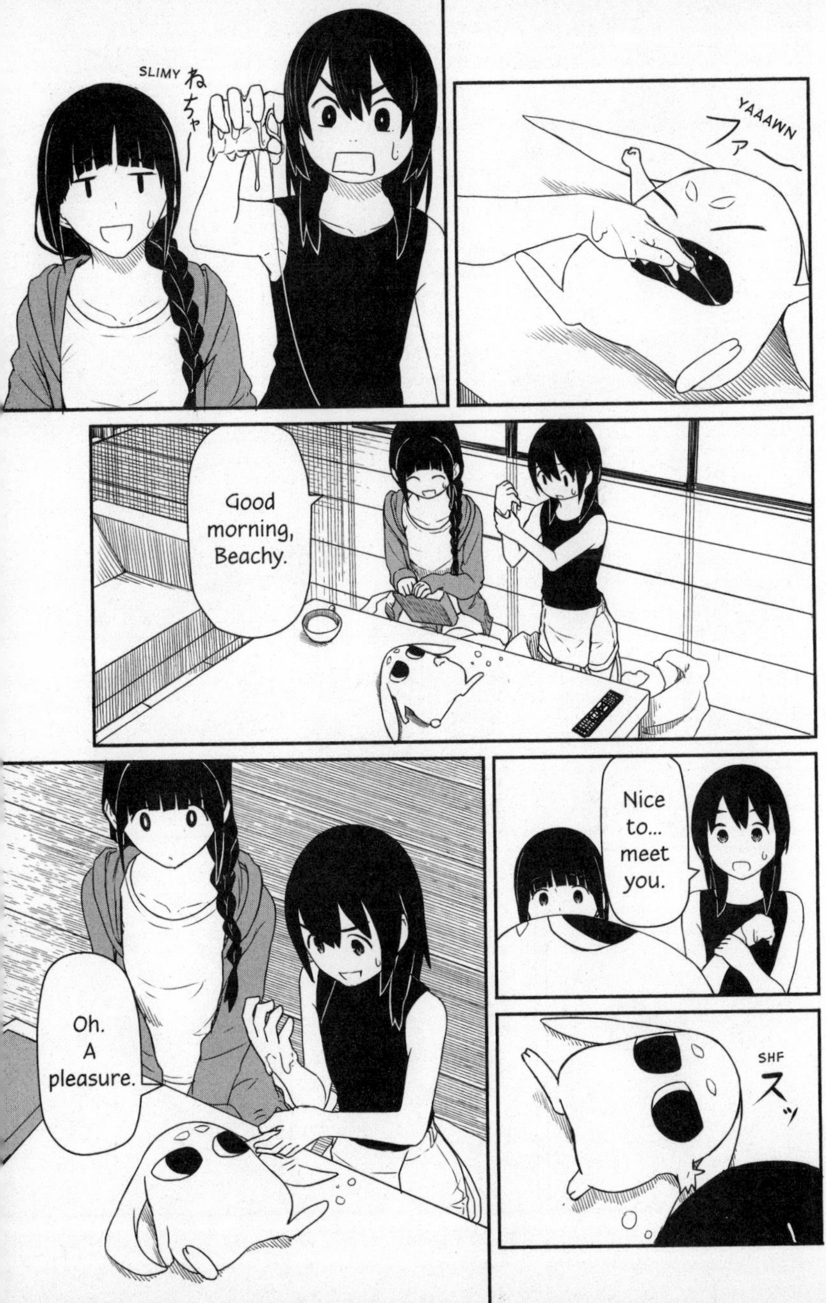
YAAAWN
ファ〜
SLIMY
ねちゃ〜
Good morning, Beachy.
Nice to... meet you.
SHF
スッ
Oh. A pleasure.

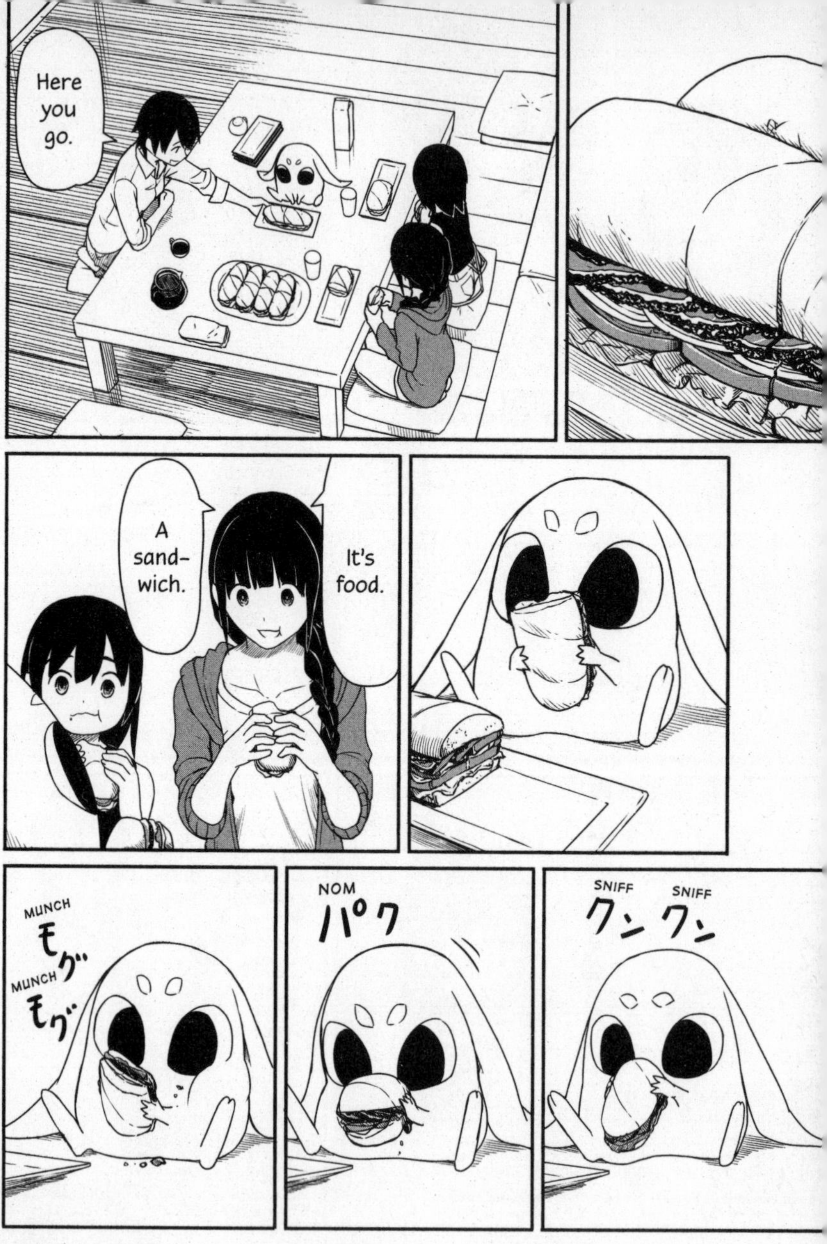

Here you go.
It's food.
A sand-wich.
SNIFF クン SNIFF クン
NOM パク
MUNCH モグ
MUNCH モグ

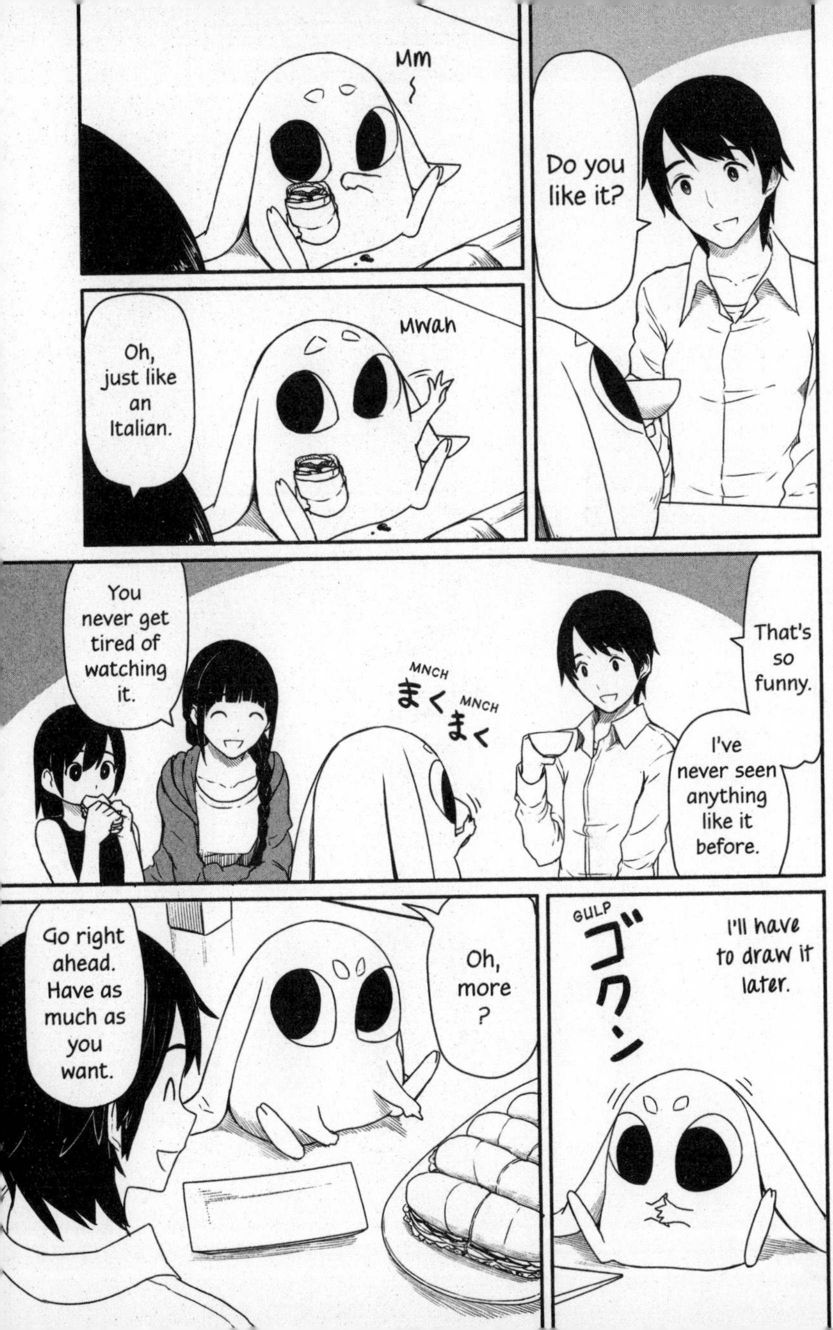

Do you like it?
Mm~
Mwah
Oh, just like an Italian.
That's so funny.
I've never seen anything like it before.
MNCH MNCH
まくまく
You never get tired of watching it.
GULP
ゴクン
I'll have to draw it later.
Oh, more?
Go right ahead. Have as much as you want.

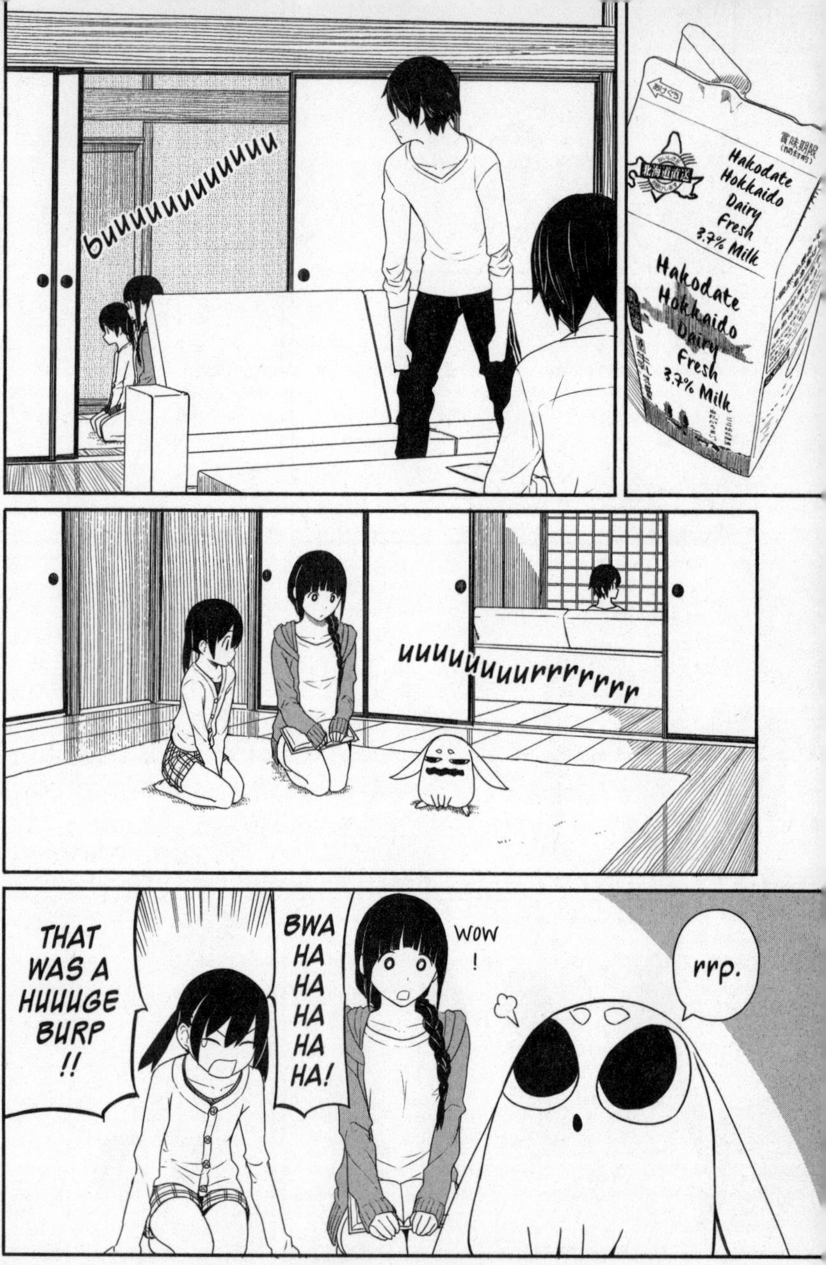
賞味期限
北海道直送
Hakodate Hokkaido Dairy Fresh 3.7% Milk
Hakodate Hokkaido Dairy Fresh 3.7% Milk
buuuuuuuuuuuuu
uuuuuuuurrrrrrr
rrp.
WOW!
BWA HA HA HA HA HA!
THAT WAS A HUUUGE BURP!!

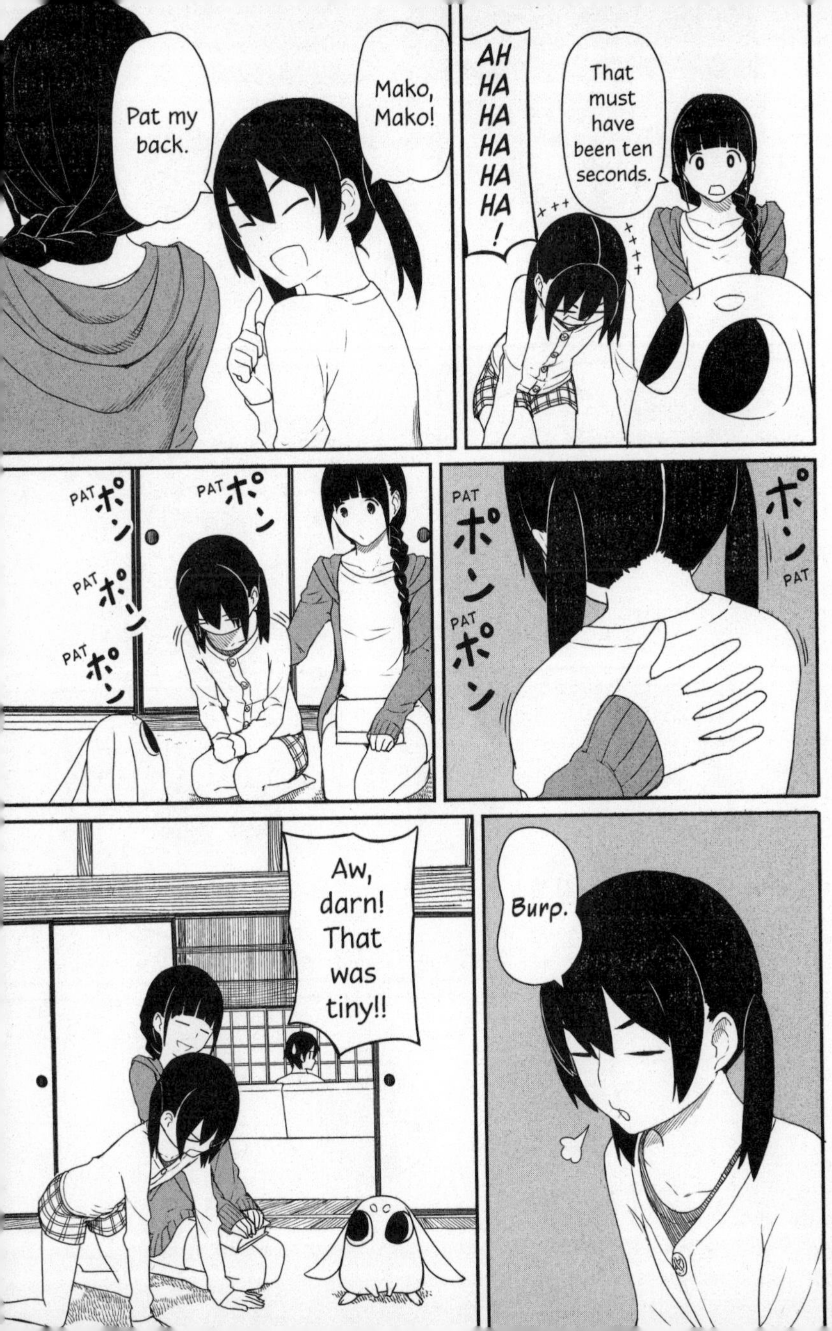
That must have been ten seconds.
AH HA HA HA HA HA!
Mako, Mako!
Pat my back.
ポン PAT
PAT ポン
PAT ポン
PAT ポン
PAT ポン
PAT ポン
PAT ポン
Burp.
Aw, darn! That was tiny!!

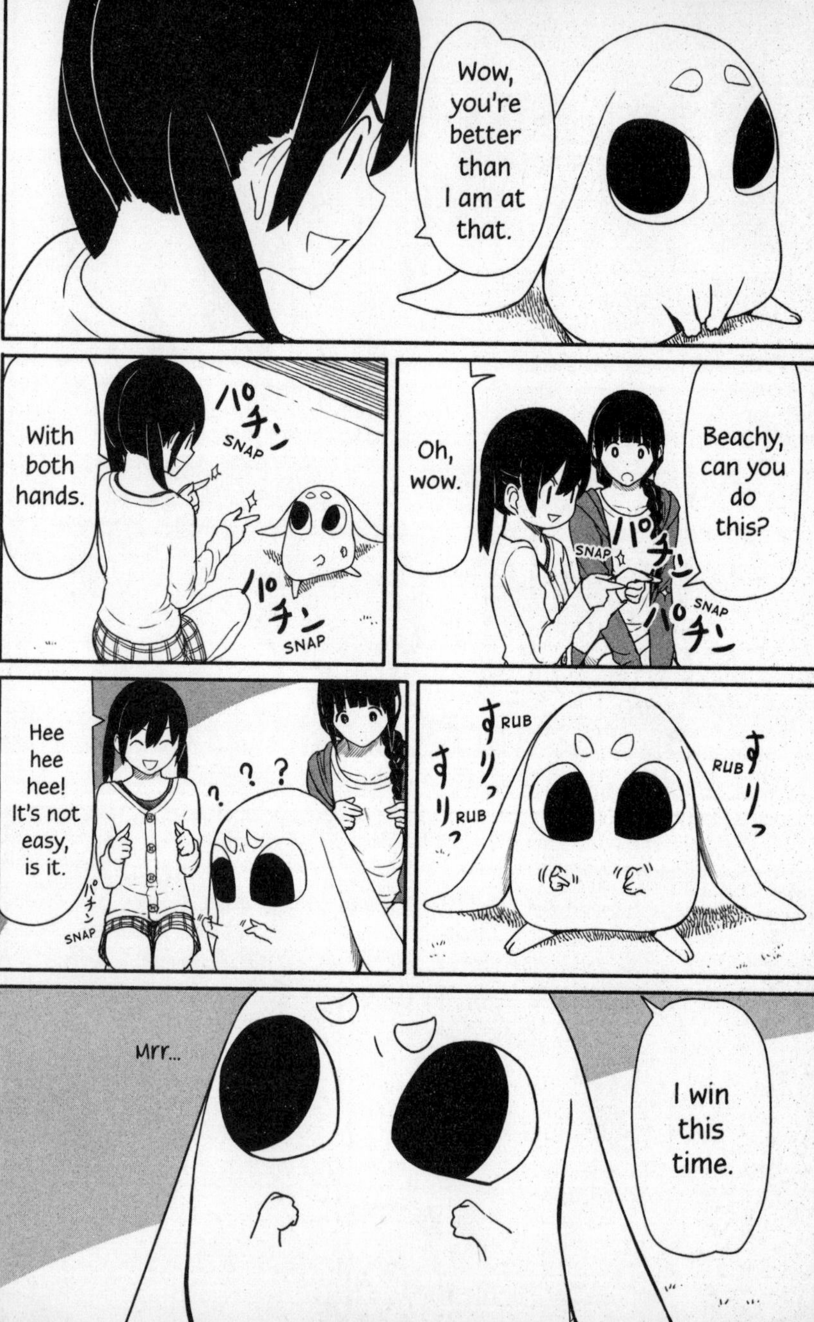
Wow, you're better than I am at that.
Beachy, can you do this?
パチン
SNAP
パチン
SNAP
Oh, wow.
With both hands.
パチン
SNAP
パチン
SNAP
すりっ
RUB
すりっ
RUB
すりっ
RUB
Hee hee hee! It's not easy, is it.
パチン
SNAP
I win this time.
Mrr...

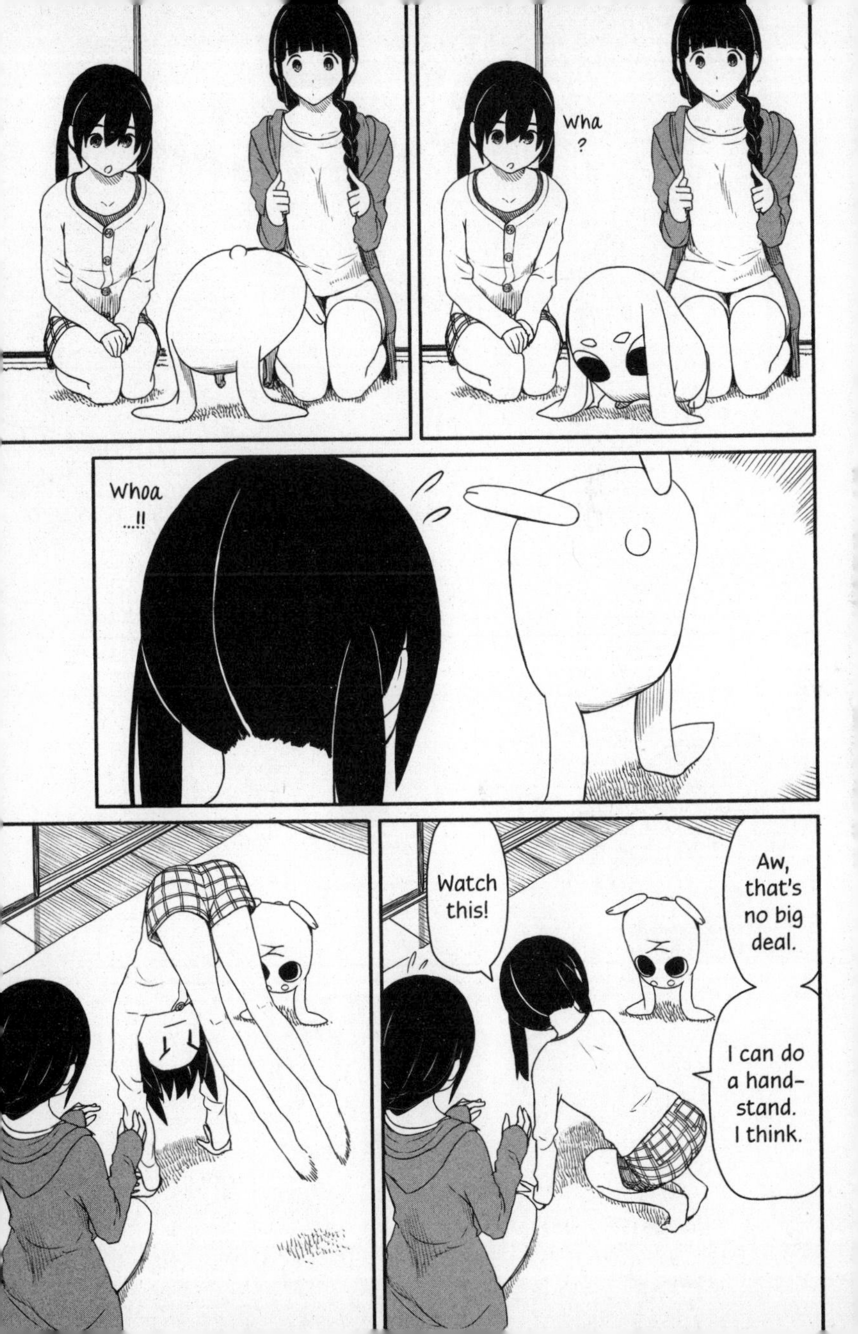
Wha ?
Whoa ...!!
Aw, that's no big deal.
I can do a hand-stand. I think.
Watch this!

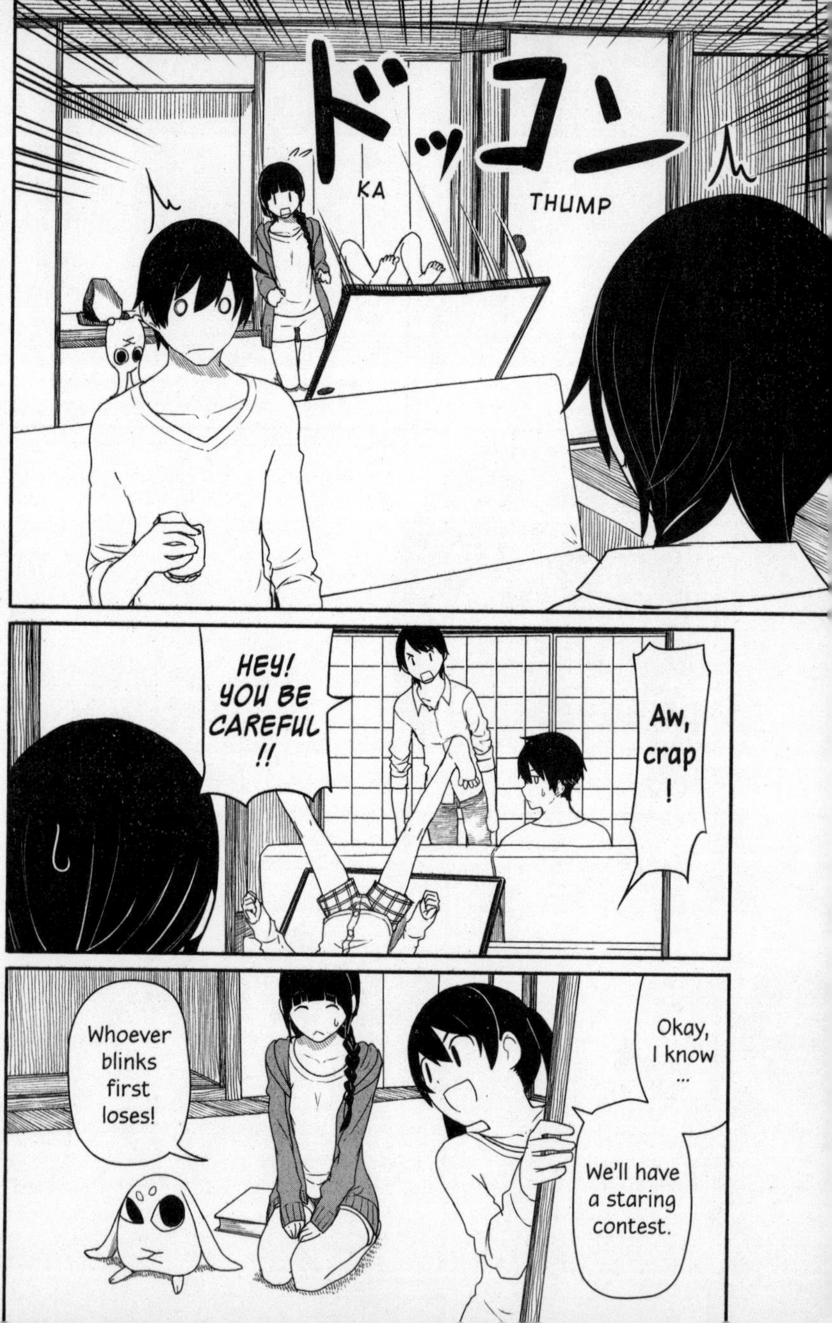
ドッコン
KA
THUMP
Aw, crap!
HEY! YOU BE CAREFUL!!
Okay, I know ...
We'll have a staring contest.
Whoever blinks first loses!

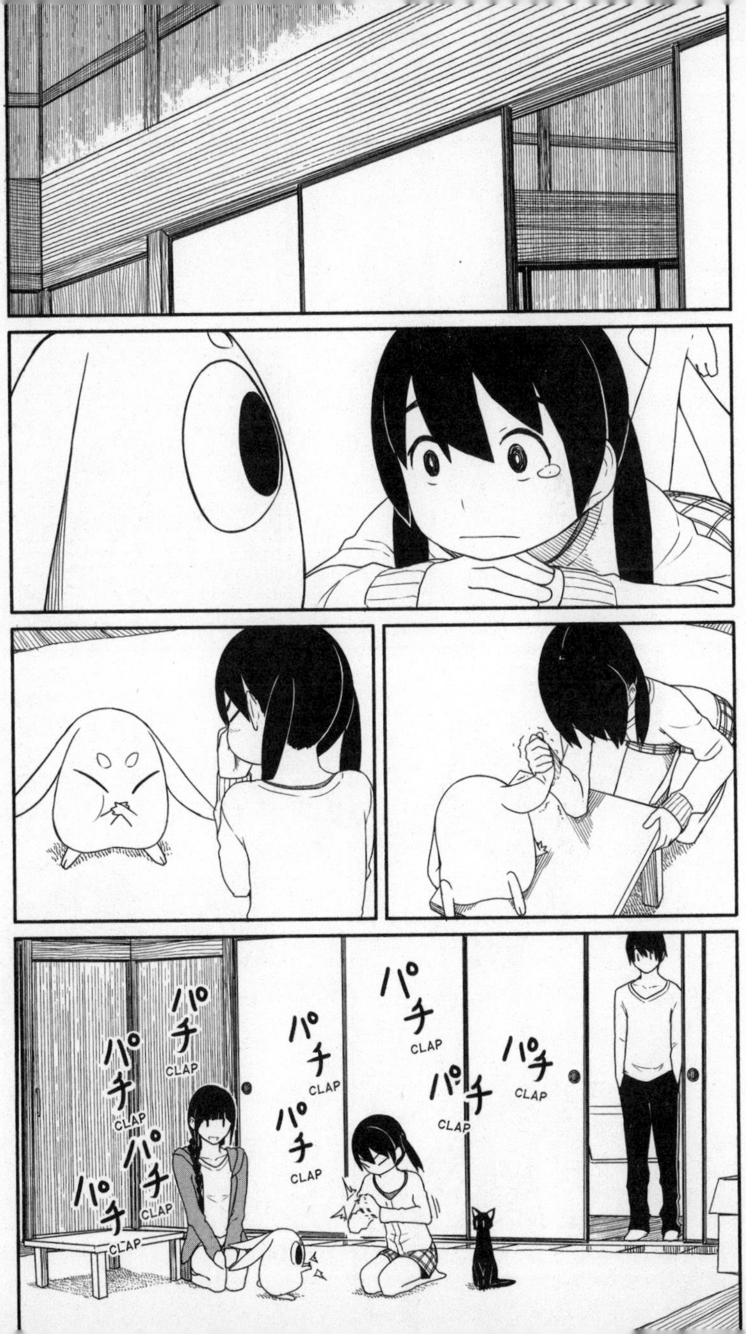
パチ
CLAP
パチ
CLAP
パチ
CLAP
パチ
CLAP
パチ
CLAP
パチ
CLAP
パチ
CLAP
パチ
CLAP
パチ
CLAP
パチ
CLAP
パチ
CLAP
パチ
CLAP
パチ
CLAP
パチ
CLAP
パチ
CLAP
パチ
CLAP

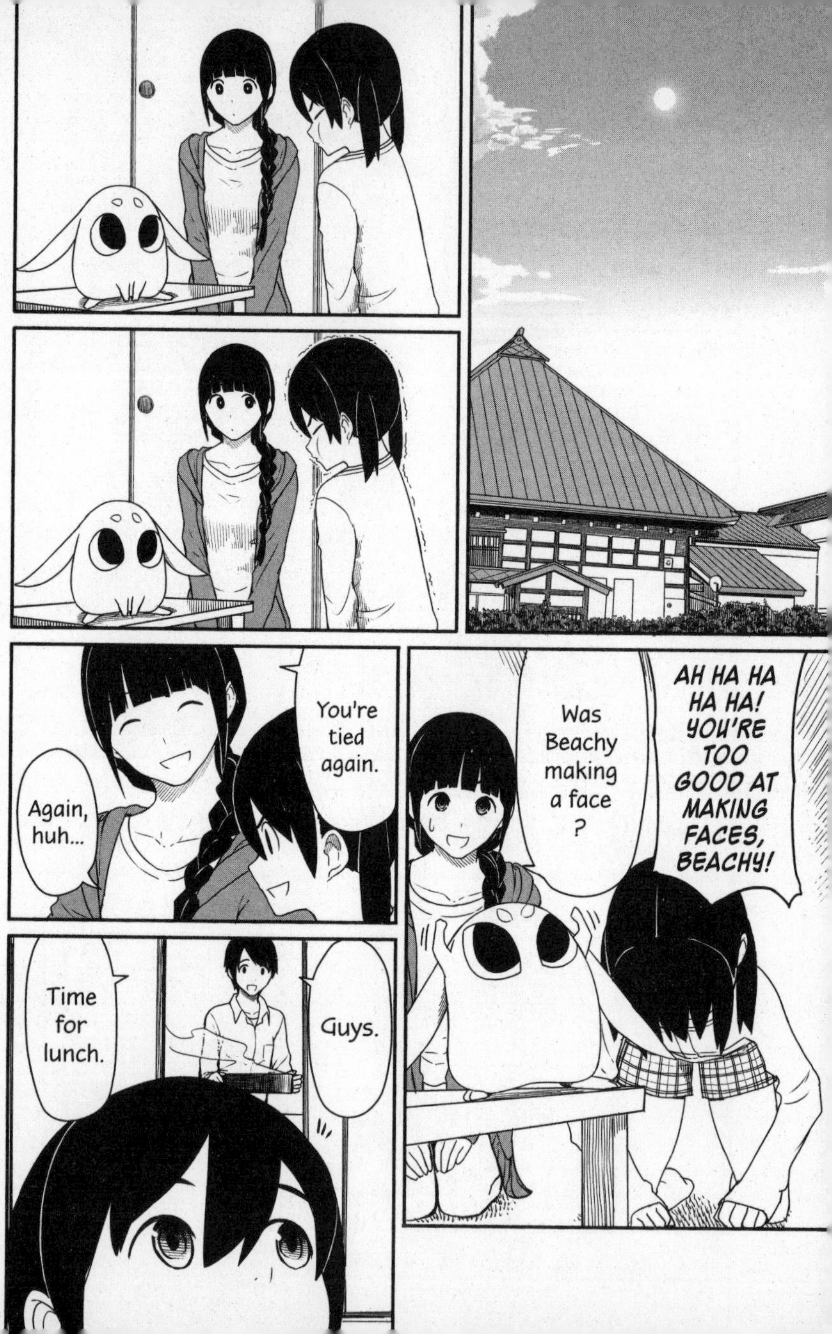
AH HA HA HA HA! YOU'RE TOO GOOD AT MAKING FACES, BEACHY!
Was Beachy making a face?
You're tied again.
Again, huh...
Guys.
Time for lunch.

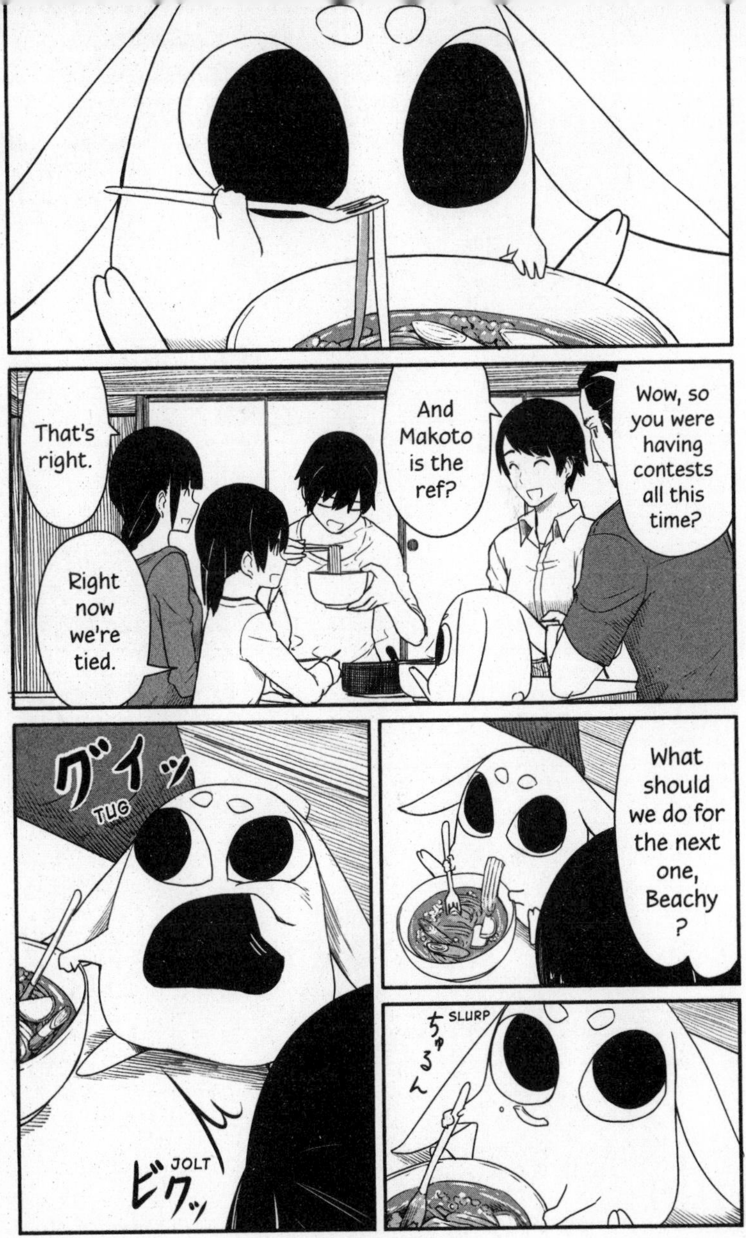
Wow, so you were having contests all this time?
And Makoto is the ref?
That's right.
Right now we're tied.
What should we do for the next one, Beachy?
ちゅるん
SLURP
グイッ
TUG
ビクッ
JOLT

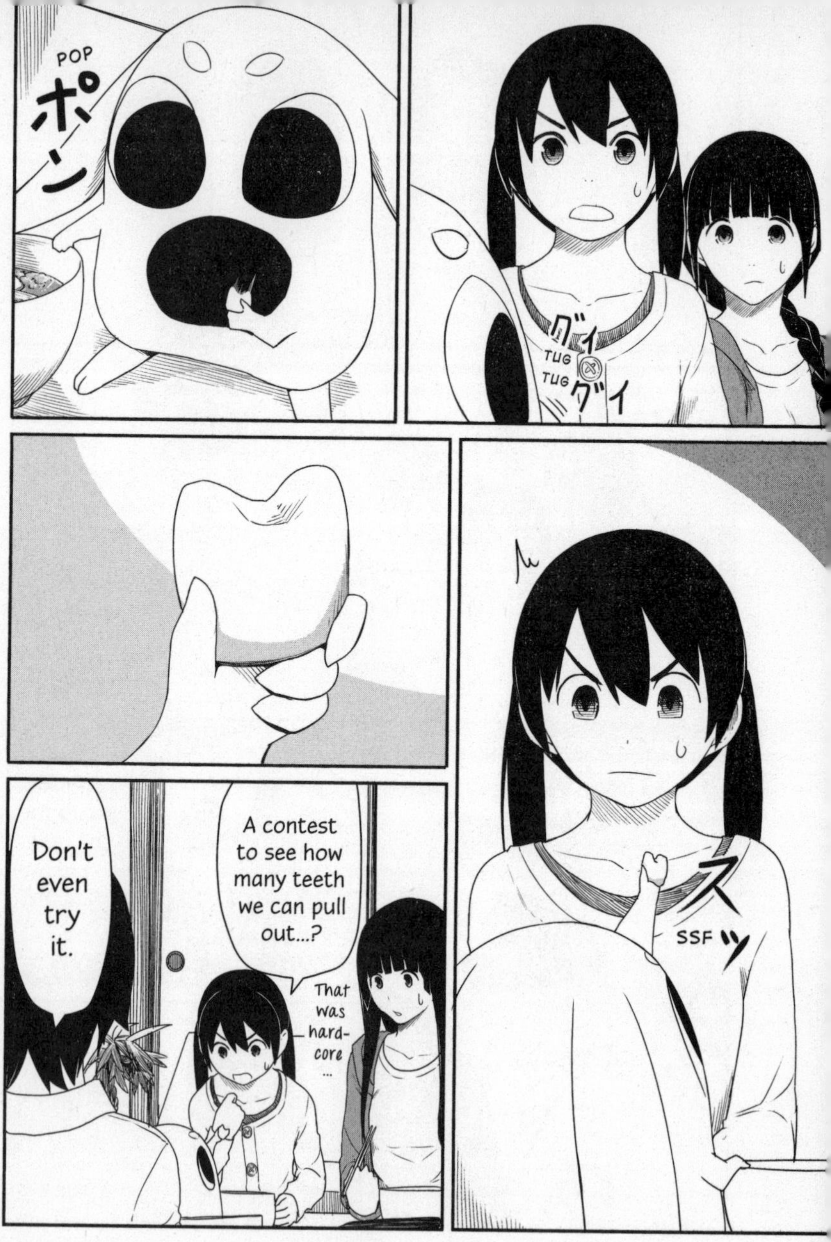
グイ
TUG
TUG
グイ
POP
ポン
ム
ス
SSF
ッ
That was hard-core ...
A contest to see how many teeth we can pull out...?
Don't even try it.

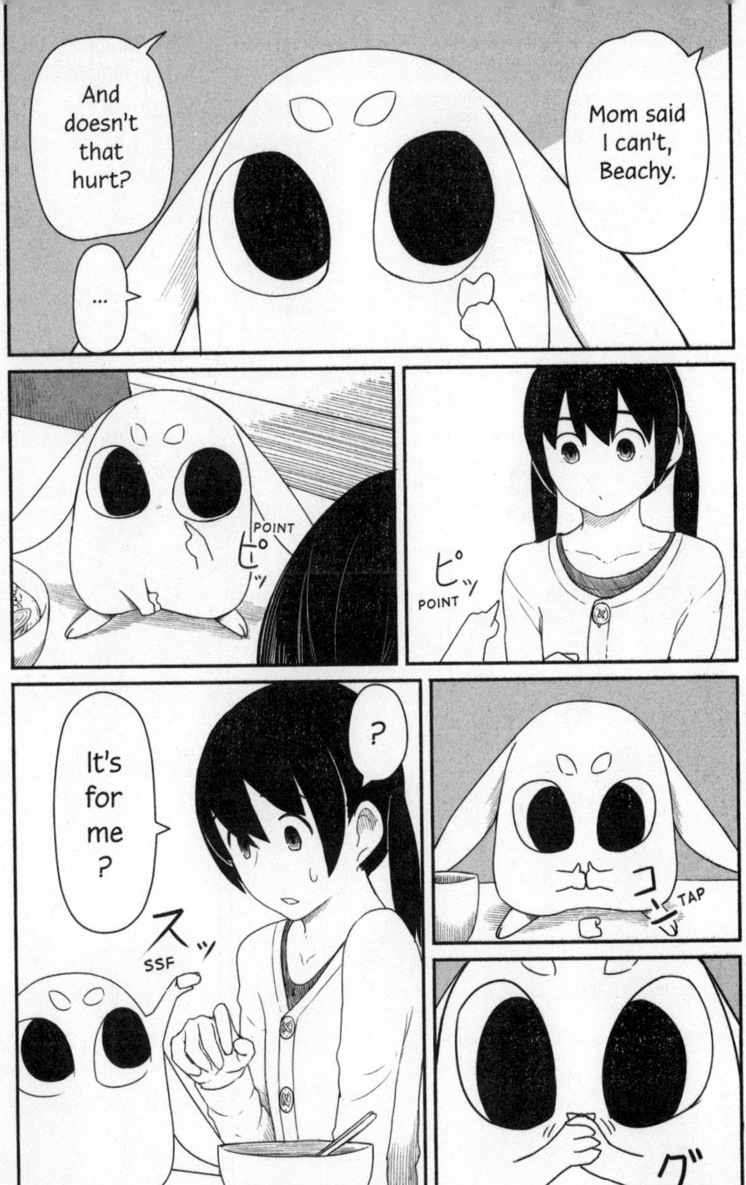
Mom said I can't, Beachy.
And doesn't that hurt?
...
ピッ
POINT
ピッ
POINT
コン
TAP
グッ
SQUEEZE
?
It's for me?
スッ
SSF

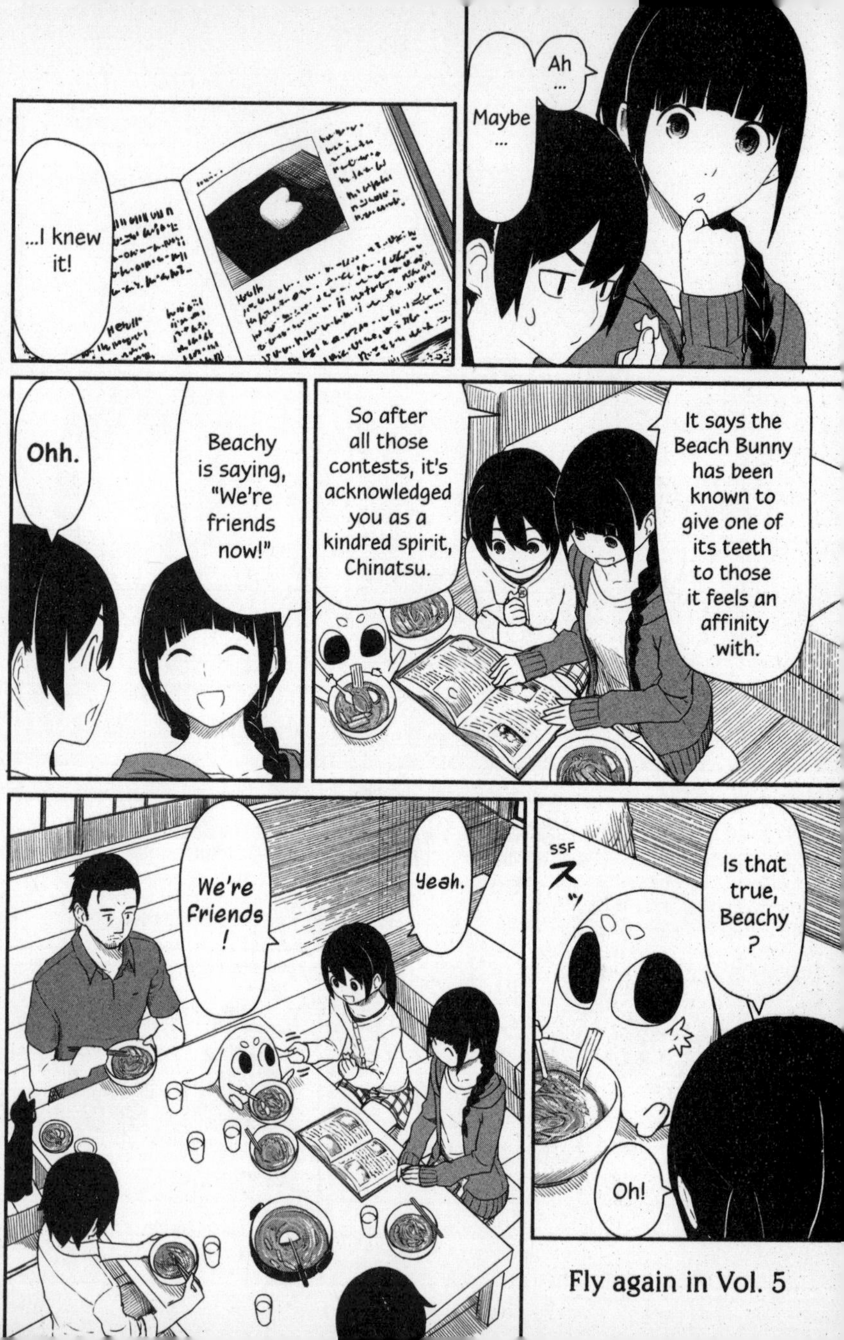
Ah ...
Maybe ...
...I knew it!
It says the Beach Bunny has been known to give one of its teeth to those it feels an affinity with.
So after all those contests, it's acknowledged you as a kindred spirit, Chinatsu.
Beachy is saying, "We're friends now!"
Ohh.
SSF
Is that true, Beachy?
Oh!
Yeah.
We're friends!

Fly again in Vol. 5

Is it okay with a tooth missing?
This says they grow back.

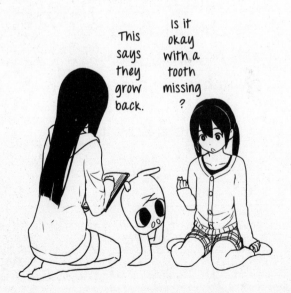

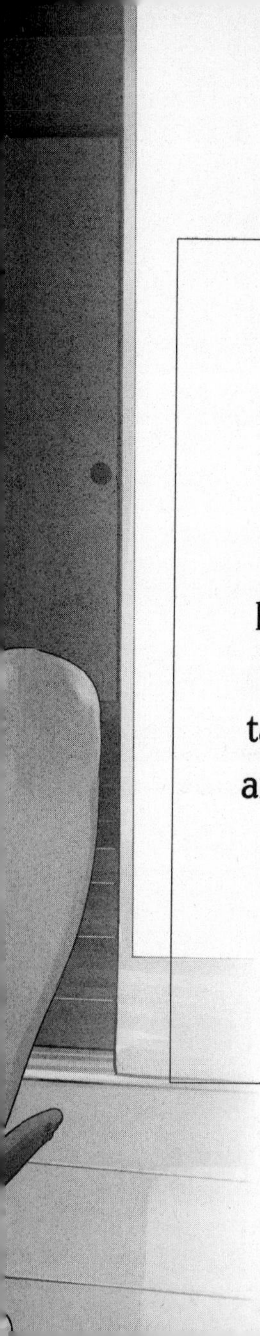

flying witch ✳ kcm flying witch preview for next volume ✳ flying witch ✳ volume

Volume 5 preview

I received my first professional commission from the Witch's Association! I'm a little unsure as to whether I'm up to the task, but I'll do my best and hopefully grow as a witch in the process!

—Makoto Kowata

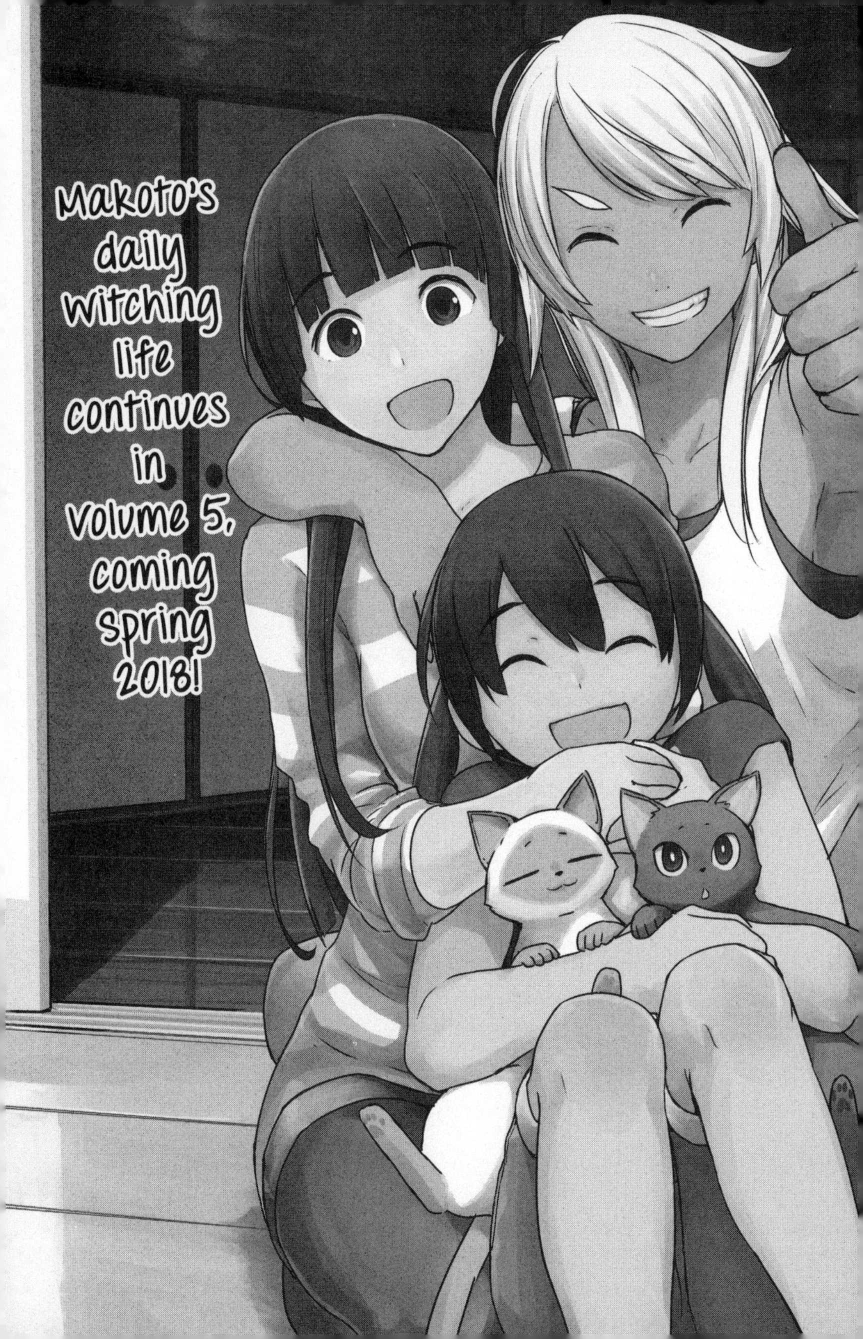
Makoto's daily witching life continues in volume 5, coming spring 2018!

Flying Witch 4

Translation - Melissa Tanaka
Production - Grace Lu
Tomoe Tsutsumi

First published in Japan in 2016 by Kodansha, Ltd., Tokyo
Publication for this English edition arranged through Kodansha, Ltd., Tokyo

Translation provided by Vertical Comics, 2017
Published by Vertical Comics, an imprint of Vertical, Inc., New York

Originally published in Japanese as *Flying Witch 4* by Kodansha, Ltd., 2016
Flying Witch first serialized in *Bessatsu Shonen Magazine*, Kodansha, Ltd., 2013-

ISBN: 978-1-945054-12-9

Manufactured in the United States of America

First Edition

Vertical, Inc.
451 Park Avenue South, 7th Floor
New York, NY 10016
www.vertical-comics.com

Vertical books are distributed through Penguin-Random House Publisher Services.